Introduction to Sports Analytics Using R

Ryan Elmore
University of Denver

Andrew Urbaczewski
University of Denver

Prospect Press

Founded in 2014, Prospect Press serves the academic discipline of Information Systems by publishing essential and innovative textbooks across the curriculum including introductory, emerging, and upper-level courses. Based in Burlington, Vermont, Prospect Press distributes titles worldwide. We welcome new authors to send proposals or inquiries to Beth.golub@prospectpressvt.com.

Editor: Beth Lang Golub
Associate Editor: Dave Williams
Production Management: Scribe Inc.
Cover Design and Illustrations: Annie Clark

eTextbook:
ISBN: 978-1-958303-06-1
Available from Redshelf, VitalSource, and Perusall

Printed Paperback:
ISBN: 978-1-958303-07-8
Available from Redshelf

For more information, visit https://www.prospectpressvt.com/textbooks/elmore-sports-analytics.

Contents

Preface

Welcome to *Introduction to Sports Analytics Using R*! We know that the topic is quite exciting to sports fans and enthusiasts, and we present this book as an opportunity to learn how to explore doing sports analytics using the R language. Our goal is to help make this learning process fun and rewarding.

Overview and Class Design

This book was designed to complement the Sports Analytics course we teach at the University of Denver. It starts with an overview of sports analytics and then provides an introduction to R programming and web scraping / data acquisition. Once those topics are covered, we go into individual sports and analytics that are useful in those sports. We could not hope to cover every technique and sport that is important to every audience, and we've chosen a selection of sports and techniques that provide a baseline to those interested in other sports for how to proceed. We conclude with a chapter on sports wagering and daily fantasy sports (DFS).

While the sports are unique, the chapters build on one another. If we introduce an R package in chapter 4 ("Baseball"), we do not reintroduce it in chapter 5 ("Basketball"), as we assume that the students will know how to load and use it in the latter chapter. We apply similar logic to coding fundamentals.

Student Preparation

This book is geared toward upper-division undergraduates and master's students. When writing this text, we assumed that students would have experience, perhaps limited, in some coding environment. This does not mean that students with zero programming experience could not complete this course; however, programming fundamentals might need to be supplemented with outside materials. We recommend Hadley Wickham's *R for Data Science* (O'Reilly, 2023; `https://r4ds.hadley.nz/`), which we reference throughout the text, as a place to find deeper information.

We do use chapter 2 as an introduction to R programming, and we try to compress into one chapter material that might take a novice programmer an entire semester to explore. We show how to use loops, conditionals, variables, and visualizations all in the "R" way—and particularly in the tidyverse environment common not just in sports analytics but in all forms of data science. This chapter can serve additionally as a refresher for those who have not coded in a while as to how to write code, but those who have never written a line of code may struggle and need more assistance.

We also expect that students have had exposure to some levels of inferential statistics and preferably some predictive statistics and classification models. For more advanced techniques, such as clustering in chapters 8 and 9, we spend more time going over the techniques. Gaussian mixture models, as covered in the soccer chapter, may be above even the students with significant statistical backgrounds. However, for techniques like ordinary least squares regression, logistic regression, and generalized additive models, we spend less time introducing the technique and assume that students are at least familiar with the basic concepts of these techniques. We also assume that students are familiar with p-values in identifying whether a variable is a significant and reliable predictor in a model. We recommend Gareth James, Daniela Witten, Trevor Hastie, and Robert Tibshirani's *An Introduction to Statistical Learning with Applications in R* (Springer, 2013; `https://www.statlearning.com`) as a reference for the statistical methods covered in this textbook.

We also recognize that students may have limited exposure to linear programming and optimization models, as covered in chapter 10. However, the concepts of selecting the optimal DFS team should be salient enough by this point in the book that students will be able to at least grasp the technique in this context.

Pedagogical Features of the Text

Consistent Chapter Format: In each chapter, we follow a consistent format. We introduce the topic (or sport), assuming that readers may know nothing about that sport. We then proceed to cover the topic, introducing what target question we are trying to answer and then showing how to acquire data, prepare data, and analyze data to get some answers to those questions.

Hands-On Approach: Rather than primarily discussing concepts and theory, we show how to do things first and then ask the students to complete them later. In a field like sports analytics, students are used to seeing the data and drawing high-level conclusions, but we get into the weeds with the students in developing the code. The code is also available for students to copy and paste from our website, as mentioned below.

Code and Pictures: We believe not just in code but also in pictures. We focus heavily on data visualization in this text. We find that students are drawn to graphically presenting their work, and when the students can show their work as a graphical representation, it makes what they do that much more valuable to nontechnical consumers of the information. The code for data analysis and visualization is presented in such a way that students should feel ready to adopt it as a baseline for their own projects and curiosities.

Research Block: Most chapters include a research block. This block talks about a sports analytics–related question that has been addressed in academia and published in peer-reviewed research, along with a link to access that published paper. These are meant to show students and faculty the types of questions that are being answered not just by teams but also by academics. We recommend that instructors choose several of these for discussion throughout the course.

Labs: Most chapters also include a lab for students to practice what they've learned. These are generally code-intensive applications for the demonstration of a single analytic question from beginning to end.

Case Studies: Most of the chapters end with a case study. Far less code-intensive than the labs, these are instances of real-world sports problems (e.g., "Adjusting to Baseball in Colorado"). These may be assigned to students to read before class and to spur a class discussion about the problems and how data might be used to address the specific situations. Several of them also ask questions that offer the opportunity for students to gather data and analyze the questions being asked. Most of these questions have no "right" answer.

Homework Exercises: There are also questions for students to answer at the end of each chapter.

Presentation of Student Work / Analytic Products

We discuss how to perform the analysis but leave the presentation up to the individual instructor. In chapter 7 ("Hockey"), we briefly cover the R Shiny app development process and how to create simple web applications to share analysis. Your class may be more interested in copying and pasting pictures to slide presentations, integrating with notebooks, or something else entirely. Whatever you choose, we recommend that you operate under the assumption that your external audience (e.g., sports professionals) knows little to nothing about R and RStudio and that students prepare to show the efforts of their work in some means that can be consumed by nontechnical parties.

Overview of Chapters

Chapter 1 is an overview of the topic. It helps explain why we study sports analytics at all, although we find most students who choose this course need little motivation. If this is a required course at your institution and some students do not have an affinity for sports, this should help explain why it is important.

Chapter 2 is an introduction to R programming. We assume that students in this class have had some experience in some coding language by the time they get to this course. It is not impossible to use this text if they haven't, but there will need to be much more work done before students are ready to progress to chapter 3—perhaps 5 weeks' worth in a 15-week semester. Students could get supplemental material from Datacamp or some other learn-to-code course. If your students already have extensive experience with R, you may find this chapter redundant and may choose to focus on other chapters. We do, however, use sports-related examples in this chapter, as it is a sports-related book, and it may be a welcome refresher for students who haven't used R in a while.

Chapter 3 teaches students how to scrape data from the web. While in most of the book, we use datasets that we supply or APIs to interface with official data provided by leagues, this shows students how to get their own data from web pages on the Internet. The web scraping techniques covered here could be used for any sort of data acquisition, but again, this is a sports analytics text, and as such, we acquire sports data. Chapter 3 is also the one that is the most likely to be "broken" because we are acquiring data from external sources and have no control over if and when any of these external providers change their formatting and/or access. We will do our best to respond to requests to fix things, but please know this is the nature of the beast in this topic.

Chapters 4–9 start the sports-specific chapters of "Baseball," "Basketball," "Football," "Hockey," "Soccer," and "Golf," respectively. We recognize that not everyone, especially depending on the geographic market, may be interested in every sport that we provide. However, with the addition of flag football to the 2028 Los Angeles Summer Olympics as well as the reintroduction of baseball at the 2021 Tokyo and 2028 Los Angeles Summer Olympics, all these sports are international enough to have athletes from around the world competing in them for Olympic medals. This being said, if the instructor wishes to skip a chapter, this is of course his or her prerogative, but note that the coding techniques build on one another, and the instructor may need to pull out the necessary material from an earlier chapter and frame it for the students. For example, at the beginning of each chapter, we show the R packages needed for that chapter, divided into two parts: one contains packages we have used in past chapters and one introduces new packages for the current chapter.

In chapters 4–9, we also tend to focus on one type of statistical analysis. We assume that students enrolled in this class have had some type of univariate statistical class, and hopefully they have at least covered some very basic multivariate, like multiple linear regression. It doesn't mean that a student can't do this if he or she has not had statistical training, but he or she will need to supplement it in some way. Also, once we cover a statistical concept in one chapter, we assume that it is known as we advance to the next chapter.

- Chapter 4 covers baseball and primarily regression, with a lot of visualization.
- Chapter 5 covers basketball and prediction, with the addition of animation to the visualizations.
- Chapter 6 covers football and simulation.
- Chapter 7 covers ice hockey and visualization, with a focus on player analysis. This is also where we introduce R Shiny and how students can publish their work on the Internet.
- Chapter 8 covers soccer and primarily clustering.
- Chapter 9 covers golf and also cluster analysis, with an emphasis on comparing disparate groups.

Chapter 10 covers wagering and DFS. We use this as the last chapter because of the ability for anyone to attempt to profit from their analysis. In the last decade, sports wagering has driven the field of sports analytics outside of team rooms and into the general public. In the wagering section, we primarily look at pricing models, while the fantasy sports section uses optimization as the tool of analysis. We recognize that not all students will have completed a course in optimization by this time, and we aim to include enough material to help the instructor explain the purpose of optimization as a tool. An instructor may wish to go back and show the use of Solver in Excel as a means of performing optimization of simple problems if this is particularly the case for his or her students.

Instructor and Student Resources

Instructor Resources:

- The `ISAR` package contains most of the data needed for this textbook. The package can be acquired at the GitHub site for the book (`https://github.com/rtelmore/isar`) and installed using methods spelled out to the students in chapter 2.
- Code files for students to copy and paste as desired, available at `https://datacolorado.com/r/isar-code/`
- Answers to the end-of-chapter labs and questions
- Slides for each chapter
- Test questions

To Access the Instructor Resources:

- Visit `https://www.prospectpressvt.com/textbooks/elmore-sports-analytics`
- Scroll to the red horizontal menu bar
- Click on **Instructor Resources**
- Click on the yellow box with **Resources Login**
- Click on the **Instructor Resources Access Request Form** and fill out the form. *Only verified faculty will receive access information.*

Student Resources:

- The `ISAR` package contains most of the data needed for this textbook. The package can be acquired at the GitHub site for the book (`https://github.com/rtelmore/isar`) and installed using methods spelled out to the students in chapter 2.
- Code files for students to copy and paste as desired, available at `https://datacolorado.com/r/isar-code/`

To Access the Student Resources:

- Visit `https://www.prospectpressvt.com/textbooks/elmore-sports-analytics`
- Scroll to the red horizontal menu bar
- Click on **Student Resources**

Errata and Potential for Errata

We wrote this book as a very real guide to performing sports analytics, including data acquisition. This means that external websites disappear or change formats, APIs break, and a number of other things could go wrong. As mentioned earlier, a particular place to pay attention would be in chapter 3 with web scraping, as "current seasons" or numbers of seasons played will change. Also in DFS in chapter 10, it is possible that the scoring methods being used by the sites may change, but the code should still work.

All of the code in this text runs and works as of February 2024, but things can change that are beyond the control of the authors. For example, we had to do a major rewrite of the hockey chapter in December 2023, as the NHL API changed and the majority of our examples no longer worked.

As you find errata, please report them to `ryan.elmore@du.edu` and/or `andrew.urbaczewski@du.edu` and we will do our best to provide working code through our GitHub site for the text, `https://datacolorado.com/r/isar-code/`.

Acknowledgments

We would like to acknowledge the efforts of countless people who helped make this text a reality.

To James Campbell, Robert Dennis, Jay Leaf, Jesse Pietz, and Jack Van Deventer, among others, we are indebted to you for your careful reading and the valuable comments you provided to improve the quality of the text.

To Ben Williams, thank you for trusting us enough to use an early version of this textbook in your classes at the University of Denver. And to the many students at the University of Denver who took our (and Ben's) sports analytics classes, thank you for your thoughts and feedback throughout the years. We would not have this text without you all.

A lot of this work was done while Ryan was on sabbatical in the Department of Statistics at the University of Auckland (the birthplace of R). Thank you, in particular, to James Curran for extending an invitation to visit, Joei Mudaliar for logistic support, and the entire department for the many conversations. Further acknowledgment goes to Te Pātaka Kōrero o Te Hau Kapua, the public library in Devonport, New Zealand, as much of the writing of this textbook took place on its second floor overlooking the Auckland Harbour. Ngā mihi.

To Angela Green Urbaczewski, thank you for your understanding as many of Andrew's evenings and weekends were sometimes occupied with writing and code review and testing information presentation formats instead of mowing the lawn or cooking as many dinners as he should have.

To Maggie Stanislawski and August Elmore, thank you for being an awesome family and a supportive bunch!

Finally, we would like to thank the following reviewers for their valuable feedback on the manuscript:

Sarah Abramowitz, Drew University
E. Cabral Balreira, Trinity University
Ryan Baranowski, Coe College
John D. Draper, The Ohio State University
Kyle Evans, Trinity College
Nicholas Gorgievski, Nichols College
Dr. Ross M. Gosky, Appalachian State University
Paul M. Holmes, Ashland University
Dr. Canchu Lin, SUNY Farmingdale
Dr. Robert McDermand, Senior Lecturer of Sports Business and Management, Stephen F. Austin State University
Dr. Bret R. Myers, Professor of Practice, Villanova University
Nakul Padalkar, Assistant Professor, Georgetown University
Mark Pahls, EdD, Senior Lecturer in Health and Human Performance, Fort Hays State University
Andrew B. Perry, Springfield College
N. David Pifer, Florida State University
Shane Sanders, Syracuse University
Judith A. Smrha, Baker University
Ryan Spalding, University of Oklahoma
Prof. Kyle Stich, St. John Fisher University, Department of Sport Management
Dr. Robert Taylor, California University of Pennsylvania
Alexander Traugutt, Elon University
Dr. Nilofar Varzgani, La Salle University, Department of Business Systems and Analytics
Jerred J. Wang, Miami University
Wenche Wang, University of Michigan

About the Authors

Ryan Elmore has been a sports fan his entire life. Some of his earliest childhood memories involve collecting and trading sports cards, playing backyard sports, and memorizing player/team statistics. He has a BS in mathematics from Morehead State University, an MS in statistics from Miami University, and a PhD in statistics from Penn State University. His current sports-related passions include hiking and backpacking with his family (Maggie and August), cycling (commuting and mountain), and watching his son develop his sports and nonsports passions.

Andrew Urbaczewski is a sports fan and numbers nerd who enjoyed putting those two passions together in creating this book. He has a PhD in management information systems from Indiana University and wrote this book while teaching at both the University of Denver and the United States Air Force Academy. He and his wife, Angela, can be found camping in the summer and watching sports in person or on TV in the winter. Andrew can also frequently be found on the golf course—purely for analytical purposes, of course. He has two grown children, Hannah and Colin, and two grown stepdaughters, Elizabeth and Catie.

Chapter 1

Introduction

> The opportunities in all sports in regard to analytics [are] growing so rapidly, the opportunities are unlimited. Technology has opened the door for infinite analytic advancement. Analytics is one of the fastest-growing job types in the market according to our research. Organizations are hiring now. This is a new career path with vast potential.
>
> —Dr. Lynn Lashbrook, president, Sports Management Worldwide

1.1 Why Sports Analytics?

If you are reading this book, you almost certainly have an interest in sports. People have engaged in sport for thousands of years, and the ancient Olympic Games that inspired our modern Olympics date back almost 3,000 years. As long as there have been athletes and competitions, there have always been those seeking to gain an edge. Some are accepted within the rules and spirit of sport, like better training methods and calendars and nutrition and technology, while others violate the rules, like secretly using equipment that has been deemed to be nonconforming with the rules of the sport or having competitors (both human and animal) use performance-enhancing drugs.

As data and computing became more plentiful and available, people turned to analytics to gain an advantage in sport. It is unclear who was the first sports analyst or who was the first team or sport to employ an analyst like we might think of today, but it is quite clear which two major inflection points caused analytics to gain traction. One of these inflection points was developed by an insider; the other was a revelation by an outsider.

1. 1977: Bill James, a graduate of the University of Kansas and a freelance writer, publishes the *1977 Baseball Abstract: Featuring 18 Categories of Statistical Information That You Just Can't Find Anywhere Else*. James used his unique (at the time) statistical analysis from box scores of the previous year's baseball games. While this self-published book sold fewer than 100 copies, it set in motion a new means for fans to analyze the performance of players and teams called sabermetrics. While many fans loved this, baseball scouts and managers, at least publicly, did not take to this new means of analysis. However, a quarter century later, it caused at least one team to think about this differently.
2. 2003: Michael Lewis's book *Moneyball* is published. Lewis's book detailed the adoption of baseball analytics techniques by the 2002 Oakland A's baseball team as they tried to rebuild from losing three players from their stellar 2001 season to teams with more resources who could pay the players more. He detailed general manager Billy Beane's pursuit of the art of winning an unfair game by using advanced analytics to identify value in players that other teams did not see. His techniques were first ridiculed by other teams and then slowly adopted. By the time the 2011 movie of the same name was released, starring Brad Pitt as Billy Beane, every team in Major League Baseball had some sort of an on-the-field analytics department.

Figure 1.1: The cover of the 1988 edition of *The Bill James Baseball Abstract*.

If you are reading this textbook, you are probably familiar with Billy Beane, Brad Pitt, and the movie *Moneyball* even if you have never heard of Bill James or Michael Lewis. Maybe that is what inspired you to look at sports through an analytical lens. Maybe you were just tired of finishing in last place in your annual fantasy football league. Maybe you need a good excuse to learn R programming and improve your mathematical modeling skills. Or maybe you have both a love of sport and an aptitude for data and mathematics and want to conspire to put the two together simply to be a more informed fan. Regardless of your personal reasons, welcome to the world of sports analytics.

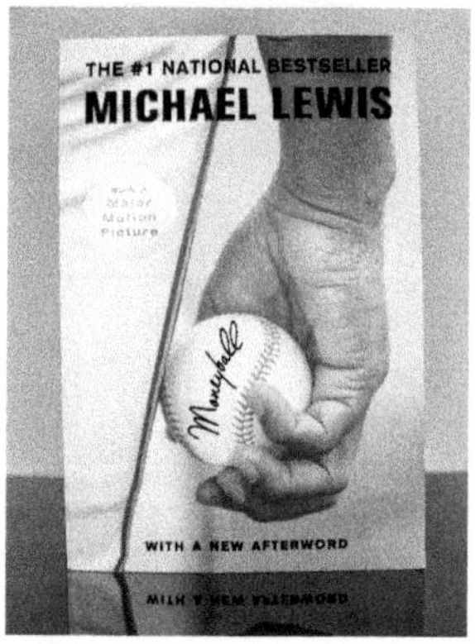

Figure 1.2: The cover of Michael Lewis's book *Moneyball*.
Source: Bill Tompkins / Getty Images

1.2 What Is Sports Analytics?

Sports analytics is the use of data and advanced mathematical methods to build models to help a player or team gain a competitive advantage on the field of play. The field of play designation is important in this context, because this subject does not encompass the analytics that a team might use to determine ticket packages, hot dog pricing, or other types of interactions with their customer base that any other entertainment product like a ballet company or theater might use.

While sports and sports reporters have long used data and frequency counts to report on players and games and the state of the team/sport, in general, sports analytics will go well beyond counting the number of home runs or calculating a free throw percentage or a goalie's save percentage. Sports analysts certainly use these statistics, and they often develop more statistics like the wins above replacement (WAR) player rating in baseball or the Corsi statistic in hockey. The difference between statistics and analytics is that analytics involves building models that are composed of statistics, and the models can be used to inform a strategy or select players in search of a competitive advantage over opponents.

1.3 Careers in Sports Analytics

Sports analytics is a highly sought-after career field. Like many jobs in sports, including players, there is a far higher demand for jobs with teams than there is a supply of the jobs. The pay structure is relatively top-heavy, also similar to the players, where a small number of stars make the majority of the salary pool and a large number of supporting cast members are working for far less than might be earned using similar analytic skills in a different field of business. Yet there is still the allure of working directly for a team that, for many people, far outweighs the compensation in salary. Fortunately, to help with the demand, there are many other jobs in sports analytics that use the tool sets we teach in this textbook but do not require that you work directly for a team.

Working for a team is the dream job for many in sports analytics. The team analyst uses data to evaluate player selection, game strategy, and situational decision-making. Jonah Hill's character Peter Brand in *Moneyball* might be the quintessential team analyst. While his position was unique at the time, most teams have some sort of analytics department, often with multiple analysts.

Career Spotlight: Team Analyst

Layne Vashro is the senior sports analyst for the Denver Nuggets of the National Basketball Association (NBA). The Nuggets won the NBA championship in June 2023, no doubt (us authors believe) in part due to their creative use of analytics. While there was time for cigars and champagne to celebrate, the NBA season being what it is, there was a very quick turnaround to preparing for the NBA draft and player evaluation and summer league games. Fortunately, he was able to spend a few minutes with us to discuss his professional life:

How did you get into your position? While I was working on my PhD in anthropology, I worked on basketball analytics as a hobby. I used basketball data as a sandbox to test statistical techniques and contribute to my passion for arguing with people online. I developed a small public presence and, through that, started receiving interest from teams. Eventually, I was able to begin doing sports analytics professionally.

What is a typical day like? The typical day varies throughout the season. For stretches, I do standard data engineering and extract-transform-load (ETL) of datasets. There are other stretches where I focus on more "academic-style" research projects or expand and maintain projections and other models. There are also times when I work with other front-office staff, working on salary-cap scenarios and assisting with player scouting. Once we get into the core decision periods (trade deadline and draft seasons), most of the days are spent in meetings exchanging information with the rest of the staff.

What are the toughest parts of your job? Most NBA analytics teams, including ours, are smaller than you see in other industries. That makes it impossible to focus only on the parts of the overall data science job where I am the most qualified. I've had to stretch my skill set further into back-end and front-end tasks than I would have expected. This is great for personal growth, but it also involves growing pains and, occasionally, slow progress.

How has your field evolved since you broke into it? Sports analysis is continually maturing. Many teams have growing staffs with more specialized roles. In addition, the technical talent across the league is always improving. When I started, *analyst* was a much looser term from a technical-skills perspective, but that is no longer the case. Now some teams with larger staffs will have people specialize more into just doing data science, data engineering, front-end development, machine learning, or a similar more compartmentalized task.

What do you see as the future of your field? In addition to continuing the growth and specialization of analytics departments noted above, the use of tracking (player position, ball position, etc.) data continues to evolve. The collection and use of tracking data has been a hot topic for a decade now, and that is not changing. We are still in an era where seemingly endless new insights can come from manipulating the spatial tracking data collected by the NBA.

What do you recommend to people who would like to break into your field? Become an expert in SQL and R and/or Python. Specialize in data engineering or front-end development and look for posted openings in those areas. These are the easiest jobs to get into on merit alone (i.e., without an internal network/connections). You will need a legitimate passion for those specific roles to be good enough, but you can also expand into other jobs within a team from that starting point.

Similar to working for a team, a league analyst works for a league or a foundation overall. The purpose of the league analyst is to better the game overall rather than improve the fortunes of one team or player over another. League analytics can be used to suggest or evaluate rule changes, player eligibility, or weather conditions toward an outcome that the league feels is in the best interest of the league and the game.

Career Spotlight: League Analyst

Michael Lopez is the senior director of data and analytics at the National Football League (NFL) headquarters in New York City. He uses data and analytics to help the NFL solve a variety of on-field problems and analyze situations, such as the impact of proposed rule changes. Here he shares some insights into his career:

How did you get into your position? There were certainly academic qualifications (master's plus PhD) that helped, but the primary reason I am in football analytics is because I was doing football analytics work before getting the job. It was my side hobby and passion, but it also provided a direct avenue into the field. Poster presentations, academic talks, and blog posts were all part of my application—unofficially, that is—as they allowed me to improve both my skills and network.

What is a typical day like? We're partially a service group (reporting on what is asked) and partially a research group (trying to uncover new trends or create new metrics). In both situations, there are short-term (hands on keyboard) and long-term (strategy and reporting) efforts that I will contribute to. Our NFL league office data group is up to eight people at this point, so there's always a lot going on in both modeling/tuning and meeting with stakeholders.

What are the toughest parts of your job? Nothing immediately stands out—we certainly have our ups and downs—but one constant challenge is that there is no playbook for many of our critical questions. There's no minor league for us to experiment with changes. Teams operate separately from the league, and for competitive reasons, they may not exactly be forthcoming with any trends that they've picked up. Moreover, there isn't a plethora of other professional sports leagues with similar issues. So we are often flying blind as we start new efforts, making data even more important—even if we cannot always justify our assumptions.

How has your field evolved since you broke into it? More data, better data, more tools, and faster tools—it's all made for a much different job than when I started. Within the last decade, the NFL has gone from primarily play-based (160 rows per game) to scouting-based (e.g., Pro Football Focus, assigning player roles, responsibilities, and performance assessment) and RFID-based (Next Gen Stats player tracking). The NFL data scientist's tool kit has needed to expand as well, from the viewpoint of not only "What model should I fit?" but also "How do I wrangle and store all of these new data?"

What do you see as the future of your field? With all the improvements made, there's still a long way to go, and we're just getting started. There's so much context around football—when Patrick Mahomes throws a touchdown pass to Travis Kelce, how much credit does each player get? The play caller? The offensive line? Et cetera, et cetera—that we'll be trying to define and account for that context for years to come.

What do you recommend to people who would like to break into your field? The best way to get started in football analytics is to do football analytics. Whether it's for a class (high school, college, grad school), a sports team (your own team, or a nearby program), a blog post, and so on, you learn a lot by doing.

There are only so many jobs available working with teams or leagues, and yet there are many more people interested in working with analytics and sports. This discrepancy sometimes induces people to go out on their own and create their own opportunities. This could be in scouting, marketing, branding, or game evaluation.

Career Spotlight: The Entrepreneur

Alex Monahan is the cofounder of OddsJam, a provider and aggregator of sports betting odds and information to its customers. As legalized sports betting began to enter many more markets in the US starting with a Supreme Court decision in 2018, he saw an opportunity to sell access to up-to-the-minute odds information to new bettors. Seeing how the markets for sports betting are similar to those for financial markets, he and his cofounder saw a gap in the market and started OddsJam. Here he describes more of his story:

How did you get into your position? I worked as a trader in financial markets. It was a lot of looking at data—numbers and markets. Sports betting is very similar. I bet for "fun" while I was a trader and started to take it more seriously as time went on. I found the more time I put into it, the more money I made. Eventually, I decided to get into the industry and utilize my technical training and trading experience. Sports betting was just legalizing across the country, and it just felt right.

What is a typical day like? There is no real typical day. Parts of my day may be spent marketing (e.g., writing articles or making YouTube videos), or I may be dealing with a product/engineering team on existing or new products.

What are the toughest parts of your job? Explaining the product to new bettors. At the end of the day, odds are a foreign language to most people. For new sports bettors, a lot of concepts that are essential are difficult to understand at first.

How has your field evolved since you broke into it? A lot more states and countries (e.g., Canada) have legalized. Also a number of different types of platforms have popped up and become popular, such as DFS [daily fantasy sports] "pick 'em" platforms (e.g., PrizePicks), especially in states where laws don't clearly allow for sports betting.

What do you see as the future of your field? The world is only getting smarter, so I do think we'll see more data-driven sports betting products and companies. I also think sportsbooks will consolidate. It's unsustainable to have this many sportsbooks in each state.

What do you recommend to people who would like to break into your field? There are tons of opportunities—just apply to them and get a start. Lots of new start-ups pop up in this industry every week. People are raising money and trying to get into the industry left and right, and that means jobs, internships, and contract opportunities.

While there are not many players who themselves get heavily involved in the data (golfers using TrackMan being notable exceptions), they may have people who work for and with them to gain an advantage through the data. Agency analysts may work for agents who represent players in negotiations with leagues and teams. These sports analysts look to show value in a way that can increase the market value of a player and may even cross over into sponsorship deals, where they show how a player can positively affect a brand. Analytics can help agents identify talent to potentially represent or understand which players they may seek to avoid. Analysts might do this full time or on a contractual basis as a consultant.

Increasingly, media outlets require analytics as well. Whether it is working for a large firm, such as FiveThirtyEight or Fox Sports, or as an individual YouTuber or blogger, an analyst can work as a reporter to show the value of data as columns are written and videos are made.

Finally, we will discuss those who use analytics under the general guise of making money by predicting the outcomes of games. We will refer to them as gamblers, though they might disagree with the use of that term, as those in this field believe that what they do is not a game of chance but rather one of skill, where they use their talents in analyzing data to predict the performance of a player or a team in a certain situation. Daily fantasy sports, as well as traditional sports wagering, provide markets for these analysts to test their models and earn or lose money based on the outputs of their models compared to actual results.

1.4 Off-the-Field Analytics

This book focuses on the analytics decisions that are made by individuals and teams directly regarding on-the-field play. Many of these same techniques can be used by sports teams and organizations for off-the-field decisions. For example, how much should a team charge for a Friday night ticket when they are playing the New York Yankees as opposed to a Wednesday afternoon game against the Oakland A's? How should a team market itself to get more fans to come to the games, where they are more likely to buy $15 beers and $10 hot dogs and pay $30 for parking, often rendering the ticket price itself inconsequential? Should a team be willing to play a college football game on a Tuesday night in order to get national TV exposure when they might not normally get it in the usual Saturday afternoon spot?

All of these are very important to the financial success of a team, and in general, the larger the attendance at a game, the greater the home-field advantage, which translates somewhat to on-the-field success. However, these analytics are beyond the scope of this textbook.

1.5 How This Book Is Organized

After this chapter, the first section of this book will introduce you to the tools we will use to perform sports analytics in the rest of the book. While you are certainly free to jump around to chapters and topics that you like and pique your interest, once we introduce a tool, method, or technique in one chapter, we will assume that you know it or can refer back to it.

Chapter 2 is an introduction to the R programming language. R is an open-source statistical programming language that is used not just in sports analytics but by analysts in business, medicine, natural resources, politics, and just about any other field that you might imagine. If you already have extensive experience with R, you may skip most of this chapter. We will also cover R Markdown and Quarto in this chapter, as it will be our preferred way of creating, documenting, and sharing R scripts with others (including you, the reader). If you are already familiar with Markdown as a means of writing documents, you should pick this up quite quickly. Chapter 2 also is an introduction to the tidyverse. The tidyverse is a collection of packages within R that adhere to a "tidy" philosophy of data management and manipulation. While it is not necessary to utilize tidyverse packages to successfully analyze data in R, you will find that its use is quite common among the more public-facing sports analysts.

Chapter 3 relates to getting data for analysis through web scraping. We assume that if you are reading this book, you know how to download an Excel or CSV file from the web to get data. Sometimes data are not provided for us in that format, but we can see them represented as tables on web pages. This chapter will show you how to retrieve data from those tables on web pages and put them into a format like a CSV file that we can then store for later use or for immediate manipulation and analysis.

Beginning with chapter 4, we will look at analytics for individual sports and situations. While chapters 2–3 show us the tools, in chapter 4, we will start applying these tools and new techniques to particular sports. So while you may be interested in examining the sports in a different order than we present them here, you may need to briefly refer back to a previous chapter if you do not understand a particular function or library.

Chapters 4–9 will cover analytics for various sports. Baseball, basketball, football, hockey, soccer, and golf will all be discussed. The data and analytics we will use in these chapters aim to solve particular problems in those sports. However, we cannot possibly show you all the analytics for each sport. Moreover, you may be inspired to try to develop your own analytics, and we hope you are! Take the techniques we show you for one sport and perhaps try them with another sport, or for different data, or for a sport we don't even discuss here.

Finally, we also include a chapter showing the use of data for fantasy sports analysis and sports wagering. We will discuss different types of popular fantasy sports games as well as sports wagers and how you might use sports analytics in those endeavors.

In each chapter, we will include a lab where you follow along with us in producing a piece of code or an output. We provide step-by-step examples, and we also show the output next to the code input. We include several challenge questions at the end of each chapter where you will have to try to create the code to deliver the solution without our tutelage.

1.6 Research Block: Do Players Get Streaky?

In each chapter, we will include a discussion about a piece of research referencing sports analytics. These will be summaries of academic studies that examine a sports-related question or a theoretical question that is addressed through the lens of sports. In this chapter, we introduce one for thought about randomness and streaks and cognitive bias.

Thomas Gilovich is a psychology professor at Cornell University specializing in research on heuristics and cognitive biases. As part of his early research, he was concerned with individuals' abilities to understand randomness in sequences. An avid sports fan whose doctoral dissertation studied the concepts of biased evaluation and persistence within the context of gambling, it was a natural fit to use sports as the domain for studying cognitive biases.

In his 1985 paper with Robert Vallone and Amos Tversky, "The Hot Hand in Basketball: On the Misperception of Random Sequences," which can be found at `https://www.sciencedirect.com/science/article/abs/pii/0010028585900106`, he conducted a series of studies involving both individuals' perceptions in a survey and statistical analysis while looking for evidence of a "hot hand" or even a "cold hand." The hot hand is used to represent the idea that a player who makes a basket is more likely to make the next basket than his base rate (think: skill level) would imply, while the cold hand implies one who misses will continue to miss at a greater-than-base rate. He examined data from both the Cornell University men's basketball team and the Philadelphia 76ers NBA team. Despite the 76ers roster including Andrew Toney, a player who was known in the media as a notorious streak shooter, his analysis found no evidence of either a hot or a cold hand.*

Gilovich concluded through his study that the hot hand effect is simply an illusion that is a limitation of people's memories. Individuals are more likely to remember a streak but yet are unable to comprehend the

* Interestingly, the only player whose current shot success rate was statistically dependent on the previous shot was Darryl Dawkins, and it was in the opposite direction (i.e., he was more likely than the base rate would imply to miss the current shot if he had made the previous one, and vice versa).

frequency with which streaks appear in random sequences. This, however, does not stop people from believing in a hot hand, even in contexts as random as roulette. Casinos take advantage of this by posting the previous results of the spins on a signboard next to the roulette wheel, encouraging people to place their bets and implying that people might want to bet against a streak continuing to occur, as there is no way that a ball could land in a red pocket yet again if it had landed in a red one on the previous six spins. (If you are unfamiliar with roulette, essentially, it is a coin flip if the ball lands in a red or a black pocket.) The casinos use a similar strategy in another essentially coin-flip game, baccarat.

The hot hand theory continues to be tested in a variety of domains and sports, including baseball, soccer, volleyball, bowling, stock market investing, and even dice games and lotteries. Indeed, the authors of this textbook published a paper in 2018 examining this effect in golf. In the nearly 40 years since Gilovich published this initial paper, the power of sports analytics not only to answer sports questions but to inform more general topics continues to expand with the volume of data available.

Figure 1.3: Andrew Toney of the Philadelphia 76ers.
Source: Public domain

1.7 Case Study: Transitioning to Analytic Thinking in Sports

Each chapter will also include a case study relative to the topic of the chapter. In this case study, you will be provided with some background material on a particular topic, incident, or dilemma within sports. Sometimes there will be direct coding exercises related to the case study, and other times there will be topics for discussion. Often you will be able to use analytics to back up your arguments, and that will be the purpose of the discussion.

Major organized professional team sports have existed for over 100 years. During that time, there have been many methods that teams have used to evaluate potential players for those teams. Some sports have the benefit of colleges or schools to do the training, while others (particularly soccer) have created their own junior divisions of their clubs to handle training internally—sometimes of children of single-digit ages. In this case study, we will focus largely on evaluating players who have reached adulthood but have not yet been made a part of a team in a top-level league.

Figure 1.4: A signboard at a roulette table.
Source: istockphoto/o-che

In sports like baseball, for over a century, major-league teams have relied on scouts to go to parts of the country and view players in high school, college, American Legion, Pony, or other organized leagues and summer leagues to identify if there are players who should be considered for signing as a part of their clubs. Increasingly, MLB teams look internationally for players, with the Dominican Republic being a hot spot for academies for teams to look for talent. These scouts will write reports based on their observations of a player and send them to team management.

In American football, in addition to scouting reports, the NFL also holds the NFL Scouting Combine, a set of workouts in the late winter in Indianapolis for college players who are eligible for the draft. At this combine, players are examined in a variety of running and jumping drills, and many parts of their bodies are officially measured. There are other examples for other sports, but it is under these watchful eyes that many of the evaluations are made.

The years of experience of the scouts are often long, and their expertise is valuable. However, scouts can be prone to human bias, falling in love with someone who "looks the part" and disregarding talent who doesn't have that look. At the end of the 20th century, one needs to look no further than quarterback Ryan Leaf, who was the 2nd player chosen in the 1998 NFL draft. At 6′ 5.5″ (196 cm) and 235 pounds (106 kg), and recently completing a brilliant junior season at Washington State University, he had the look of the prototypical quarterback. The Indianapolis Colts had the first pick of the draft that year and ultimately chose Peyton Manning, who was a similar size and had an extremely successful college career. Manning ultimately won five NFL MVP awards and two Super Bowls and was inducted into the NFL Hall of Fame in 2021, while Leaf played in a total of 25 games over four years and is widely regarded as one of the biggest NFL "busts" of all time. Moreover, two years later, it was not until the 199th pick that the New England Patriots selected Tom Brady in the draft. While tall, he was considered slight of build (for an NFL quarterback) and slow and had a mediocre collegiate career. However, he played 22 NFL seasons; won a total of seven Super Bowls, five Super Bowl MVPs, and three NFL MVP awards; and is often referred to as "The GOAT"—an acronym meaning "Greatest of All Time."

Scouting is not a perfect science, of course, and there can always be some freak injury that derails a highly regarded prospect or someone with little exposure from a small school who winds up being quite successful. Analytics offer a tool set that can be used for player evaluation that can help teams not be blinded by a human bias. While the models that teams use for player evaluation may include some of the data from scouting reports, they may also include other inputs, many of which could be proprietary to the team. Analytic models are also designed to reduce the influence of human bias. This does not mean that a team should always defer to whatever answer the computer spits out, but a model's prediction of player success is another data point that a team can use, along with contract considerations, for example.

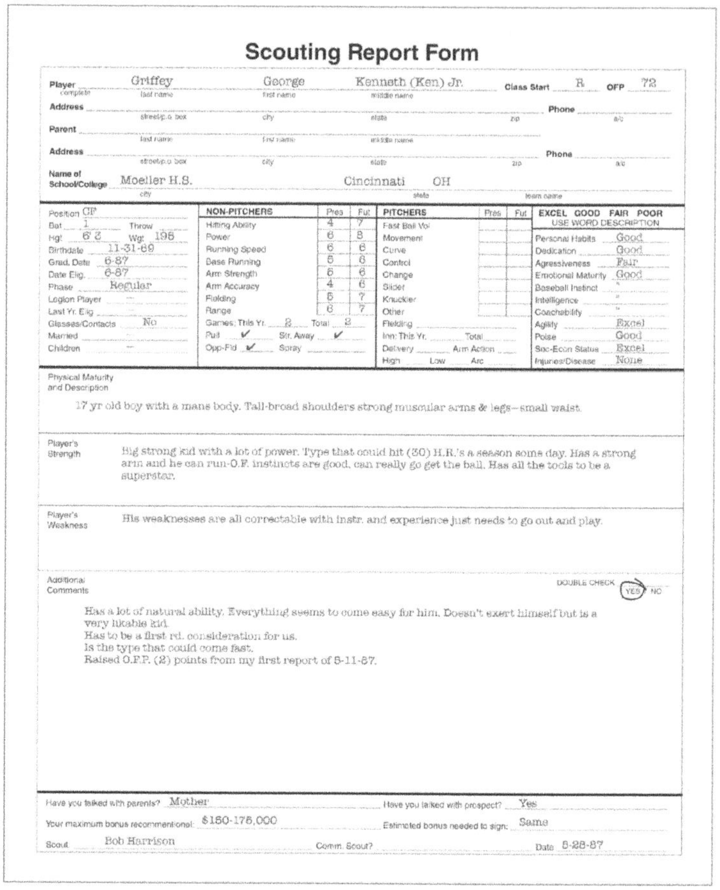

Scouting Report Form

Player (complete): Griffey (last name) George (first name) Kenneth (Ken) Jr. (middle name) Class Start R OFP 72

Address (street/p.o. box, city, state, zip) Phone (a/c)

Parent (last name, first name, middle name)

Address (street/p.o. box, city, state, zip) Phone (a/c)

Name of School/College: Moeller H.S. (city) Cincinnati OH (state) (team name)

Position CF
Bat 1 Throw
Hgt 6'3 Wgt 198
Birthdate 11-31-69
Grad. Date 6-87
Date Elig. 6-87
Phase Regular
Legion Player —
Last Yr. Elig —
Glasses/Contacts No
Married —
Children —

NON-PITCHERS	Pres	Fut
Hitting Ability	4	7
Power	6	8
Running Speed	6	6
Base Running	5	6
Arm Strength	6	6
Arm Accuracy	4	6
Fielding	5	7
Range	6	7

Games: This Yr. 2 Total 2
Pull ✔ Str. Away ✔
Opp-Fld ✔ Spray

PITCHERS	Pres	Fut
Fast Ball Vel		
Movement		
Curve		
Control		
Change		
Slider		
Knuckler		
Other		

Fielding
Inn: This Yr. Total
Delivery Arm Action
High Low Arc

EXCEL GOOD FAIR POOR — USE WORD DESCRIPTION

Personal Habits	Good
Dedication	Good
Agressiveness	Fair
Emotional Maturity	Good
Baseball Instinct	"
Intelligence	"
Coachability	"
Agility	Excel
Poise	Good
Soc-Econ Status	Excel
Injuries/Disease	None

Physical Maturity and Description: 17 yr old boy with a mans body. Tall-broad shoulders strong muscular arms & legs—small waist.

Player's Strength: Big strong kid with a lot of power. Type that could hit (30) H.R.'s a season some day. Has a strong arm and he can run-O.F. instincts are good, can really go get the ball. Has all the tools to be a superstar.

Player's Weakness: His weaknesses are all correctable with instr. and experience just needs to go out and play.

Additional Comments: DOUBLE CHECK YES (circled) NO

Has a lot of natural ability. Everything seems to come easy for him. Doesn't exert himself but is a very likable kid.
Has to be a first rd. consideration for us.
Is the type that could come fast.
Raised O.F.P. (2) points from my first report of 5-11-87.

Have you talked with parents? Mother — Have you talked with prospect? Yes
Your maximum bonus recommendation: $150-175,000 — Estimated bonus needed to sign: Same
Scout Bob Harrison — Comm. Scout? — Date 5-28-87

Figure 1.5: Reproduction of Ken Griffey Jr.'s scouting report while attending Moeller High School in Cincinnati, Ohio (1987).

If the 21st century is considered to be the time when analytic thought first began to pervade front offices in sports teams, perhaps we can test if it improves the ability of teams to select players.

(a) (b) (c)

Figure 1.6: Three American football quarterbacks drafted in the late 1990s: Peyton Manning, Ryan Leaf, and Tom Brady.

Sources: (a) Rick Stewart / ALLSPORT via Getty Images; (b) Jonathan Daniel / Allsport via Getty Images; (c) Rick Stewart / Allsport via Getty Images

1.8 Questions for Consideration

1. Compare the draft position of NFL Hall of Famers who began their NFL careers in 2001 and later with those who began their careers in 2000 or prior. Can you see if there is any improvement in the ability of teams to select successful players in the age of analytics? You can find a list of players in the NFL Hall of Fame at `https://en.wikipedia.org/wiki/List_of_Pro_Football_Hall_of_Fame_inductees` and a list of their draft positions at `https://www.profootballhof.com/heroes-of-the-game/hall-of-famers-by-draft-round/`. Note that the NFL draft has varied in the number of players allowed to be selected over the years, but since 1994, it has been seven rounds and approximately 225–50 players selected.
2. Other than examining the players who are in the Hall of Fame, what other metrics might you use to see how successful the teams in the NFL have been in evaluating players?
3. Is there any one team that you think is better at evaluating prospective players than average? Or worse? To what might you attribute this perceived skill in player evaluation or lack thereof?
4. If you were building a model to predict a player's success in the NFL, what do you think should be the variables included in that model? Are there variables that might be popular but you would not include? Why?

Chapter 2

Introduction to R

> Computer programming is quickly becoming an essential career skill. Learning to code is a fantastic opportunity equalizer—if you're good at it, it can help you achieve your dreams.
>
> —US Senator Cory Booker
>
> Whether you want to uncover the secrets of the universe, or you just want to pursue a career in the 21st century, basic computer programming is an essential skill to learn.
>
> —Stephen Hawking

2.1 Background

If you are reading this book, you may have experimented a bit with R or at least heard of R, but you might not consider yourself an expert. That's OK. If you were, you may have chosen a different book! In this section, we will introduce you to the R programming language that you will use later in this text for performing the analytics you need to answer your sports-related questions.

In this book, we will reference R and also helper applications for R. If you get confused among all this terminology, please refer to the definitions below:

1. **R:** From the R Project's website, "R is a free software environment for statistical computing and graphics. It compiles and runs on a wide variety of UNIX platforms, Windows and MacOS."
2. **RStudio:** From the Posit (formerly RStudio) website, "RStudio is an integrated development environment (IDE) for R and Python. It includes a console, syntax-highlighting editor that supports direct code execution, and tools for plotting, history, debugging, and workspace management. RStudio is available in open source and commercial editions and runs on the desktop." RStudio works on Mac, Windows, and Linux.
3. **R Markdown:** Posit's flavor of the Markdown language.
   3.1. **Quarto:** From Posit's website, "Quarto is a multi-language, next generation version of R Markdown from Posit, with many new features and capabilities. Like R Markdown, Quarto uses knitr to execute R code, and is therefore able to render most existing Rmd files without modification."

The beauty of R is that it is almost infinitely expandable. While we take a particular approach to programming in R, you may find later that you are more comfortable with a different approach, or prefer other packages to the ones we use, or use something else that makes you more productive and confident. This is entirely OK! We do not want you to become a slave to the tool, and some of the techniques we show you and use ourselves you may not feel that you need at all.

2.2 R Software

R is the statistical programming language that we will use in this book. It's great for statistical programming because it was developed by statisticians! It is often referred to as the lingua franca of statistics. On the other hand, it's not great for general-purpose programming because it was developed by statisticians. It is based on a prior statistical programming language called S used in a commercial software called S-PLUS. R, however, is open source and freely available to anyone to download and install and use without restriction.

2.3 RStudio

Just having the R interpreter installed on your computer is probably not enough to make you an efficient and successful coder. An integrated development environment (IDE) helps coders work within the environment, see sample outputs, easily install add-ons, and manage projects and additional features to make coding better. You may have worked with IDEs in other languages such as Visual Studio, Jupyter, or Xcode. The most popular IDE for R, and the one we will use throughout this book, is RStudio, an open-source IDE maintained by Posit. It will work on your laptop, or you can access RStudio through a web browser if it is installed on a server. This book assumes you will be using it locally on your personal computer, but it is nice to know that if your datasets and/or processing needs become too large for your PC or Mac, the transfer to a server is quite easy.

2.4 Getting Your Machine Ready to Follow along with This Book

Computer Requirements

Whenever doing data analysis, the size of your data files and the complexity of your models and the amount of patience you have are all contributors to the amount of computing power you need. But you don't need the latest and greatest machine to do most of the work. For example, this book is being written in R Markdown on a four-year-old Apple MacBook Pro, and all of the data analysis for this textbook (not to mention the authors' research agendas) is done on this same class of computer. If your computer supports HDMI video output, it likely is modern enough to run the analyses we cover in this book.

All of the scripts we are using here are also largely platform agnostic. By that, we mean that the examples we show here were done on a Mac, but they all run the same and look almost identical if you are using Mac, Windows, or Linux. So don't feel like you need to go and buy a different computer to complete these examples.

Installing R

To write code or scripts in R, all you need is a text editor. However, for the scripts to actually run, we need to have R (and possibly R packages) on our machines so that it can interpret our scripts and give us the output that we expect. To obtain the latest version of R, go to the R Project's website at `https://r-project.org` (see figure 2.1) and read the "Getting Started" paragraph. Specifically, click on the "Download R" link and choose a server that is located near you. All of these servers are mirrors of the Comprehensive R Archive Network, or CRAN, which you can access through the menu on the left side of figure 2.1. You will see CRAN again later in this chapter as we work with different software packages that are available as add-ons to R.

Once you have selected a server near you, choose the version of R that works with your computer (PC/Mac/Linux), and then on the following page, choose the "Latest Release." This will download the R installation file onto your computer as a `.pkg` file (Mac) or an `.exe` file (Windows). If you are using Linux, there are several versions of R available depending on what distribution of Linux you have.

Figure 2.1: Screenshot of the R Project's home page for downloading R.

It is a bit more complicated than the install for Mac or Windows, but we are supposing that if you are running Linux on your machine, then you probably know what to do from here.

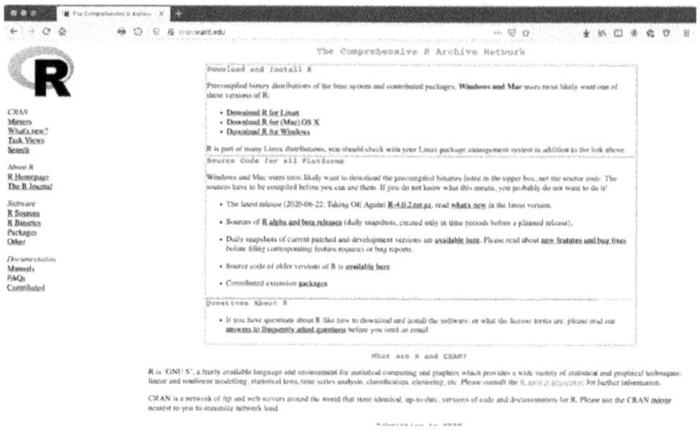

Figure 2.2: Screenshot of the Comprehensive R Archive Network.

Installing RStudio

The RStudio IDE that runs on top of R can be downloaded from the Posit website at `https://posit.co/download/rstudio-desktop/`. From here, the installation is straightforward, and in fact, you can find instructions on installing R there as well. Be aware that you are downloading the correct version (e.g., Mac or Windows) for your particular machine.

The authors are using RStudio for Mac, version 2023.06.1+524, but RStudio is designed to run the same anywhere. Of course, software continually changes, and we cannot ensure that on the day you read this text, RStudio or the accompanying screenshots will still look the same or even exist.

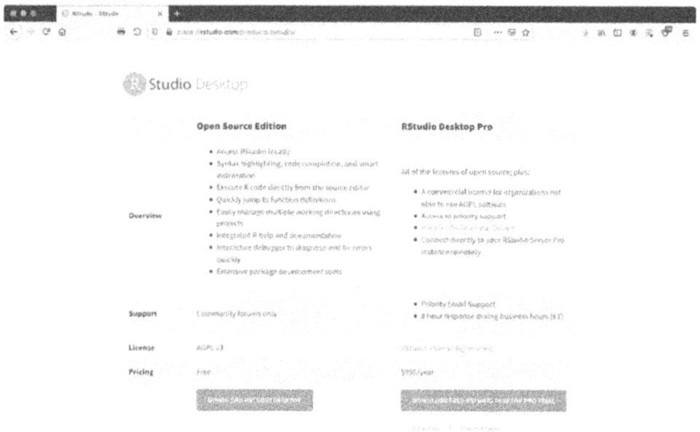

Figure 2.3: Screenshot of the RStudio desktop page.

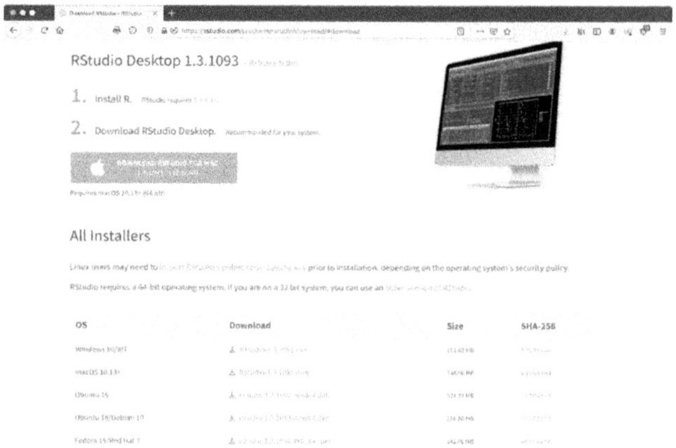

Figure 2.4: Screenshot of the RStudio download page.

Starting RStudio

Once you start RStudio on your computer, it looks quite plain, and you may be wondering what to do. Hopefully, figure 2.5 can help you out.

On the left side, you will see the console. Later, when you are writing scripts or working with datasets, you will be able to see those scripts and datasets in the upper-left corner above the console, and you can switch between them as they show up as different tabs. On the upper-right side, you will see the environment, which will show you the names of datasets and values of any objects that are currently open and available. You will also see tabs showing your history of commands, any connections you may have open, and the ability to view a tutorial if you install the `learnr` package. Below that, you will see another window with a list of files, views of any plots

Figure 2.5: Start-up windows for RStudio.

you may have created, a package manager for installing packages, access to R documentation, and more access to presentations.

You should see a greater-than sign and a cursor in the console window. The console window acts as the R interpreter, or REPL (read-evaluate-print-loop). For example, you can type 2 + 2 and it will tell you the answer is 4:

```
2 + 2
```

```
[1] 4
```

As a point of good practice, we recommend creating a new R Project (File → New Project) for each class, analysis project, or independent R session that you might use. An R Project is a collection of all related files and datasets used in that analysis. You can find more information related to R Projects in chapter 8 of the excellent book *R for Data Science* by Hadley Wickham, available at `https://r4ds.hadley.nz`.

Figure 2.6: Another view of RStudio as the authors were working on chapter 9.

2.5 R Packages

We will use the following R packages to complete the coding topics in this chapter. Normally when you write your R scripts, the first thing in the script at the top loads the packages (libraries) that you need for the script to run. In each following chapter, we will have a section at the beginning loading all of our packages as well as introducing any new packages that we have not used already in this book, but for this chapter, we list them here:

```
library(remotes) # used to install R packages from github repositories
library(ISAR) # the authors' package to accompany this textbook
library(Lahman) # a lot of baseball data
library(dplyr) # tidyverse package for manipulating data
library(ggplot2) # tidyverse package for data visualization
```

Installing R Packages

When we installed R and RStudio, we also installed the "base" R setup. One of the benefits of using R, particularly when working with sports data and analyses, is the rich ecosystem of user-contributed add-ons referred to as packages. To see a list of the packages installed on your system (in a library), click on the "Packages" tab in the bottom-right corner of RStudio. Some of the packages you may need to complete your projects (including the ones above!) may not yet be installed on your computer, and thus you will need to acquire and install them.

Many coders who write R packages choose to have them hosted on CRAN, and they can be installed on your system (or project) using the `install.packages()` function. Or more simply in RStudio, click on the Install option on the "Packages" tab, type the name of the package that you want to install, and RStudio will install it (using the `install.packages()` function), along with any other packages that your desired package needs to run as long as you leave the "Install Dependencies" box checked.

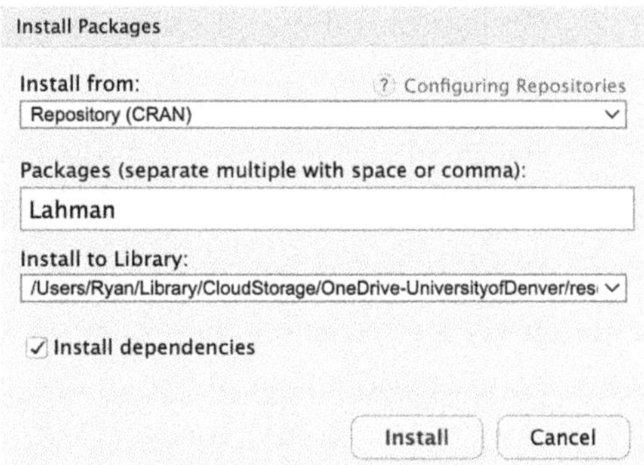

Figure 2.7: The package install window in RStudio. Note that this shows us installing the `Lahman` package.

Packages can be distributed to users in other ways. For example, packages that are hosted on GitHub are usually installed using the `install_github()` function within the `remotes` or `devtools` packages. There is similar functionality for projects that are hosted on other sites such as Bitbucket and GitLab.

While we could choose to make available every one of the thousands of packages that have been made available on every R script we write, we choose not to use them all every time because of resource constraints on our computers (and to relieve that constraint adds a constraint to our wallets!). Therefore, we choose the necessary packages for each R script that we write, and we make them available to our script through the `library()` function, generally placed at the beginning of our scripts. This tells R that for this script, we want to use a package that we have previously installed on our computer (in addition to base R) and to make its data and functions available for the script. For example, the following code (with comment lines that begin with the hashtag) will install the `remotes` package and then the `ballr` package from GitHub:

```
# Install the remotes package
install.packages("remotes")
# Load remotes to my library for use in this R session
library(remotes)
# Install the ballr package from github
install_github("rtelmore/ballr")
# Load ballr to my library for use in this R session
library(ballr)
# Alternatively, install without loading remotes to the
#  library, i.e., using the install_github function without
#  loading remotes.
remotes::install_github("rtelmore/ballr")
```

Note we illustrate using `install_github()` whether the `remotes` package is loaded or not. The latter `remotes::install_github()` is referred to as calling a function along with its associated namespace. You will see code online using functions with and without their namespace. We will adopt the practice of loading packages (and hence their functions) and drop the namespace when calling functions throughout the remainder of this textbook. Note that it is never wrong to use the package name first when calling a function, and in fact, it may be a good idea, since multiple packages could have the same function name and you want to be certain that R is choosing the function you expect from the package you expect. However, we have made certain in this textbook that there will be no function name conflicts, and for the sake of brevity, we drop the package name in the code that we write.

R Package for This Book: ISAR

We have provided an R package named `ISAR` to supplement this textbook. The R package contains data that are used throughout the text. The ISAR website located at `https://datacolorado.com/r/isar/` is the resource for up-to-date information related to the text (e.g., errata), the latest development version of the R package, and additional information. As discussed earlier, you can install the R package `ISAR` from CRAN or by using the `remotes` package for the latest developmental version:

```
install.packages("ISAR")
## or
remotes::install_github("rtelmore/ISAR")
```

Once you have installed this package, it can make a number of datasets available for your use after you make it available with the `library(ISAR)` command. You can see them by clicking in the "Environment" tab in the upper-right corner of RStudio, and then clicking on "Global Environment" and choosing `package:ISAR`. This will show you all the datasets currently available, as shown in figure 2.8.

2.6 Programming in R

R Style Guides

Because you will almost certainly never be working by yourself, it is a good practice to adopt a coding style and stick with it. This way, when you share code with others, import code, publish packages, or search for help on sites like `StackOverflow.com`, your code will be written and consumed in a way that others understand. Initially, a choice of coding style may not be obvious; however, it will improve your coding habits as you mature in this field. The two most commonly used style guides are the tidyverse style with its guide located at `https://style.tidyverse.org` and the Google style described at `https://google.github.io/styleguide/Rguide.html`. We will, for the most part, adopt the tidyverse guide in this book, and later in this chapter, we will cover our approach to implementing tidy principles into our code.

Figure 2.8: RStudio window pane showing the datasets that are available in the `ISAR` package.

The Console

As shown in the example in a previous section ("Starting RStudio"), we can type code into R and have it return immediate output to us. Or we can combine many lines of code into a script and run the entire script at once. While most of this book will focus on script writing, there are times when we may just need a quick answer to a question or to verify that something is working correctly in our environment. This is when we use the console.

For example, we can type math operations into the console and get immediate answers. We refer to this as using R as a calculator. R uses the standard +, -, *, /, and ^ operators for addition, subtraction, multiplication, division, and exponentiation, respectively. We will first learn how to use the console for a REPL style of programming before writing scripts for later use.

2.7 Data Storage in R

Numbers in R

As with most variables we will see later, R provides much flexibility in the way it handles numbers and variables. Numbers in R are treated as general numeric objects—that is, as a double precision floating point real number. There is no need to specify a particular number of decimal places for storage. However, there may be times when you will need to store a number specifically as an integer. To do that, use the `L` suffix when working with a number. For example, `x <- 1` creates an object `x` containing `1` as a floating point real number, whereas `x <- 1L` creates `x` with `1` stored as an integer. Continue reading for more about the `<-` assignment operator.

Variables and Assignment

We can create variables or, in general, objects in R using the standard notation of `variable_name <- value`. The `<-` symbol is often referred to as the R assignment operator. The equal sign, =, will also work, but we suggest using the `<-` notation, as it is used throughout much of the R programming world. It is shaped to look like a left-pointing arrow to denote that you are taking the expression on the right and assigning it to the variable or object on the left.

```
field_goals <- 2
4*field_goals
```

```
[1] 8
```

```
pts_by_field_goals <- field_goals*3
pts_by_field_goals
```

```
[1] 6
```

Objects and variables need to abide by the same naming conventions in most other languages. For example, they cannot begin with a number, cannot contain special characters like & or @, and cannot contain spaces.

Basic Objects

Many modern programming languages are object oriented. This means that they are designed to work with objects and inherit other objects' properties, encapsulate the object, or exhibit polymorphism. If you have programmed extensively in C++ or Java, you are likely familiar with these concepts; however, this section will not be a theoretical debate or explanation of object orientation. Just know that for here, most of the ways we import, manipulate, or export information will be as an object.

Basic objects in R can take on distinctive classes, or what you might think of as a data type in a database. We have discussed two of them, real numbers and integers, already. Others include logicals (yes/no, binary), character/strings, dates, and a host of others for specialized use cases. Except for integers, as described, objects do not need to be explicitly typed, although we will show how to do this later. R does its best to automatically create the appropriate type of object when we create it.

Examples of scalar (vectors of length 1) objects include the following:

```
pitch <- "ball"
pitch_count <- 115
```

Vectors

Vectors are sequences of scalars and are often used as the basis for data analysis. If you are familiar with arrays from other programming languages, think of a vector as a one-dimensional array. R uses the `c()` function to combine items into a structure, which in this case is a vector. Examples of different types of vectors are given in the following code chunk:

```
## vector of character Team Names for the NL West division
##  in baseball
nl_west_teams <- c("Arizona Diamondbacks",
                   "Colorado Rockies",
                   "Los Angeles Dodgers",
                   "San Diego Padres",
                   "San Francisco Giants")

## vector of numbers, specifically Nikola Jokic's FG PCT,
##  3PT FG PCT, and FT PCT during the 2023 NBA playoffs
jokic_shooting_slash <- c(0.58, 0.42, 0.84)
## vector of logicals, whether the Denver Broncos made the
##  playoffs or not from 2015-2022.
broncos_playoffs <- c(TRUE, FALSE, FALSE, FALSE, FALSE, FALSE, FALSE, FALSE)
```

R uses a 1-based indexing system, meaning that, for example, the first element in a vector is indexed by the number 1. You can access individual elements of a vector using the `[]` notation—for example,

```
broncos_playoffs[1:2]
```

```
[1]  TRUE FALSE
```

or

```
jokic_shooting_slash[c(1, 3)]
```

```
[1] 0.58 0.84
```

Again, vectors generally contain elements of the same data type. If you mix data types, you will get a vector of the least restrictive data type. Generally, that means characters, and you can't do math on characters! If you need to be sure you are working with a certain data type, use one of the `as` functions to be sure it is of that data type. Be careful when turning numerics into integers; `as.integer()` will truncate any value after the decimal rather than round it to the nearest integer. You can use `as.numeric()`, `as.logical()`, and `as.character()` to do similar conversions. Below is an example where the par rating on a hole in golf is obviously an integer, so we would want R to recognize that as we work with the data:

```
## Assign Par by hole at Cherry Hills Country Club to be an integer
cherry_hills_par <- c(4.0, 4.0, 4.0, 4.0, 5.0, 3.0, 4.0, 3.0, 4.0,
                      4.0, 5.0, 3.0, 4.0, 4.0, 3.0, 4.0, 5.0, 5.0)
as.integer(cherry_hills_par[18])
```

```
[1] 5
```

Matrices

A matrix in R is a two-dimensional array indexed by rows and columns. We use matrices when we want to look at information that might normally be in a table. The `matrix()` function creates a matrix for us as we specify the number of rows (`nrow`) and columns (`ncol`) for the matrix as well as how to read the data (`byrow`). See the example below, which records the scores for each of the four rounds for Collin Morikawa, Paul Casey, and Dustin Johnson at the 2020 PGA Championship at TPC Harding Park:

```
## 3x4 matrix and populate it with the scores for the three players
## for each of the four rounds.
pga_2020_top_three <- matrix(c(69, 69, 65, 64,
                               68, 67, 68, 66,
                               69, 67, 65, 68),
                             nrow = 3, ncol = 4, byrow = TRUE)
pga_2020_top_three #print the matrix to the console
```

```
     [,1] [,2] [,3] [,4]
[1,]   69   69   65   64
[2,]   68   67   68   66
[3,]   69   67   65   68
```

We can also use the `colnames()` and `rownames()` functions to name our rows and columns. This may help us remember what these elements represent:

```
colnames(pga_2020_top_three) <- c("round_1", "round_2",
                                  "round_3", "round_4")
rownames(pga_2020_top_three) <- c("Morikawa", "Casey", "Johnson")
pga_2020_top_three #print the matrix to the console
```

```
         round_1 round_2 round_3 round_4
Morikawa      69      69      65      64
Casey         68      67      68      66
Johnson       69      67      65      68
```

Matrices, similar to vectors, are 1-based. That is, the first column is referenced as column 1 and the first row as row 1. We mention this because several popular languages—for example, Python—are 0-based, where the first row and column are referenced by 0. Similar to the indexing in vectors, we can use the `[rows, columns]` notation to access specific elements in a matrix. If we want Casey's scores from the 2020 PGA Championship (second row) or just his third- and fourth-round scores, we could access both, as shown below:

```
pga_2020_top_three[2, ]
```

```
round_1 round_2 round_3 round_4
     68      67      68      66
```

```
pga_2020_top_three[2, c(3, 4)]
```

```
round_3 round_4
     68      66
```

Lists

If you want to create a vector-like structure that will hold (and retain) data items with different data types, you can use a list. We can create them using the `list()` function. Here is a list that holds information related to William "Wild Bill" Karlsson, a forward in the National Hockey League (NHL) who played on the 2023 Stanley Cup champion Vegas Golden Knights:

```
wild_bill <- list("William", "Karlsson", "1/8/1993", "Forward",
                  "Left", "Vegas Golden Knights", "Sweden", 14,
                  39, 53)
wild_bill
```

```
[[1]]
[1] "William"

[[2]]
[1] "Karlsson"

[[3]]
[1] "1/8/1993"

[[4]]
[1] "Forward"

[[5]]
[1] "Left"

[[6]]
[1] "Vegas Golden Knights"

[[7]]
[1] "Sweden"

[[8]]
[1] 14

[[9]]
[1] 39

[[10]]
[1] 53
```

Factors

Factors resemble vectors, but they are generally used for storing categorical variables. For example, the numerals 0 and 1 can be used to represent female and male categories, but those integers are not nearly as descriptive as the words *female* and *male*. As another example, consider downhill skiing, where races might be downhill, downhill combined, slalom, giant slalom, and the super-G. We can classify a skier's results by using the `factor()` function and, within it, the `c()` function to combine the various data items into the factor. Then we can use the `table()` function to print the number of times each level appears in our factor data:

```
races <- factor(c("downhill", "superg", "downhill", "gs", "slalom",
                  "slalom", "dcombined"))
races
```

```
[1] downhill  superg    downhill  gs        slalom    slalom    dcombined
Levels: dcombined downhill gs slalom superg
```

Data Frames

A commonly used data structure in R is referred to as a data frame. Data frames generally have observations indexed by rows, with measured variables as columns. Data frames are constructed using the `data.frame()` function:

```
df <- data.frame(balls = c(4, 2, 0, 1, 2, 1, 0, 3, 2),
                 strikes = c(0, 2, 2, 1, 1, 2, 1, 2, 2),
                 pitches = c(4, 5, 3, 2, 3, 3, 1, 6, 4))
df
```

```
  balls strikes pitches
1     4       0       4
2     2       2       5
3     0       2       3
4     1       1       2
5     2       1       3
6     1       2       3
7     0       1       1
8     3       2       6
9     2       2       4
```

You can access individual fields within a data frame using the `$` notation. Or, similar to a matrix as defined earlier, you can use 1-based referencing and use `[row, column]` notation. For example, the `pitches` variable or the first three pitches in the `pitches` variable (from `df`) can be accessed in the following manner:

```
df$pitches
```

```
[1] 4 5 3 2 3 3 1 6 4
```

```
df[1:3, "pitches"]
```

```
[1] 4 5 3
```

Missing Values

We would love to believe that our datasets are always going to be perfectly clean and complete, but in reality, we know that there will always be some data wrangling to do. One common challenge in sports analytics, and analytics in general, is handling missing data. When we try to read data and insert it into a list or a matrix and something is missing, R needs to tell us. It does this through two closely related but different notations: `NA` and `NaN`. `NA` is short for "Not Available," or purely missing, while `NaN` indicates that a value is attempting to be represented that is "Not a Number" (e.g., division by zero). `NA`s and `NaN`s will show up in your vectors and matrices as you read and manipulate data. This can be a sign that your calculations were erroneous, and doing more calculations on them may just muddle things more, so be careful! We will demonstrate how to deal with these when we come across the issues later in the text.

2.8 Coding Techniques

Loops

You would be hard-pressed to think of a programming language that does not provide a methodology for repeating a task a specified number of times. One of the more powerful features of computers is their ability to do the same repeated tasks multiple times much more quickly than humans without fatigue or random errors.

In R, the `for` loop will suffice for most of your looping needs. In an R script, `for` loops use an iterator variable and assign it successive values to execute the loop a stated number of times. These loops are then frequently used for iterating over the elements of an object (list, vector, etc.) and accomplishing the task on each of those elements.

```
for (i in 1:5){
  print(i)
}
```

```
[1] 1
[1] 2
[1] 3
[1] 4
[1] 5
```

In the above case, `i` is the iterator, and the loop runs five times, once for each value of `i` in the sequence defined using the notation `1:5`. The loop then prints the value of `i` to the console. This is a simple example to demonstrate the concept of looping in R. If we change the number 5 to the number 2,000, the loop would run 2,000 times and print the numbers 1–2,000 to the console. In general, the form of a `for` loop should have the following structure (note that this pseudocode chunk is not executable, and if it is sent to the console exactly as written, you will get an error):

```
for (i in something) {  # decide how many times you want the loop to execute
  some code             # the code that we want to repeat i times
}
```

Sometimes we do not know beforehand the number of iterations we want the loop to run. Suppose we want to add the preface "Andrew competed in the" to the factors in the skiing example given earlier. We could simply create a loop and use the `paste()` function—for example,

```
races <- factor(c("downhill", "superg", "downhill", "gs", "slalom",
                  "slalom", "dcombined"))
for (race in races) {
  statement <- paste("Andrew competed in the", race)
  print (statement)
}
```

```
[1] "Andrew competed in the downhill"
[1] "Andrew competed in the superg"
[1] "Andrew competed in the downhill"
[1] "Andrew competed in the gs"
[1] "Andrew competed in the slalom"
[1] "Andrew competed in the slalom"
[1] "Andrew competed in the dcombined"
```

Remember that everything you want the loop to execute must be enclosed in the curly braces.

Conditional Evaluation

Within R, sometimes we want our script to do one of two different things depending on the particular situation being evaluated. For example, if the last basket was scored by the home team, then cheer; otherwise, boo. This is what we call a conditional because we are evaluating a situation and executing a block of code or not depending on the results of that condition. The type of condition we just described above is called an if-then-else structure:

```
if( logical_condition ) {
 # execute code if the condition is true
}
 # Continue with the rest of the script
```

R then evaluates the condition within the script. If the condition is true, then the code within the braces will be executed. If the condition is false, the program continues following the closing curly brace. We can add alternative instructions with the `else` clause:

```
if(condition) {
  # execute code that runs when the condition is true
} else {
  # execute code that runs when the condition is false
}
  # Continue with the rest of the script
```

You can nest `if` statements by using the `else if` statement:

```
if ( condition_1 ) {
  # execute code that runs when condition1 is true
} else if ( condition_2 ) {
  # execute code that runs when condition1 is false but condition2 is true
} else {
  # execute code that runs when both condition1 and condition2 are false
}
  # Continue with the rest of the script
```

In addition to if-then-else constructs, R supports the evaluation of code while a condition is met using the `while` function. Be careful when using `while` logic, as you can easily get stuck in a never-ending loop! A simple `while` loop is provided next:

```
while (logical_condition) {
  # Only evaluate this code while the logical_condition is
  #  TRUE.
}
```

2.9 Exploratory Data Analysis in R

Descriptive Statistics

As you might expect, R includes many built-in functions to compute basic descriptive statistics. Several of these functions are described in table 2.1.

It is best to illustrate these functions using a real dataset. In this case, let us consider the `Batting` dataset in the `Lahman` package. The `Lahman` package was installed at the beginning of this chapter and provides a set of tables (as `data.frames`). The tables come from the Lahman Baseball Database for baseball statistics available at `http://seanlahman.com/download-baseball-database/`. Once the package is installed, load the package into your current R session using the `library()` function. In the following code chunk, notice the use of the `str()` function on `Batting` immediately after loading the `Lahman` package. The `str()` function is used to display the structure of objects in R. In this case, R shows us that the `Batting` object is a data frame and shows us the variables in the data frame. The == is a logical operator that evaluates to `TRUE` if the logic is satisfied and `FALSE` otherwise. In this case, we are selecting rows satisfying `COL` and `2022` in the `teamID` and `yearID` columns, respectively:

Table 2.1: Basic statistical functions in R

Function	Description
max(x)	Maximum value in object x
min(x)	Minimum value in object x
mean(x)	Mean value of object x
median(x)	Median value of object x
quantile(x, 0.25)	First quartile of object x
quantile(x, 0.75)	Third quartile of object x
IQR(x)	Interquartile range of object x
sd(x)	Standard deviation of object x
var(x)	Variance of object x
summary(x)	Summary measures of object x

```
str(Batting)
```

```
'data.frame':   112184 obs. of  22 variables:
 $ playerID: chr  "abercda01" "addybo01" "allisar01" "allisdo01". . .
 $ yearID  : int  1871 1871 1871 1871 1871 1871 1871 1871 1871 1871 . . .
 $ stint   : int  1 1 1 1 1 1 1 1 1 1 . . .
 $ teamID  : Factor w/ 149 levels "ALT","ANA","ARI",..: 136 111 39 142 111 56 111 24 56 24 . . .
```

```
 $ lgID    : Factor w/ 7 levels "AA","AL","FL",..: 4 4 4 4 4 4 4 4 4 4 . . .
 $ G       : int  1 25 29 27 25 12 1 31 1 18 . . .
 $ AB      : int  4 118 137 133 120 49 4 157 5 86 . . .
 $ R       : int  0 30 28 28 29 9 0 66 1 13 . . .
 $ H       : int  0 32 40 44 39 11 1 63 1 13 . . .
 $ X2B     : int  0 6 4 10 11 2 0 10 1 2 . . .
 $ X3B     : int  0 0 5 2 3 1 0 9 0 1 . . .
 $ HR      : int  0 0 0 2 0 0 0 0 0 0 . . .
 $ RBI     : int  0 13 19 27 16 5 2 34 1 11 . . .
 $ SB      : int  0 8 3 1 6 0 0 11 0 1 . . .
 $ CS      : int  0 1 1 1 2 1 0 6 0 0 . . .
 $ BB      : int  0 4 2 0 2 0 1 13 0 0 . . .
 $ SO      : int  0 0 5 2 1 1 0 1 0 0 . . .
 $ IBB     : int  NA NA NA NA NA NA NA NA NA NA . . .
 $ HBP     : int  NA NA NA NA NA NA NA NA NA NA . . .
 $ SH      : int  NA NA NA NA NA NA NA NA NA NA . . .
 $ SF      : int  NA NA NA NA NA NA NA NA NA NA . . .
 $ GIDP    : int  0 0 1 0 0 0 0 1 0 0 . . .
```

```
rox_batting <- subset(Batting, teamID == "COL" & yearID == 2022)
```

Given the importance of manipulating data within data frames, we return to the idea of indexing. Suppose we want to select the `AB` (at bats) column for baseball players, which is the seventh column of `Batting`. There are a number of ways that you can do this in base R—for example, `Batting$AB` or `Batting[, "AB"]`, or `Batting[, 7]`. The numeric indexing applies to both rows and columns. For example, if we want the first five observations from the second and fourth columns of `Batting`, we can access this information by issuing `Batting[1:5, c(2, 4)]`. Recall that `1:5` and `c(2, 4)` are just vectors of length five and two, respectively. For two generic vectors, `v1` and `v2`, we can get the `v1` rows and `v2` columns from `Batting` by `Batting[v1, v2]`. You can define indexing vectors in quite a few unique ways in order to extract data from a data frame.

We will examine the data for the Colorado Rockies in 2022. The last line in the previous code chunk creates a new data frame using the `subset()` function. The function is read as "Create a subset of the `Batting` data frame consisting of data for only the Colorado Rockies (`teamID == "COL"`) for the year 2022 (`yearID == 2022`)." You may want to know the dimensions of your data frame (or matrix) or the length of an arbitrary vector. The `dim()` function returns the number of rows and then columns, while `length()` returns the number of columns for a single row or the length of a vector in the data frame.

```
dim(rox_batting)
```

```
[1] 43 22
```

```
length(rox_batting)
```

```
[1] 22
```

As mentioned earlier, base R is equipped to handle basic (and advanced) statistical analysis and includes a host of built-in functions. The following code shows the mean, median, and standard deviation of home runs for the 2022 Colorado Rockies. We can obtain the IQR, variance, or a host of other statistical measures in a similar manner (see table 2.1):

```
mean(rox_batting$HR)
```

```
[1] 3.465116
```

```
median(rox_batting$HR)
```

```
[1] 0
```

```
sd(rox_batting$HR)
```

```
[1] 6.525951
```

Creating Plots for Data Exploration

Given the mean and median home runs hit by Rockies players in the 2022 season are 3.47 and 0, respectively, the distribution is likely to be skewed to the right, with quite a few players recording 0 home runs. You can use the `hist()` function to view the histogram of home runs (or whatever variable). Graphics within R are almost infinitely customizable. Here we create a histogram with custom x- and y-labels and a main title. Note that we use the = sign when assigning arguments within a function a particular value—for example, `main = "Home Runs by Player: 2022 Rockies"`. We do not use the arrow, or `<-`, assignment operator within functions for argument assignment. Figure 2.9 is an example of a base R figure:

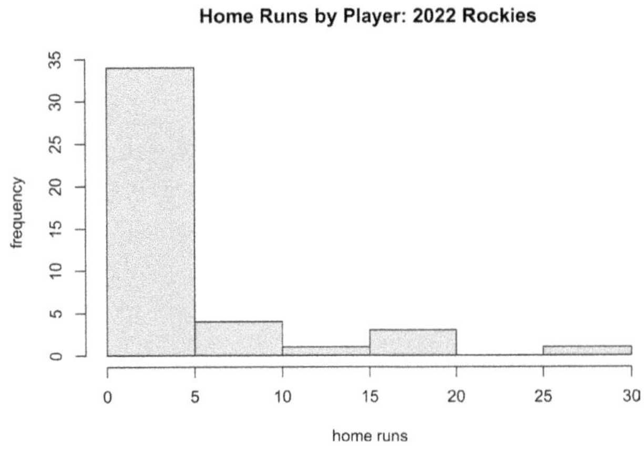

Figure 2.9: Home runs by player for the 2022 Colorado Rockies.

```
hist(rox_batting$HR,
     main = "Home Runs by Player: 2022 Rockies",
     xlab = "home runs",
     ylab = "frequency")
```

Suppose we are interested in the relationship between home runs (HR) and runs batted in (RBI) for the 2022 Rockies. The `plot()` function will display these data as a basic scatterplot. In this case, we illustrate a basic scatterplot, and we add axis labels in the same way as we did in the histogram. We denote the data to be used for the x- and y-axes, and we also use the `pch` argument to state how we want each point to appear in the scatterplot (16 is a solid black dot; feel free to experiment with others from 0 to 25). Finally, we show the least squares regression line of RBI regressed on HR and overlay it on the plot by using the `lm()` and `abline()` functions in figure 2.10. The `grid()` function adds grid lines to our plot:

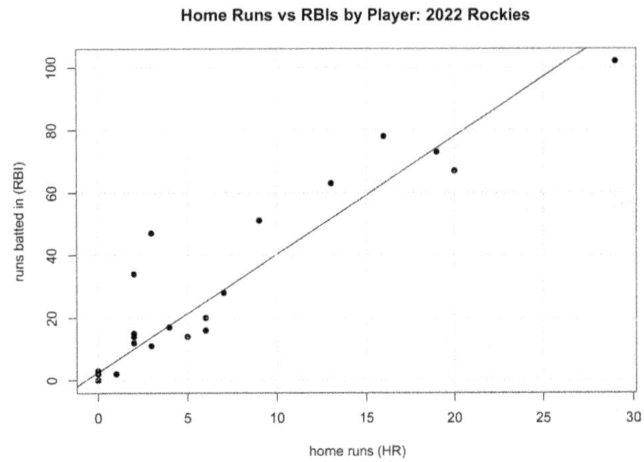

Figure 2.10: Scatterplot of home runs (x) and runs batted in (y) for the 2022 Colorado Rockies.

```
plot(x = rox_batting$HR,
     y = rox_batting$RBI,
     main = "Home Runs vs RBIs by Player: 2022 Rockies",
     xlab = "home runs (HR)",
     ylab = "runs batted in (RBI)",
     pch = 16)
rox_regression <- lm(RBI ~ HR, data = rox_batting)
abline(rox_regression, col = "black")
grid()
```

2.10 R Markdown or Quarto

When you write programs in R, hereafter referred to as scripts, you may wish to share your work with friends and colleagues. The more you document your code with comments, the easier it will be for others to understand what you did. Consider the following block of R code. We could simply save the following code as an R Script, perhaps titled `baseball.R`:

```
## The Lahman package includes several datasets including one
##  named Batting. We will subset the data to include only data
##  from the Colorado Rockies.
df <- subset(Batting, teamID == "COL")
## Compute the total number of home runs per year
df_by_year <- aggregate(HR ~ yearID, data = df, FUN = sum)
plot(x = df_by_year$yearID,
     y = df_by_year$HR,
     type = "b",
     pch = 16,
     xlab = "year",
     ylab = "home runs")
grid()
```

While you likely do not understand all of the syntax here yet, you probably notice that it is just a mash-up of R code and natural language comments. That was intentional and illustrates what `.R` files are all about: R code and comments. We used the comments to provide a narrative to the code. However, that's suboptimal at best when it comes to delivering a report along with code. Fortunately, there are better ways of weaving a story into a code-based file, and that's usually through the use of "literate programming" principles. That is, we can write a document (or slideshow, dashboard, etc.) while we program . . . and, really, does it get any better than that? Perhaps you have used something similar such as Jupyter notebooks with other languages like Python.

One of the ways to implement literate programming in R is to use a variant of Markdown called R Markdown. Note that the file extension for an R Markdown document is `.Rmd` as opposed to `.R` for a pure R file. One of the primary benefits (among many) to this style of programming is that your work should be fully reproducible at the completion of your project—that is, a colleague should be able to reproduce your analysis, your write-up, and even your formatting if you share the `.Rmd` file (and data) with them.

As mentioned, R Markdown is a variant of John Gruber's text markup language Markdown, adapted specifically for R projects by Posit. Quarto is Posit's next generation of R Markdown that you may also run across. As such, it helps to understand a little bit about Markdown. For now, know that R Markdown allows the user to keep all of your analysis code, output, and thoughts/comments/conclusions in a single document. In addition, R Markdown can be used to produce reports (Word, PDF, HTML, GitHub docs), dashboards, and slides, among other types of output—that is, R Markdown is extremely flexible as a tool.

2.11 R Markdown File

In order to create a new R Markdown document (`.Rmd` file), go to `File` → `New File` → `R Markdown` within RStudio. An example of this process is shown in figure 2.11.

A default template will show up in your text editing window within RStudio. The template is customizable for your own needs, but it requires a little hacking around to do this.

R Markdown Document Structure

R Markdown documents (in the most basic form) will have three parts:

1. YAML. Header information that includes title, author, date, and output type (e.g., PDF or HTML) at a minimum. An example YAML section might look like the following text:

```
---
title: "R Markdown, RStudio, and R"
author: "Ryan Elmore"
date: "29 Aug 2023"
output:
  pdf_document
toc: TRUE
---
```

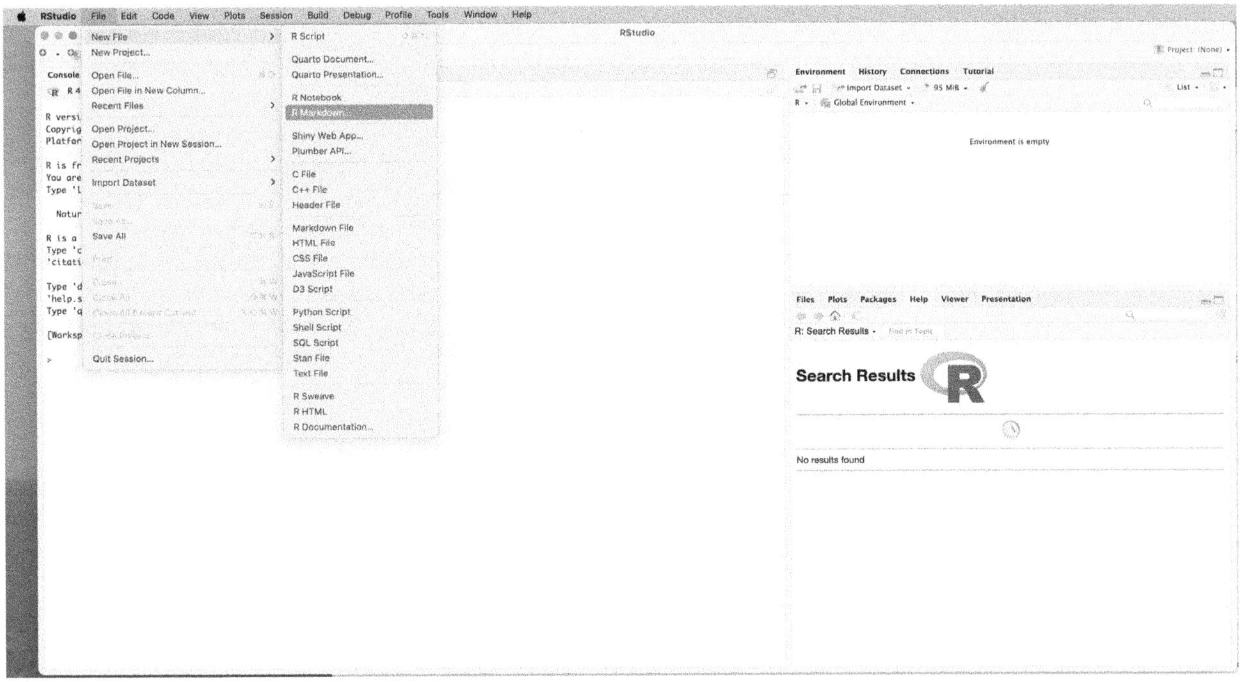

Figure 2.11: RStudio screenshot showing how to create a new R Markdown file.

2. Markdown code. Section headings, lists, comments, conclusions, and so on are all written in Markdown. There are many references online for learning about Markdown. We recommend as a reference *The Markdown Guide* found at `https://www.markdownguide.org`, but if you find a different one that you like better, by all means, use it!
3. R code. The actual R part of your `.Rmd` document is embedded within what we refer to as "code chunks." R can be placed inline—for example, `mean(rnorm(50))` would evaluate the mean of 50 random normal numbers within the document (e.g., 0.19). The other way to insert R into a document is to include a stand-alone chunk by using the three-backticks method, such as the following:

````
```{r, eval = FALSE}
## R CODE GOES HERE
```
````

In the simple example above, we used the `eval = FALSE` argument so that the code would actually appear when we printed this textbook. Because we are writing this using R Markdown, the code would have tried to run (and as a result, left only a blank space, since there is nothing to execute) instead of printing the code block so that we could show it to you.

The only actual R code in that previous text chunk is contained on the lines between the three backticks, or the text `## R CODE GOES HERE`. We usually organize `.Rmd` documents in the following order:

1. YAML heading
2. R code chunk at the top of the document to load necessary packages
3. Code chunk to import any necessary data
4. Text and R code chunks throughout the rest of the document as necessary

Recently, a newer literate programming language called Quarto has appeared. Quarto offers more flexibility and customization than R Markdown and is probably worth diving straight into if you are not familiar with either. The basic mechanics are similar to an R Markdown file described above. We include a mention of Quarto here, as you might encounter `.qmd` file types on your R journey.

2.12 Introduction to the Tidyverse

One of the benefits of using R is the vast number of user-contributed packages for specialized data analyses. This leads to many different software design choices made by the various authors, and as a result, programmatic principles from package to package may be wildly divergent. An attempt to unify the disparate nature of design standards for R package development resulted in what is now known as the tidyverse. As mentioned on the tidyverse website at `https://www.tidyverse.org`, "The tidyverse is an opinionated collection of R packages designed for data science. All packages share an underlying design philosophy, grammar, and data structures." The remainder of this textbook will rely on the bits and pieces from the tidyverse to guide the R programming. You can load the entire catalog of R packages that make up the tidyverse using `library(tidyverse)` or just load certain packages as you go—for example, `library(dplyr)`—as we do in this chapter. We will generally adopt the latter style and only load packages as necessary.

It is worth noting that there is immense merit in using and learning the base R language. We believe, however, that the unified syntax presented in the tidyverse allows us to focus on the data wrangling, analysis, and output rather than peculiar programming requirements in base R. If by some chance you are already familiar with base R, you can easily find online guides for transitioning from base R into the tidyverse style. We like the recommendations provided by Hadley Wickham in chapter 27 of his *R for Data Science* book, available at `https://r4ds.hadley.nz`.

Data Manipulation

Earlier in this chapter, we discussed how to work with data in data frames. For the rest of this chapter, we will be working with data frames, largely from the Lahman Baseball Database. As mentioned previously, Sean Lahman created a valuable resource of historic baseball data. We will refer back to the code given at the beginning of this chapter and describe the `dplyr` syntax using the `Batting` table in Lahman.

A key difference in using the tidyverse instead of base R is the way that we assign data to R objects. Instead of using the `data.frame` object as in base R, the tidyverse relies heavily on the `tibble` object. A tibble is a more general data structure and is technically a superclass of the `data.frame`. Whereas a data frame typically includes data such as numeric or character-valued vectors as columns, a tibble can include almost any object as elements in its columns—for instance, functions or the output of functions. As an example, suppose we want to create an object named `df` using the `Batting` data as a tibble. The output of `str()` executed on `df` shows that this object is a tibble with 112,184 rows and 22 columns. It also shows us the values of the first few rows for each column to help us with basic data exploration. Note also that the resulting object is also a data frame:

```
df <- tibble(Batting)
str(df)
```

```
tibble [112,184 × 22] (S3: tbl_df/tbl/data.frame)
 $ playerID: chr [1:112184] "abercda01" "addybo01" "allisar01" "allisdo01". . .
 $ yearID  : int [1:112184] 1871 1871 1871 1871 1871 1871 1871 1871 1871 1871 . . .
 $ stint   : int [1:112184] 1 1 1 1 1 1 1 1 1 1 . . .
 $ teamID  : Factor w/ 149 levels "ALT","ANA","ARI",..: 136 111 39 142 111 56 111 24 56 24 . . .
 $ lgID    : Factor w/ 7 levels "AA","AL","FL",..: 4 4 4 4 4 4 4 4 4 4 . . .
 $ G       : int [1:112184] 1 25 29 27 25 12 1 31 1 18 . . .
 $ AB      : int [1:112184] 4 118 137 133 120 49 4 157 5 86 . . .
 $ R       : int [1:112184] 0 30 28 28 29 9 0 66 1 13 . . .
 $ H       : int [1:112184] 0 32 40 44 39 11 1 63 1 13 . . .
 $ X2B     : int [1:112184] 0 6 4 10 11 2 0 10 1 2 . . .
 $ X3B     : int [1:112184] 0 0 5 2 3 1 0 9 0 1 . . .
 $ HR      : int [1:112184] 0 0 0 2 0 0 0 0 0 0 . . .
 $ RBI     : int [1:112184] 0 13 19 27 16 5 2 34 1 11 . . .
 $ SB      : int [1:112184] 0 8 3 1 6 0 0 11 0 1 . . .
 $ CS      : int [1:112184] 0 1 1 1 2 1 0 6 0 0 . . .
 $ BB      : int [1:112184] 0 4 2 0 2 0 1 13 0 0 . . .
```

```
$ SO     : int [1:112184] 0 0 5 2 1 1 0 1 0 0 . . .
$ IBB    : int [1:112184] NA NA NA NA NA NA NA NA NA NA . . .
$ HBP    : int [1:112184] NA NA NA NA NA NA NA NA NA NA . . .
$ SH     : int [1:112184] NA NA NA NA NA NA NA NA NA NA . . .
$ SF     : int [1:112184] NA NA NA NA NA NA NA NA NA NA . . .
$ GIDP   : int [1:112184] 0 0 1 0 0 0 0 1 0 0 . . .
```

One of the key pieces of the tidyverse, and one that we use regularly, is the `dplyr` package. Per the tidyverse website, the `dplyr` package provides a "grammar of data manipulation, providing a consistent set of verbs that help you solve the most common data manipulation challenges." The main verbs are `mutate()` for defining new columns, `select()` for selecting columns, `filter()` for row-wise subsetting, `summarize()` for returning summary statistics (often in the aggregate), and `arrange()` for organizing the result of the data manipulation.

The following code chunk is an example of using these verbs, or functions, to perform a common data manipulation task. The first line in the code chunk redefines the `Batting` object (initially a data frame) as a tibble and names it `df`. The output of that operation is then piped (`|>`) into the next line of code—in this case, a `filter()` from `dplyr`—to restrict our attention to particular teams (`filter`). That is, we are filtering out every row except for the rows containing the Colorado Rockies and Florida/Miami Marlins data (`filter` is a row-wise operation). We then pipe that output into the `dplyr` `mutate()` function to change `teamID` into a character-valued variable and to unify the `teamID` for Miami. Next, we group the tibble by `year` and `team` and then `summarize()` the data by calculating the sum of the home runs per year for both the Colorado Rockies and the Florida/Miami Marlins. That summarized variable is defined as `team_hr`:

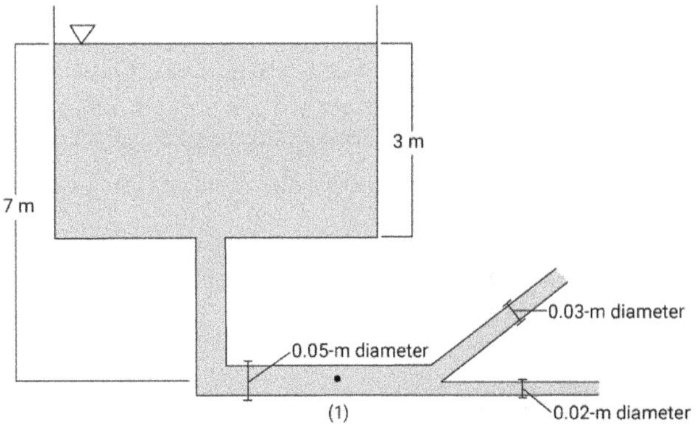

Figure 2.12: An illustration of plumbing, or pipes.

```
df <- tibble(Batting) |> ## Assign Batting to df as a tibble
  filter(teamID %in% c("COL", "MIA", "FLO")) |>
  mutate(teamID = as.character(teamID), # Change teamID to a string
         teamID = ifelse(teamID == "FLO", "MIA", teamID)) |> # FLO to MIA
  group_by(teamID, yearID) |> ## Group by team and year
  summarize(team_hr = sum(HR)) ## sum total HR
head(df)
```

```
# A tibble: 6 × 3
# Groups:   teamID [1]
  teamID yearID team_hr
  <chr>   <int>   <int>
1 COL      1993     142
2 COL      1994     125
3 COL      1995     200
4 COL      1996     221
5 COL      1997     239
6 COL      1998     183
```

For reasons that will become more apparent throughout the text, `dplyr` and other packages in the tidyverse rely heavily on the pipe operator, `|>`. Think of the pipe as a way of telling the script to *then* do something, as if it stands for the word *then*. The pipe is used to direct output from the left-hand side of the pipe into the first argument on the right-hand side. A metaphor would be the reservoir in your town, which goes through a water main pipe along the highway, which then goes into a smaller pipe on your street, which then goes to a smaller pipe at your curb, and so on until you get the water that you want at your kitchen faucet. Pipes in R work in a similar manner.

The `%in%` construct is a vectorized logical operator. So after we have created `df`, we need to filter it by `teamID`. Since we have multiple values for `teamID` that we want to include in our filtered results, we use the `filter()` function and tell it to only include `teamID` that was `%in%` the vector that followed. In this case, only return Colorado (COL) and Miami (MIA), but since the Miami Marlins were called the Florida Marlins when they first began play in 1993, we need to include Florida (FLO) as well or we will only return more recent results for that franchise.

You may also notice the `ifelse()` function. In section 2.6, we introduced how R evaluates conditional statements using the if-then-else (or `else if`) connotation. Here we use the `ifelse()` function, which is very similar to how the =IF function works in Excel. In this code, we are telling the script that if `teamID` is equal to FLO, then mutate it to MIA; otherwise, leave it as it is.

The verb functions offered by `dplyr` give us a "grammar" for performing these same operations. In our opinion, this makes our code much more readable and digestible for an R novice.

Joining Datasets

Both base R and the tidyverse offer an array of functions to join data from different tables in ways that might be familiar to you, particularly if you know SQL or have some database experience. For example, the `dplyr` package offers `left_join()`, `right_join()`, and `inner_join()`, among other functions, and base R generally relies on its `merge()` function. Here we provide an example that shows joining two datasets from the `Lahman` package. First, consider the `AllstarFull` object and note that player first and last names are not present in the dataset:

```
names(AllstarFull)
```

```
[1] "playerID"     "yearID"       "gameNum"      "gameID"       "teamID"
[6] "lgID"         "GP"           "startingPos"
```

Those fields are given in the `People` object, however. If we would like the first and last names (along with additional information) of the 2022 Major League Baseball All-Stars, we can join the two datasets together using the following pipes:

```
mlb_all_stars_2022 <- AllstarFull |>
  filter(yearID == 2022) |>
  left_join(People, by = "playerID") |>
  select(nameFirst, nameLast, startingPos, teamID, lgID, bats, throws)
head(mlb_all_stars_2022)
```

```
  nameFirst    nameLast startingPos teamID lgID bats throws
1     Shane McClanahan           1    TBA   AL    L      L
2 Alejandro        Kirk           2    TOR   AL    R      R
3  Vladimir    Guerrero           3    TOR   AL    R      R
4    Andres     Gimenez           4    CLE   AL    L      R
5    Rafael      Devers           5    BOS   AL    L      R
6       Tim    Anderson           6    CHA   AL    R      R
```

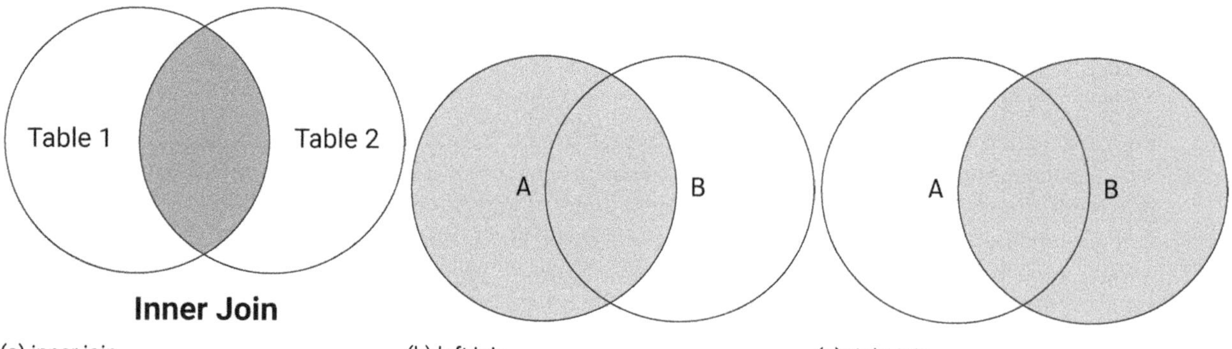

(a) inner join (b) left join (c) right join

Figure 2.13: Examples of three types of joins available in the `dplyr` package.

Creating Figures Using ggplot()

Previously, we used the plot() function in R. This functionality is included in the base R packages. From now on, we will use the ggplot() function, part of the ggplot2 package and the tidyverse. The ggplot() is built with the idea of Leland Wilkinson's "grammar of graphics" in mind and, thus, is similar to the way that dplyr provides a grammar of data manipulation.

In particular, ggplot() relies on layers in constructing figures. You first define a plot object by setting up the data to be plotted. Next, you can systematically apply layers to the object in order to display the data. For example, you can apply a layer of points or lines using geom_point() or geom_line() if you are interested in a scatterplot with lines connecting the points. Finally, the grammar allows for the easy customization of colors, groups, and so on by specifying different aesthetics.

As an example of using ggplot2, let's plot the data that we summarized previously by initially defining a plot object p. We will illustrate the layering effect with a series of figures as each layer is added. In doing this, we declare that ggplot() will use the tibble df for its data, and aesthetics (aes) include yearID and team_hr as the x- and y-variables, respectively. We then add layers to that object p by using the +. Here, we want to show each data point using a geom_point() and connect them using a geom_line(). Since we want to show a side-by-side comparison of the Rockies and the Marlins, we will use a facet_grid with (~ teamID) columns for each value of teamID and use labs() to create labels for the x- and y-axes, a title for the graph, and a subtitle for the graph and force it to output in black and white:

```
p <- ggplot(data = df, aes(x = yearID, y = team_hr, col = teamID))

p + geom_point() +
  scale_color_brewer(palette = "Set1") +
  labs(x = "Year",
       y = "Home Runs",
       title = "Home Runs by Year",
       subtitle = "Colorado Rockies and Miami Marlins"
  ) +
  theme_bw()
```

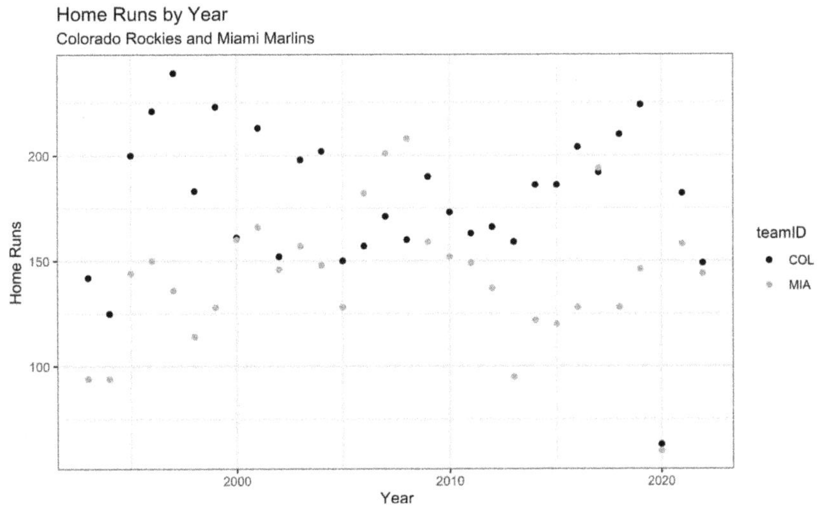

Figure 2.14: A basic ggplot using only the geom_point layer.

```
p <- ggplot(data = df, aes(x = yearID, y = team_hr, col = teamID))

p + geom_point() +
  geom_line() +
  scale_color_brewer(palette = "Set1") +
```

```
  labs(x = "Year",
       y = "Home Runs",
       title = "Home Runs by Year",
       subtitle = "Colorado Rockies and Miami Marlins"
  ) +
  theme_bw()
```

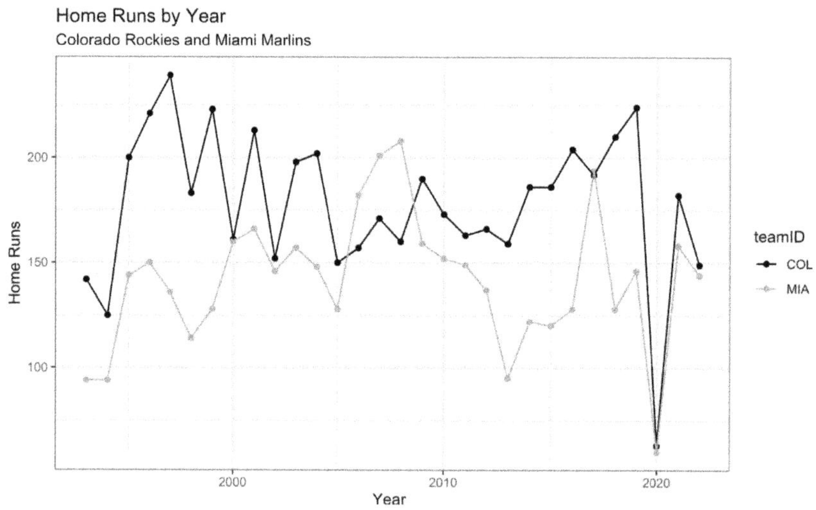

Figure 2.15: A `ggplot` with both points (`geom_point`) and lines (`geom_line`) layers.

```
p <- ggplot(data = df, aes(x = yearID, y = team_hr))

p + geom_point() +
  geom_line() +
  facet_grid(~ teamID) +
  labs(x = "Year",
       y = "Home Runs",
       title = "Home Runs by Year",
       subtitle = "Colorado Rockies and Miami Marlins"
  ) +
  theme_bw()
```

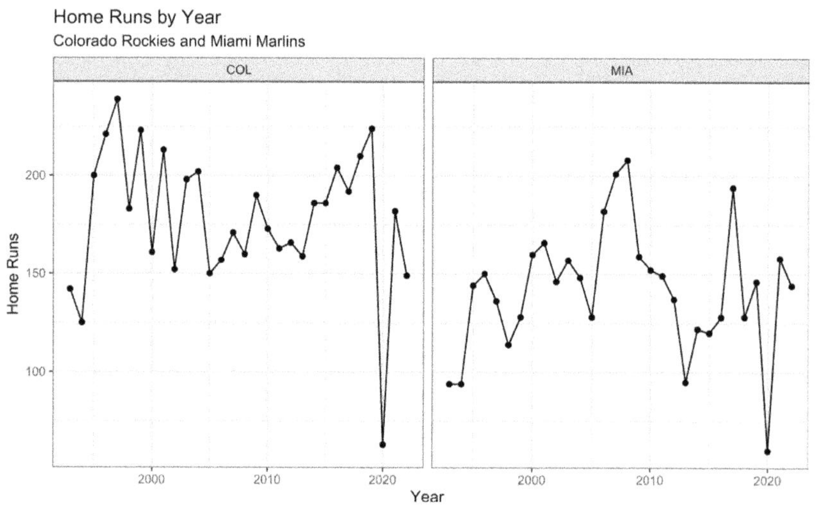

Figure 2.16: A `ggplot` with both points (`geom_point`) and lines (`geom_line`) layers, and we show individual panes, or facets (`facet_grid`), for each team.

2.13 Getting Help

If you need help with a particular function—for example, the `mean()` function—you can call the `help()` or ? functions with "mean" as their argument. In either case, the R documentation file associated with the function of interest is displayed in the "Help" window within RStudio. On the other hand, you may just need help with a particular topic such as "plotting." If this is the case, you can pass the "plotting" string to the `help.search()` function to search all of R's documentation for topics and/or functions related to plotting as shown below. You can also search websites such as Stack Overflow using the R tag for assistance with R questions.

```
help(mean)
?(mean)
help.search("plotting")
```

Debugging Your Code

Source: istockphoto / PeskyMonkey

Like in all programming languages, eventually, you are going to make mistakes. These mistakes could be syntax errors, where the interpreter cannot understand your code, or logic errors, where your code runs but gives you output that is incorrect for what you are hoping to analyze. Unfortunately, this is one of the most frustrating parts of coding, as finding the source of these errors and fixing them is not always obvious. We will walk you through several ways you may begin to debug your code.

If your R code results in your code not running and an error message in red text appearing in the console, it is likely that you are not the first person to encounter this error. Figure 2.17 shows an error message that is fairly straightforward to fix. However, many others may be somewhat confusing. Our recommendation for handling errors that do not have an obvious fix is to begin by searching the Internet for that error message. There is a reasonable chance that you will be able to find how others fixed this error, particularly on sites like `StackOverflow.com`. In your search term, include as much detail as you can from the error message, but to get the best match, you might refrain from including variable names specific to your code.

If you can identify where the error is in your code from the error messages, go to that section and start there. R might not tell you exactly where your error is occurring, because it will try to run through as many lines of code as it can before finally refusing to run. For example, you may have forgotten a quotation mark in line 20, but the interpreter doesn't know that and will try to run through your code as long as it can until it is finally too confused to run anymore, and that might not be until down in line 26.

Once you've found the error but see that the fix is not obvious, you may try several strategies to isolate the error. This is often a process of trial and error and may be quite frustrating, but debugging is partly detective work, and you may have to begin eliminating possibilities. One way to do this is to try to rewrite the section of code where you are getting errors and then introduce bits of complexity line by line. For example, we all know that `print("hello world")` will easily run no matter what. We may not need to get to that level of simplicity, but perhaps you see where we are going with this strategy. Instead of deleting troublesome sections of code, try commenting out lines by using the hashtag (#) and then run your code to see if you are getting the expected results. Then you can re-add blocks of code easily rather than trying to remember what you had there previously.

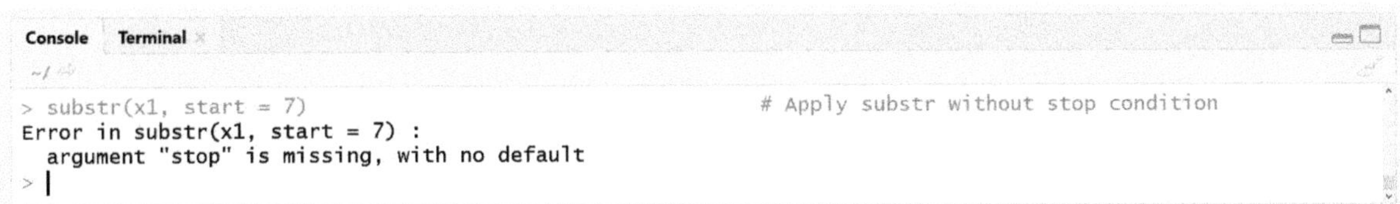

Figure 2.17: An example error message printed to the console window in RStudio.

As you add lines of code, you might use `print()` to print values to the console, and that way, you can check to see if they match what you expect. You can use `head()` to see if the data frame you are expecting is really what the R interpreter is examining. You may have other strategies that you identify as you become more proficient at coding.

Moreover, on the occasions where your instructor allows this, don't be afraid to ask one of your classmates! It's possible that they have encountered similar errors and know how to fix them.

2.14 Conclusion

R is so powerful that we could not begin to cover all of its features in a book of this length, much less a single chapter of that book. We provide you here with the basics of R to give you enough to get started and build some confidence with R. We know that for many of you, R is scary, and staring at a blinking cursor trying to remember what line of code to write is a bit daunting. We try to alleviate some of that fear here and instead open your eyes to the power built into R. We will introduce many new functions, libraries, and outputs in the following chapters where we tackle different problems. This chapter, however, can serve as a reference for all the basics going forward.

While it is certainly possible to write code any way you want that will give you a correct answer, we also introduced a set of R frameworks to help standardize your approach to writing code, retrieving data, massaging data, and generating output. Using the tidyverse will help you in working with other analysts, integrating code segments between projects, and setting up a methodology for approaching new projects. It will also help you benefit from others' work as new features and functions are added to the tidyverse.

2.15 Lab: Introduction to R with Lahman Data

Throughout this text, we will include follow-along labs at the end of each chapter. This will allow you to go through a problem from beginning to end, first as we describe our strategy and then as we turn it into R code to get the desired answers. It gives you a chance to practice the material covered in this chapter (and most likely, previous chapters).

In this lab, we will explore the sport of baseball through data from the Lahman database. Recall that we use the database by installing the R package of the same name. We will focus on the two tables related to individual hitting (`Batting`) and pitching (`Pitching`) statistics. Choose at least two teams—for example, the Colorado Rockies and the New York Yankees. Note that the `teamID` for these two teams are "COL" and "NYA," respectively.

1. Subset the `Pitching` table in the `Lahman` package to include data from only those two teams. How many rows are contained in the original `Pitching` data frame as well as the subsetted data?
2. Compute the total number of wins for each team in the 2022 season. Check your answer against `baseball-reference.com` or your favorite resource for baseball information. Hint: Base R might use `help(aggregate)`.
3. Plot the total number of wins by year for each team on the same plot. Use only data from 1990 to the present.

Let us now shift gears to the `Batting` data available in the `Lahman` package. Slugging percentage (SLG) is a baseball metric that computes a player's total bases per at bat. Total bases is defined as

$$TB = singles + 2 \times doubles + 3 \times triples + 4 \times (home\ runs)$$

4. Create two new vectors for total bases (TB) and slugging percentage (SLG) for the two teams chosen above. Note that some players will have `NaN` due to zero `AB`s.
5. Plot the average `SLG` for one of your teams from 1990 through 2022.
6. Note that question 5 is asking for the average `SLG` and not the team `SLG`. So now, plot the team `SLG` by year since 1990.

2.16 Exercises

1. What is the function in base R for constructing a histogram?
2. List at least two places where R packages are hosted. How can you install packages into your R library from these two sources?
3. Install and load the `ISAR` R package. The following questions are related to the `masters` data that are visible when you load `ISAR` into your library. The `masters` data are related to the scoring during the 2019 Masters Tournament.
4. How many rows and columns are in the `masters` dataset?
5. Compute a histogram of total scores.
6. Customize the histogram given in the previous question. (a) Add "total" to the x-label. (b) Add an appropriate title. (c) Add a vertical dashed line at the mean value of total scores.
7. Report the players who recorded the lowest score in each round (rounds 1–4).

Chapter 3

Web Scraping

> If we have data, let's look at data. If all we have are opinions, let's go with mine.
>
> —Jim Barksdale
>
> You can have data without information, but you cannot have information without data.
>
> —Daniel Keys Moran
>
> In God We Trust; All Others Bring Data.
>
> —Unknown

3.1 R Packages

To complete the work in this chapter, we will use some packages that we introduced in the previous chapter:

```
library(dplyr)
library(ggplot2)
```

In addition to the above R packages, we will also introduce a few new packages to help us with web scraping:

```
library(xml2) # allows us to interact with web pages by parsing XML
library(rvest) # helps us to harvest (scrape) data from web pages
library(janitor) # a set of tools to examine and clean dirty data
```

3.2 Getting Sports Data

In the previous chapter, we discussed how to code in R and then how to write our scripts using the tidyverse. We even looked at the `Lahman` package, which has a horde of historical data about baseball. Of course, there are many other datasets and sources available for sports analytics, and we examine where and how to obtain them.

One reason that sports analytics has become so popular in the 21st century is the sheer volume of data about them that are collected and published. Data are readily available about players, teams, coaches, conferences, leagues, arenas, plays, and a myriad of other sport-specific characteristics. When combined with the publication and distribution ease of the Internet, these data are often readily available to anyone perusing the websites of sports-related entities.

Just because we can see data on a web page, however, does not mean that they are available in a format that we can use for analysis in R or other programs. HyperText Markup Language (HTML), the language in which web pages are produced, does not integrate natively with most other statistical analysis programs. Trying to save a web page and then open it in Excel, or even copying and pasting the data elements, tends to be unreliable at best. So if we wish to take advantage of these vast data resources, we need to develop a more comprehensive strategy to get those data into a format we can use.

One way we could take web data and put them into files for analysis in R would be to manually type in the data that we see on the screen into a data file. This will work, but it is tedious, time consuming, and prone to transcription error, so we would prefer not to use this method. This chapter is about automating the process of pulling the data items we wish to collect from a web page or series of web pages. We call this process web scraping.

A Caveat

Web pages might change! Given the fact that they change (in some cases, often), the code that is presented in this chapter for scraping a website might produce different results over time. The authors tested this code in December 2023.

3.3 Web Scraping and Ethics

Before we go any further, we must mention that the practice of web scraping can be controversial. Some websites welcome the practice, others turn a blind eye, and yet others even put in active countermeasures to try to prohibit someone from scraping the data for use off of the hosting website. We suggest that if you are scraping data from a website, you should at least try to find out if scraping is actively discouraged on the site and, if so, avoid scraping on that property.

A relatively simple way to check the rules on scraping a particular website is to examine its affinity toward web scrapers and automated crawling of the site. It will list its preferences in a file in its root folder called robots.txt. These are instructions from the website to automated programs, like web crawlers for search engines, that tell these programs what directories and files it gives its permission to be downloaded and indexed and which ones it does not want to be indexed through the use of the disallow nomenclature. Here are the contents of the robots.txt file from NFL.com in June 2023 (see `https://www.nfl.com/robots.txt`):

```
User-agent: *
Disallow: /_ctv/
Disallow: /_fantasy-app/
Disallow: /_libraries/
Disallow: /_mobile-app/
Disallow: /_mobileview/
Disallow: /_phs/
Disallow: /_sponsors/
Disallow: /account/
Disallow: /nfl-films-beta/
Disallow: /search/
Sitemap: https://www.nfl.com/sitemap-index.xml

User-agent: Mediapartners-Google
Disallow: /stats/player-stats/*
```

As an example, suppose we want to scrape the Hockey Reference website. It is good practice, and indeed very much encouraged, to first examine their robots.txt file, located at `https://www.hockey-reference.com/robots.txt`. If you are unable to decipher the contents of this file and what each line represents, you could always follow up with an email to the site's host, which is exactly what we did for the websites presented in this textbook.

3.4 Web Document Structure

Before we can understand how to get the data out of a web page, we need to understand the structure of a web page. Web pages are HTML documents, which are somewhat akin to Markdown documents in that they are written as plain text with instructions for displaying the text within the documents. Each chunk of text is called a node, and each node is encapsulated within a pair of tags, which are represented between < and > characters. So that is to say that `<sample>` and `</sample>` are the tags that mark the beginning and ending of a node.

There are many different tags, such as <p> for a paragraph, <b> for bold, `<i>` for italic, and `<u>` for underline. However, we need to concern ourselves especially with the tags that are used to display data tables, as the data we seek will most often be stored in a table. Table 3.1 presents a list of common table-related tags and descriptions.

Tables have rows, and the rows have cells. The cells can be either header cells or data cells. A sample table from `https://w3schools.com` that we might scrape could look like the following:

```
<table style="width:100%">
  <tr>
    <th>Firstname</th>
    <th>Lastname</th>
    <th>Age</th>
  </tr>
  <tr>
    <td>Jill</td>
    <td>Smith</td>
    <td>50</td>
  </tr>
  <tr>
    <td>Eve</td>
    <td>Jackson</td>
    <td>94</td>
  </tr>
</table>
```

Table 3.1: Commonly used table-related tags in HTML documents

Tag	Description
<table>	Defines a table
<caption>	Defines a table caption
<th>	Defines a header cell in a table
<tr>	Defines a row in a table
<td>	Defines a data cell in a table
<thead>	Groups the header content in a table
<tbody>	Groups the body content in a table
<tfoot>	Groups the footer content in a table
<col>	Specifies column properties for each column within a <colgroup> element
<colgroup>	Specifies a group of one or more columns in a table for formatting

Note that this table has the attribute "style," and it is set to "width:100%." This means that the table will by default expand or contract to exactly fill the screen of the viewer. Many other attributes are available for `<table>` and other tags as well.

3.5 Web Scraping in R

As mentioned in section 3.1, we will be using the `rvest()` package (like "harvest") to implement web scraping techniques. If you try to run code and get error messages about a particular function not being found, be sure that you have all the packages mentioned in section 3.1 both installed in RStudio and made available to the script by having their boxes checked in the "Packages" tab in RStudio's lower-right corner. If it is not installed, click on the "Install" box and type in the name of the package. Then select it from the list and click on "Install." Once it is installed, check the box in the list of the installed packages to make it available to your script. Then in the top of your script when you are declaring the packages that you need to make your script work, add a line for `rvest` along with ones for `dplyr()` and `ggplot()`.

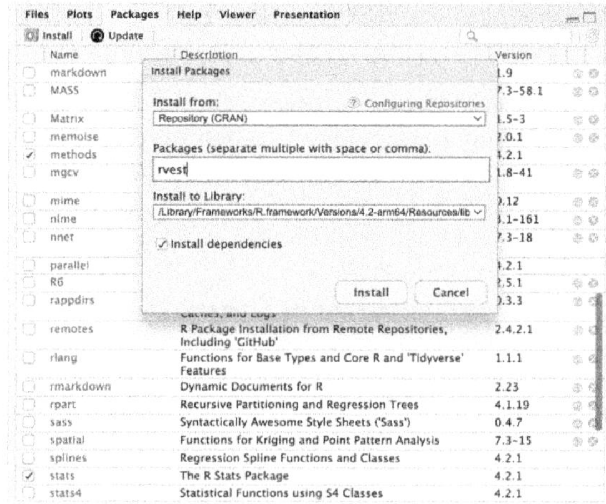

Figure 3.1: Installing the `rvest` package.

3.6 Scraping NHL Data

As an example of web scraping, we will look at how we might obtain NHL data from the web and convert them into a format where we can analyze them. To do this, we will look at the website `hockeyreference.com` and attempt to get all of the data Hockey Reference collects for the 2022–23 Colorado Avalanche players and put them into data frames we can analyze in R. To achieve this goal, we would like to complete the following two specific tasks:

other web browsers will allow you to see this as well but will have their own method for displaying the page source). A new tab will open displaying the HTML code. The page for the Colorado Avalanche 2022–23 season is over 5,000 lines long! We need to find where the roster table is in this document.

Since tables are contained in HTML nodes (or tags) that contain `<table>`, we need to search for *table* in the document. Just searching for the word *table* will return over 100 results, but if you instead search for `<table` (without the > sign, since there are many variables within the table tag, but it will always start with `<table`), it will return only the tables. Go through the results until you find the one related to rosters. You will see that it has `id=roster` in the tag as an attribute of the table, meaning that the document refers to that table by the ID *roster*.

Now we are ready to get the information for our players. In the following code block, we read the website's HTML as described and then identify the tag in the roster table using the `html_nodes()` function to identify the table with the desired tag, using `xpath` and indicated in this case by `"roster"`. The third line extracts the `href` (hypertext reference) attributes in the table, which in this case will be the unique links to each player's information on hockey-reference.com:

```
links <- pg |>
  html_nodes(xpath = '//*[(@id = "roster")]//a') |>
  html_attr('href')
```

Now that we can examine the structure of the URLs that hold the player-specific information, we can run the code below to acquire a specific player's information. You may notice that this could break depending on the time at which you are trying to scrape the data. If you are getting something that looks unusual, try to decipher what got scraped instead of what you were hoping for and adjust accordingly:

```
url <- paste("https://www.hockey-reference.com", links[27], sep = "")
mac_tbs <- rvest::read_html(url) |>
  rvest::html_table()
mac_tb <- mac_tbs[[3]]
mac_tb <- mac_tb |>
  janitor::clean_names() |>
  dplyr::filter(!(season %in% c("Career", "82 Game Avg.")))
```

You may also notice that we clean up the data a bit as well using the `janitor()` package's `clean_names()` function. In particular, `clean_names()` removes symbols from column names (e.g., +/–), changes the names to lowercase, and does other formatting representative of generally accepted programming practices. Finally, we run a filter from the `dplyr()` library to get the information for their season and career.

We can wrap the code given above into a function so that we can download those player links for any team:

```
get_hrc_player_links <- function(team, year = 2023){
  url <- paste("https://www.hockey-reference.com/teams/",
               team,
               "/",
               year,
               ".html",
               sep = "")
  pg <- read_html(url)
  links <- pg |>
    html_nodes(xpath = '//*[(@id = "roster")]//a') |>
    html_attr('href')
  teams_data <- pg |>
    html_table()
  teams_data <- teams_data[[3]] |>
    bind_cols(tibble(links = links))
  return(teams_data)
}

col_data <- get_hrc_player_links("COL", year = 2023)
```

1. Download the roster table into a format we can use for R.
2. Obtain the information from the individual player links.

As of this writing, this information can be found on the web at `http://www.hockey-reference.com/teams/COL/2023.html`. Of course, this could change at a moment's notice, as we have no control over that website directly, which is a problem that analysts face in obtaining data repeatedly.

```
team <- "COL"
year <- 2023
url <- paste("http://www.hockey-reference.com/teams/",
             team,
             "/",
             year,
             ".html",
             sep = "")
pg <- read_html(url)

tables <- pg |>
  html_table()
```

At this point, you may want to visit the website for this particular page and see what we are trying to put into a data frame for R analysis. Open a web browser and go to `https://www.hockey-reference.com/teams/COL/2023.html`. We can see by scrolling that this is a very long page with a few hyperlinks near the bottom of our initial view to help us jump to the information we want. If we click on the link for "Roster," it will take us farther down the page to the roster table. There are also hyperlinks for each player in the table. If we want to see information about Nathan MacKinnon, we can click on his name. But for now, it is this table that we want to scrape.

It may help you also to look at the page source. You may recall that HTML is simply a markup language, a cousin to R Markdown that we discussed in the previous chapter. HTML provides a web browser with instructions on how to display the text contained within the document. To view the raw document code that the page creator used, you can right-click on the page and choose "View Page Source" (in Google Chrome;

```
www.espn.com > Response

<!DOCTYPE html>
<html class="no-icon-fonts" lang="en">
<head>
    <meta http-equiv="content-type" content="text/html; charset=UTF-8" />
<meta http-equiv="x-ua-compatible" content="IE=edge,chrome=1" />
<meta name="viewport" content="initial-scale=1.0, maximum-scale=1.0, user-scalable=no">
<meta name="referrer" content="origin-when-cross-origin">
<link rel="canonical" href="https://www.espn.com" />
<title>ESPN - Serving Sports Fans. Anytime. Anywhere.</title>
<meta name="description" content="Visit ESPN for live scores, highlights and sports news. Stream exclusive games on ESPN+ and play fantasy sports." />
<link rel="manifest" href="/manifest.json">
<meta property="fb:app_id" content="116656161708917" />
<meta property="og:site_name" content="ESPN.com" />
<meta property="og:url" content="https://www.espn.com" />
<meta property="og:title" content="ESPN - Serving Sports Fans. Anytime. Anywhere."/>
<meta property="og:description" content="Visit ESPN for live scores, highlights and sports news. Stream exclusive games on ESPN+ and play fantasy sports." />
<meta property="og:image" content="https://a1.espncdn.com/combiner/i?img=%2Fi%2Fespn%2Fespn_logos%2Fespn_red.png"/>
<meta property="og:image:width" content="1200" />
<meta property="og:image:height" content="630" />
<meta property="og:type" content="website" />
<meta name="twitter:site" content="espn" />
<meta name="twitter:url" content="https://www.espn.com" />
<meta name="twitter:title" content="ESPN - Serving Sports Fans. Anytime. Anywhere."/>
<meta name="twitter:description" content="Visit ESPN for live scores, highlights and sports news. Stream exclusive games on ESPN+ and play fantasy sports." />
<meta name="twitter:card" content="summary">
<meta name="twitter:app:name:iphone" content="ESPN"/>
<meta name="twitter:app:id:iphone" content="317469184"/>
<meta name="twitter:app:name:googleplay" content="ESPN"/>
<meta name="twitter:app:id:googleplay" content="com.espn.score_center"/>
<meta name="title" content="ESPN - Serving Sports Fans. Anytime. Anywhere."/>
<meta name="medium" content="index" />

<!-- Indicate preferred brand name for Google to display -->
<script type="application/ld+json">
    {
        "@context": "https://schema.org",
        "@type":    "WebSite",
        "name":     "ESPN",
        "url":      "https://www.espn.com/"

          ,"potentialAction": {
              "@type": "SearchAction",
              "target": {
                  "@type": "EntryPoint",
                  "urlTemplate": "https://www.espn.com/search/_/q/{search_term_string}?ex_cid=google_sitelinks"
              },
              "query-input": "required name=search_term_string"
          }
```

Figure 3.2: Example of a website's source code, or page source.

Warnings versus Errors

Note that in some of our scraping code, as well as other code within the textbook, you might see a warning printed along with the output in the console window. A warning will alert the user that something went wrong, but the execution of the code will continue without harming the end result. On the other hand, an error will halt the execution of the code.

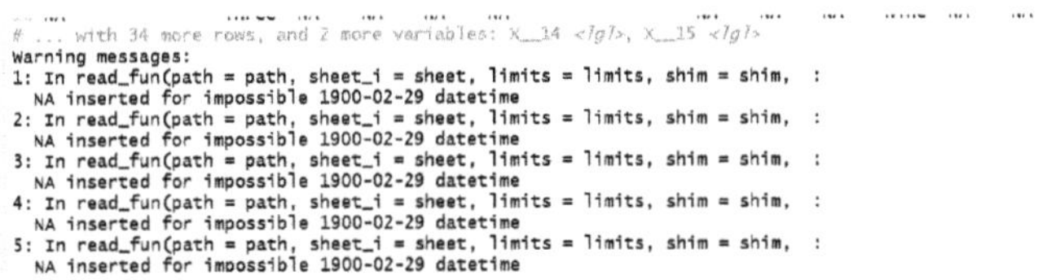

```
# ... with 34 more rows, and 2 more variables: X__14 <lgl>, X__15 <lgl>
Warning messages:
1: In read_fun(path = path, sheet_i = sheet, limits = limits, shim = shim,  :
  NA inserted for impossible 1900-02-29 datetime
2: In read_fun(path = path, sheet_i = sheet, limits = limits, shim = shim,  :
  NA inserted for impossible 1900-02-29 datetime
3: In read_fun(path = path, sheet_i = sheet, limits = limits, shim = shim,  :
  NA inserted for impossible 1900-02-29 datetime
4: In read_fun(path = path, sheet_i = sheet, limits = limits, shim = shim,  :
  NA inserted for impossible 1900-02-29 datetime
5: In read_fun(path = path, sheet_i = sheet, limits = limits, shim = shim,  :
  NA inserted for impossible 1900-02-29 datetime
```

Figure 3.3: A warning message in R.

3.7 Writing a Custom Function

Loops and Web Scraping

You can already see the power of web scraping. But what if we want to expand this? In the example in section 3.6, the logic we use may seem a bit tedious for creating a single URL for Colorado Avalanche players. However, what if we wanted data not from one team and one season but from multiple teams and multiple seasons? In chapter 1, we showed how to use loops for executing the same code a certain number of times. Let's say that we wanted to get the Colorado Avalanche and Dallas Stars information for the 2021–22 and 2022–23 seasons. To do this, we need to iterate over two teams and two seasons. We can then take the code that we created earlier and put it inside of a loop so that it can be repeated as many times as necessary. This process will be much cleaner if we write a custom function so that we only need to write the code once and have it repeat for each team. Let's call that function `get_nhl_roster(team, season)`. This function will then return to us the roster for the year that we specify as the first argument and the team that we specify in the second argument. It also sets a default of 2023 for the year so that if we do not supply an argument for year, it will give us the 2023 roster:

```
get_nhl_roster <- function(team, season = 2023){
  url <- paste("http://www.hockey-reference.com/teams/",
               team, "/", season, ".html", sep = "")
  tb <- read_html(url) |>
    html_table()
  tb <- tb[[3]]
  return(tb)
}
```

To test that the function works, let's pull just the Colorado Avalanche data from 2023 and put it into a data frame called `col_df`:

```
col_df <- get_nhl_roster(team = "COL", season = 2023)
```

Well, that seemed to work. So now let's run it in the loop. We will have two loops, one for the two teams that we placed inside of the vector teams, and inside of that loop, we will have another loop that pulls the data for each of the seasons we requested when we created the vector years. The below example will give us all of the data for Colorado first, and then it will retrieve the data for Dallas:

```
teams <- c("COL", "DAL")
years <- 2022:2023
for(i in seq_along(teams)){
  for(j in seq_along(years)){
    tb <- get_nhl_roster(teams[i], years[j]) |>
      mutate(team = teams[i],
             year = years[j])
    if(exists("results")){
      results <- rbind(results, tb)
    } else (results <- tb)
  }
}
```

So now we have written all of the team data from Colorado and Dallas to the data frame `results`, and we can use this in future analysis.

3.8 Conclusion

You probably knew that data about sports were available on the web before you picked up this book. While we showed you in earlier chapters how to install libraries that included data, such as the Lahman Baseball Database, we have now shown you how to bring in data from other places on the web to use for analysis.

Having these skills will be quite valuable for you. This text cannot possibly cover all the data sources available on the Internet—either in library format or on all the web pages that have data currently—and furthermore, there will likely be additional libraries and datasets and web pages published every year. We have only scratched the surface of what is even available within `rvest()`. To find out more about `rvest()`, scan the website `https://rvest.tidyverse.org`. This chapter gives you the skills to use other data to answer the analytics questions that are interesting to you!

3.9 Lab: Web Scraping Hockey Data

Write a function (call it `get_player_url()`) that takes team and year as inputs/arguments and returns the player names, positions, and URLs from `hockey-reference.com` for that team/year combination.

Use this function to scrape the basic statistics for Nathan MacKinnon's and Mikko Rantanen's careers. Plot shots on goal (SOG) normalized by time on ice (TOI) as a function of their age. You will need to do the following:

1. Get the URLs using your function.
2. Use `read_html` on the URLs.
3. Pipe that result to `html_table`.
4. Rename the tibble using something like `names(player_stats) <- player_stats[1, ]`.
5. Clean the names.
6. Filter the rows as necessary.
7. Mutate the individual `dfs` to add a column for the player's name.
8. Combine the data using `bind_rows`.
9. Make sure the columns of data are of type numeric; otherwise, it won't plot.
10. Plot it.

3.10 Exercises

To complete these exercises, you will need to scrape a subset of data from the Hockey Reference website.

1. What team won the Stanley Cup in 2017 (use Google)? Find the player who had the highest percent Corsi value on that team. Interpret the value.
2. Find the correlation between the Corsi percent and Fenwick percent using the entire dataset. Filter out all `NAs` (use `na_omit`).
3. Use the function from this chapter's lab and scrape Connor McDavid's and Leon Draisaitl's career statistics. Write a short report comparing these two players.

Chapter 4

Baseball

> I think the discovery of new analytics is never-ending. I think there will always be things to research, always new discoveries that we make in baseball alone—let alone all the other sports.
>
> —John Dewan, founder, STATS Inc.
>
> What we assume that the teams should know, but never seem to get, is that you're paying [players] for the future, not the past.
>
> —Abraham Wyner, Wharton statistics professor
>
> Baseball is 90% mental. The other half is physical.
>
> —Yogi Berra

4.1 R Packages

We will use the following R packages in this chapter that we have used in previous chapters:

```
library(dplyr)
library(ggplot2)
library(Lahman)
```

We will also introduce these packages, which we have not yet used. If you do not have them installed yet on your computer (and you probably don't!), refer to the instructions in chapters 2 and 3 on how to install packages. As of October 2023, `baseballr` must be installed from GitHub. You will need to use the `install_github()` function from the `remotes` package in order to install `baseballr`, as shown below:

```
install_github("BillPetti/baseballr")
library(ggcorrplot) # used with ggplot2 to visualize correlation matrices
library(broom) # converts statistical objects into Tibbles
library(baseballr) # scrapes data and calculates baseball metrics
library(lubridate) # eases the process of working with dates
library(mgcv) #enables GAM modeling and smoothness estimations
```

4.2 Introduction

Major League Baseball (MLB), as Michael Lewis subtitled in his 2003 book *Moneyball*, is an unfair game. Despite the efforts of other professional sports leagues to level the ability to acquire players, such as through salary caps, baseball has never created this hard limit. For example, in 2023, the payroll of the highest-spending team, the New York Mets, at approximately $343 million, was more than five times as high as the team with the lowest payroll, the Oakland Athletics, at approximately $62 million. In fact, the six highest payrolls in 2023 were from the two teams from New York, the Los Angeles Dodgers, and teams from Dallas, Philadelphia, and San Diego, cities that rank first, second, ninth, sixth, and eighth by population in the US. These teams stand to make much more money from ticket sales, media rights, merchandise sales, and other ancillary income than teams in places like Pittsburgh, Baltimore, and Oakland, which occupy the last three spots in payroll. Once free agency took place in the mid-1970s and player salaries climbed exponentially, teams in these larger markets could afford to pay players much higher salaries than those in the smaller markets.

Moreover, salaries of players in the MLB are fully guaranteed. If a player signs a 10-year contract and his performance diminishes after 2 years, the team is obligated to honor that contract throughout its lifetime, even if the player is cut from the team. Making a mistake with a player whose performance declines can be an anchor around a team's neck for years. Famously, Bobby Bonilla receives more than $1 million from the Mets every July 1 through 2031 even though he hasn't played for the team since 2000.* If owners of teams in places like Oakland expected to compete with those in the massive media markets, they would have to rely on something besides their checkbooks.

This is where analytics came into play. Oakland general manager (GM) Billy Beane and his assistant GM, Paul DePodesta, viewed the game differently and evaluated players on how they could make contributions to the team by creating runs or creating outs. They looked for players who were otherwise overlooked by conventional baseball personnel because they didn't pass the "eye test," or look like what was presumed to be a professional baseball player. They used this to great advantage in the early part of the 21st century, until other teams caught up. There continue to be innovations on this strategy, as you will read later in this chapter with the Houston Astros, and there are always new statistics to be measured as teams look for an edge.

(a) (b)

Figure 4.1: Billy Beane and Paul DePodesta.
Sources: (a) Muboshgu / CC BY 2.0; (b) Bill Sheridan / CC BY 2.0

So why baseball and analytics? Baseball players, coaches, and administrators need to be able to evaluate players for performance and game situations for the optimal strategy to score the most runs in nine innings and win the game. In the first four chapters of this book, we have introduced you to sports analytics, a programming language and methodology for working with sports data, and how to acquire data to analyze from different sources. Over the next several chapters, we will look at individual sports, not just baseball, and how to wrangle and analyze data related to those sports for advanced analysis. The first time we use a technique, we will explain more about it, but the subsequent times that we use it, we will assume you have seen it before. If you have jumped ahead to a particular chapter and do not understand a particular function or technique that is being used, refer back to previous chapters (and the index) to see where you might find out about that technique.

4.3 If You Don't Know Anything about Baseball

Baseball, often known as the American Pastime, is a game played between two teams of nine players where the object is to score more runs than your opponents. Legend has it that the game was invented by Abner Doubleday in the 1830s, but it is almost certainly derived from the English game of cricket and a more closely related game called rounders. It is also unique among sports in that the defense is the team that actually touches the ball, while the offense attempts to hit the ball where the defense cannot catch it or field it.

The defense throws (pitches) the ball toward an offensive player, who then attempts to hit the ball with a bat. The nine defensive players then attempt to catch the ball before it touches the ground or to touch the player with the ball as the player runs toward first base, and then second base, and then third base, before arriving back where he started at home plate. If he reaches home plate, the offense scores one point (called a run); if he does not, it is called an out. When the defense records three outs, the teams change sides and the defense goes on offense and vice versa. An inning consists of each team taking a turn on offense and defense. The team with the most runs at the end of nine innings is the winner.

* In December 2023, Shohei Ohtani signed a 10-year, $700 million contract with the Los Angeles Dodgers, almost doubling the previous largest contract in MLB history. This contract will have $680 million deferred, payable $68 million annually on July 1 from 2034 to 2043. July 1 will certainly then become known as Shohei Ohtani Day.

Obviously, this is an oversimplification of the game, but it gives you the basics of the game. A more complete explanation of the game is available at `https://www.wikihow.com/Play-Baseball`.

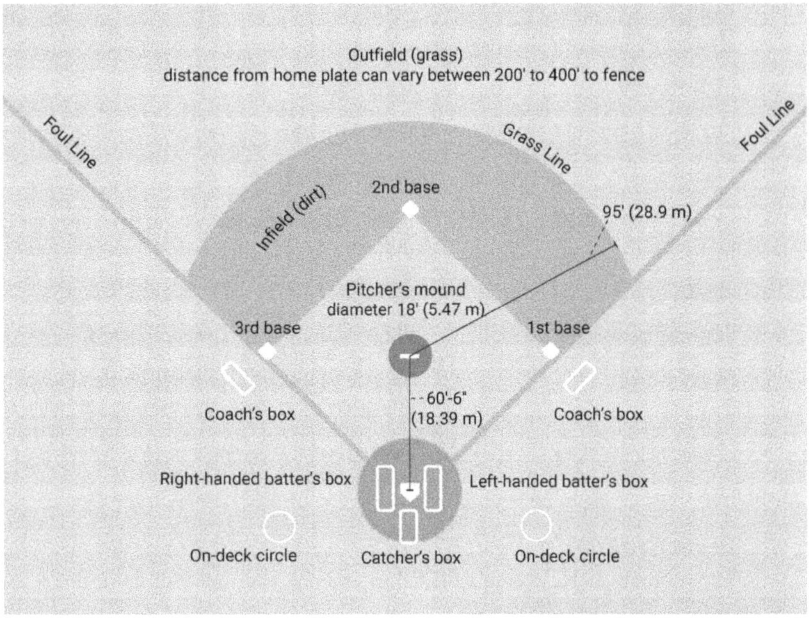

Figure 4.2: Baseball field.

4.4 Sabermetrics

More than a century's worth of analysis in baseball changed with the insights of Bill James and his publication of the *Bill James Baseball Abstract* in the late 1970s. In lieu of the traditional metrics used to evaluate players like batting average, runs, and runs batted in or, for pitchers, wins, earned run average, and strikeouts, James stressed new metrics like runs created, Pythagorean win percentage, and game score. He termed his approach to examining baseball players and teams *sabermetrics*, a nod to the Society for American Baseball Research. While many baseball purists dismissed James's work as a sideshow to the real analysis of baseball players by "baseball people," today's baseball teams employ teams of analytics professionals to use mathematics, predictive analytics, and optimization to assist them in fielding the team with the best chance to win and in making in-game decisions that lead to the best chances to win.

Figure 4.3: Bill James.
Source: Colette Morton and Dan Holden / CC BY-SA 2.0

Many people know nothing more about sports analytics than what they may have gleaned while watching the 2011 movie *Moneyball*. In that movie, Bill James was referenced with derision in the scene where the scouts assemble to discuss which players the Oakland A's should sign for the 2002 season. In the time since that season chronicled in the movie, the analysts have certainly not replaced the scouts in the evaluation of players, but every team has and uses analysts and far more complex analytics.

This chapter shows you how to use some of those metrics that have been popularized in the last two decades—and perhaps even create some of your own!

4.5 Basic Baseball Metrics

Historical Metrics

For the first 100-plus years of baseball, baseball players were measured largely by a few basic offensive and defensive metrics. However, with the advent of computers and sabermetrics and analytics, more advanced metrics were created.

Table 4.1: Early metrics used in baseball analytics	
Offensive	**Defensive**
Batting average: hits / at bats	Wins: the pitcher who was pitching when the offense took the lead for good
Home runs	Innings pitched
Runs batted in (RBI)	Earned run average: the number of earned runs per nine innings that a pitcher allowed the offense to score
Walks	Strikeouts
On base percentage (OBP)	WHIP: (walks + hits) / (innings pitched)
Runs scored	Saves: a pitcher who came into the game when his team led by three or fewer runs and pitched effectively for at least one inning and his team wins the game
Slugging percentage (SLG): TB/AB	Fielding percentage: percentage of time that a player handles the ball in the field and does not make an error

Runs Created

Runs created (RC), one of Bill James's original metrics, is defined as

$$\text{runs created} = \frac{\left(hits + BB + HBP\right) \times TB}{AB + BB + HBP},$$

where BB = walks; HBP = hit by pitch; AB = at bats; and TB = total bases. Runs created is an estimate of how many runs should have been scored by a player or a team. This can be important when evaluating a player, or a team, for consideration in the future. For example, if we are considering adding a player to our team, one metric we might use to evaluate that player is to see how many runs he might be responsible for creating for our team and compare that to other players we might want to add to our team.

How can we utilize the Lahman Baseball Database introduced earlier in this text to compute this metric? Let's create a tibble for team data since 1970:

```
team_df <- tibble(Teams) |>
  filter(yearID >= 1970)
head(team_df)
```

```
# A tibble: 6 × 48
  yearID lgID  teamID franchID divID  Rank     G Ghome     W     L DivWin WCWin
   <int> <fct> <fct>  <fct>    <chr> <int> <int> <int> <int> <int> <chr>  <chr>
1   1970 NL    ATL    ATL      W         5   162    81    76    86 N      <NA>
2   1970 AL    BAL    BAL      E         1   162    81   108    54 Y      <NA>
3   1970 AL    BOS    BOS      E         3   162    81    87    75 N      <NA>
4   1970 AL    CAL    ANA      W         3   162    81    86    76 N      <NA>
5   1970 AL    CHA    CHW      W         6   162    84    56   106 N      <NA>
6   1970 NL    CHN    CHC      E         2   162    80    84    78 N      <NA>
# i 36 more variables: LgWin <chr>, WSWin <chr>, R <int>, AB <int>, H <int>,
#   X2B <int>, X3B <int>, HR <int>, BB <int>, SO <int>, SB <int>, CS <int>,
#   HBP <int>, SF <int>, RA <int>, ER <int>, ERA <dbl>, CG <int>, SHO <int>,
#   SV <int>, IPouts <int>, HA <int>, HRA <int>, BBA <int>, SOA <int>, E <int>,
#   DP <int>, FP <dbl>, name <chr>, park <chr>, attendance <int>, BPF <int>,
#   PPF <int>, teamIDBR <chr>, teamIDlahman45 <chr>, teamIDretro <chr>
```

One problem you may notice is that singles (one-base hits) are not traditionally explicitly recorded separately, and Lahman follows that ontology. We will need to know that number when we calculate total bases. How can we compute singles? Let's create a new column, X1B, and calculate it as the number of hits less the sum of doubles, triples, and home runs. Let us also do a bit of cleaning with the HBP column to make sure that a missing value for hit by pitch is interpreted as a zero. Finally, we will then add a column for RC using the defined formula and plot it against the actual runs scored by each team in each year:

```
rc_df <- team_df |>
  mutate(HBP = ifelse(is.na(HBP), 0, as.numeric(HBP)),
         X1B = H - X2B - X3B - HR, #singles
         TB = X1B + 2*X2B + 3*X3B + 4*HR, #total bases
         RC = (H + BB + HBP)*TB/(AB + BB + HBP))
head(rc_df)
```

```
# A tibble: 6 × 51
  yearID lgID  teamID franchID divID  Rank     G Ghome     W     L DivWin WCWin
   <int> <fct> <fct>  <fct>    <chr> <int> <int> <int> <int> <int> <chr>  <chr>
1   1970 NL    ATL    ATL      W         5   162    81    76    86 N      <NA>
2   1970 AL    BAL    BAL      E         1   162    81   108    54 Y      <NA>
3   1970 AL    BOS    BOS      E         3   162    81    87    75 N      <NA>
4   1970 AL    CAL    ANA      W         3   162    81    86    76 N      <NA>
5   1970 AL    CHA    CHW      W         6   162    84    56   106 N      <NA>
6   1970 NL    CHN    CHC      E         2   162    80    84    78 N      <NA>
# i 39 more variables: LgWin <chr>, WSWin <chr>, R <int>, AB <int>, H <int>,
#   X2B <int>, X3B <int>, HR <int>, BB <int>, SO <int>, SB <int>, CS <int>,
#   HBP <dbl>, SF <int>, RA <int>, ER <int>, ERA <dbl>, CG <int>, SHO <int>,
#   SV <int>, IPouts <int>, HA <int>, HRA <int>, BBA <int>, SOA <int>, E <int>,
#   DP <int>, FP <dbl>, name <chr>, park <chr>, attendance <int>, BPF <int>,
#   PPF <int>, teamIDBR <chr>, teamIDlahman45 <chr>, teamIDretro <chr>,
#   X1B <int>, TB <dbl>, RC <dbl>
```

```
p <- ggplot(data = rc_df,
            aes(x = RC, y = R))
p + geom_point(alpha = .15) +
  geom_smooth(method = "lm", col = "black") + ## similar to trendline
  labs(x = "runs created", y = "actual runs") +
  theme_bw()
```

Figure 4.4 suggests that we could probably reliably predict a team's runs based on its runs created value. In other words, we can calculate a linear regression model between R and RC. If you don't know what linear regression is or how to calculate it, be sure to see a textbook such as *Applied Linear Regression Models* by Kutner, Nachtsheim, and Neter (available at `https://books.google.com/books/about/Applied_Linear_Regression_Models.html?id=1BqCAAAACAAJ`) for a primer. In this case, we will use the `lm()` function to create a regression model object (`rc_r_lm`), with runs (R) as the dependent variable and runs created (RC) as the independent variable. In familiar statistical terms, this model is written as

$$R = \beta_0 + \beta_1 RC + \varepsilon.$$

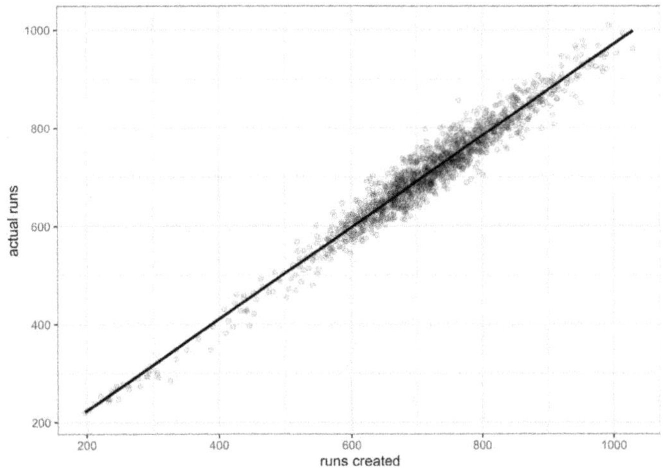

Figure 4.4: Calculated runs created (x) versus actual runs for all teams since 1970.

```
rc_r_lm <- lm(R ~ RC, data = rc_df)
summary(rc_r_lm)
```

```
Call:
lm(formula = R ~ RC, data = rc_df)

Residuals:
    Min      1Q  Median      3Q     Max 
-83.032 -16.480  -1.704  16.547 106.469 

Coefficients:
             Estimate Std. Error t value Pr(>|t|)    
(Intercept) 36.632419   4.040103   9.067   <2e-16 ***
RC           0.934785   0.005586 167.347   <2e-16 ***
---
Signif. codes:  0 '***' 0.001 '**' 0.01 '*' 0.05 '.' 0.1 ' ' 1

Residual standard error: 25.49 on 1472 degrees of freedom
Multiple R-squared:  0.9501,	Adjusted R-squared:   0.95 
F-statistic: 2.801e+04 on 1 and 1472 DF,  p-value: < 2.2e-16
```

The resulting estimated regression equation is

$$\hat{R} = 36.63 + 0.93RC,$$

where $\hat{R}$ is referred to as "R-hat," or the estimated value of R.

We can use this equation to predict a team's average runs for a given value of runs created. Note that the predicted values for each observation in the `rc_df` dataset can be obtained using the `predict()` function. We illustrate this concept by showing runs, runs created, and the predicted value of runs for the 2022 Colorado Rockies. The following code appends the predicted values to the `rc_df`, filters for the 2022 season, and selects `R`, `RC`, and `R_hat` using the following code:

```
rc_df |>
  mutate(R_hat = as.vector(predict(rc_r_lm))) |>
  filter(yearID == 2022, teamID == "COL") |>
  select(R, RC, R_hat)
```

```
# A tibble: 1 × 3
      R    RC R_hat
  <int> <dbl> <dbl>
1   698  699.  690.
```

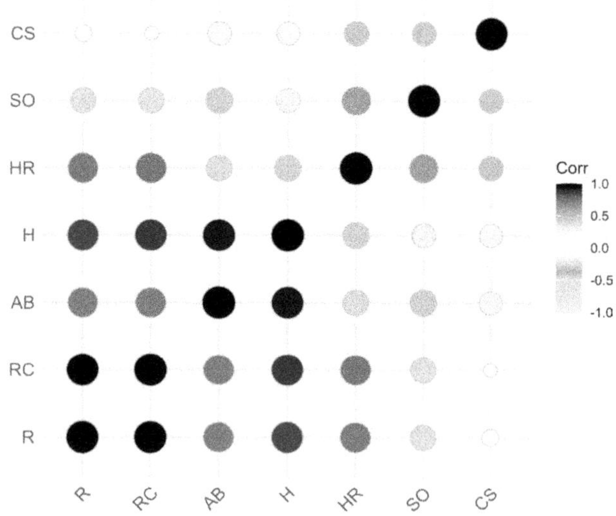

Figure 4.5: Correlation matrix for runs, runs created, at bats, hits, home runs, strikeouts, and times caught stealing a base.

In the case of the 2022 Colorado Rockies, 36.632419 + 0.934785 × 699.3997 = 690.4208 average runs. The difference between the observed value of runs, 698, and the predicted value, 690.4207, is referred to as the *residual* error. We will explore linear regression in more detail in the next section of this textbook.

Next we can check how well `RC` correlates with other team-based metrics. We will use the `cor()` function to create a correlation matrix between runs, runs created, at bats, hits, home runs, strikeouts, and number of times caught stealing (CS). We will visualize this correlation matrix using the `ggcorrplot()` function in the `ggcorrplot` package:

```
cor_mat <- cor(dplyr::select(rc_df, R, RC, AB, H, HR, SO, CS))
ggcorrplot(cor_mat, method = "circle",
          colors = c( "#2c7bb6", "#ffffbf", "#d7191c"))
```

We see strong correlations between RC and other forms of offensive production, and unsurprisingly, we see a negative correlation between RC and CS. What may further pique our interest, however, is that there is a modest positive correlation between the number of strikeouts and RC. Could it be that the team that swings for the fences is more likely to score enough runs so that additional strikeouts can be tolerated? Or is this just a function of having more at bats? And what about BB and HBP? These are problems you might consider analyzing.

4.6 Linear Regression

Rather than just looking at the correlation between runs and runs created, consider predicting runs scored in a season (per player) based on home runs using a simple linear regression model (see figure 4.6). To be consistent with other examples within this text, we will

- exclude anyone with less than 100 ABs so as to not have our model unduly influenced by non-full-time position players,
- visually examine the relationship between R and HR by creating a scatterplot, and
- use the `lm` method of geometric smoothing to create a line of best fit.

This is similar to adding a trendline to a scatterplot in Microsoft Excel if you are familiar with that process.

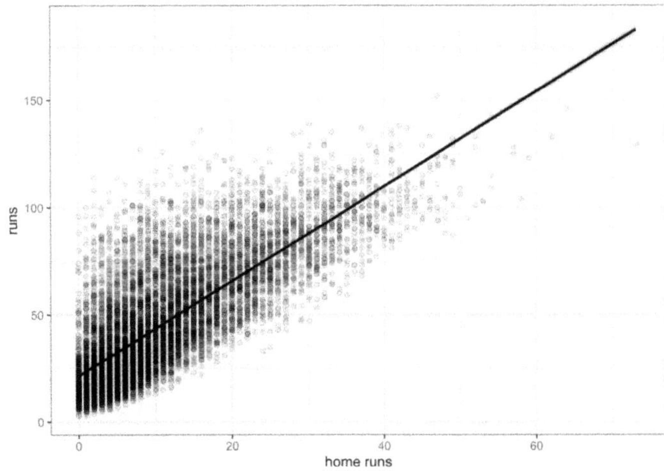

Figure 4.6: Home runs (x) versus runs scored (y) by player since 2000 in the Lahman database.

```
df_batting <- Batting |>
  filter(yearID >= 2000, AB >= 100)
p <- ggplot(data = df_batting,
            aes(x = HR, y = R))
p + geom_point(alpha = .15) +
  geom_smooth(method = "lm", col = "black") +
  labs(x = "home runs", y = "runs") +
  theme_bw()
```

In order to see the actual equation, we can run the actual linear regression model:

```
lm_batting_1 <- lm(R ~ HR,
                   data = df_batting)
summary(lm_batting_1)
```

```
Call:
lm(formula = R ~ HR, data = df_batting)

Residuals:
    Min      1Q  Median      3Q     Max 
-53.939 -12.693  -4.328   8.884  88.095 

Coefficients:
            Estimate Std. Error t value Pr(>|t|)    
(Intercept) 21.48112    0.26959   79.68   <2e-16 ***
HR           2.21175    0.01817  121.76   <2e-16 ***
---
Signif. codes:  0 '***' 0.001 '**' 0.01 '*' 0.05 '.' 0.1 ' ' 1
```

```
Residual standard error: 17.78 on 10061 degrees of freedom
Multiple R-squared:  0.5957,    Adjusted R-squared:  0.5957
F-statistic: 1.483e+04 on 1 and 10061 DF,  p-value: < 2.2e-16
```

So how do we interpret the parameters of this model? When a player has zero home runs, the average number of runs scored by that player is 21.481, the y-intercept. Similarly, we expect that for each additional home run that a player hits, the average number of runs scored by that player will increase by approximately 2.212 runs.

We know that any point estimate or prediction from an estimated regression model has error. Therefore, we may wish instead to communicate a confidence interval for the parameters of our models using the `confint()` function. This lets us state with a given level of confidence that our parameter is between a lower bound and upper bound. In the following example, we use $\alpha = .01$, or a 99% level of confidence that the true value of our parameter is between the lower and upper bounds, or in the case of the slope and intercept parameters in our model, we have the following:

```
confint(lm_batting_1, level = .99)
```

```
                0.5 %   99.5 %
(Intercept) 20.786575 22.17567
HR           2.164953  2.25855
```

Suppose we want to store the results of our predicted values from our model with the actual data. You can calculate the predictions and append them directly onto your original data frame as a new column. Here we create the column `pred_R` to store the values of predicted runs next to the actual runs and home runs:

```
df_batting_new <- df_batting |>
  mutate(pred_R = predict(lm_batting_1))
head(df_batting_new)
```

```
   playerID yearID stint teamID lgID   G  AB   R   H X2B X3B HR RBI SB CS  BB
1 abbotje01   2000     1    CHA   AL  80 215  31  59  15   1  3  29  2  1  21
2 abbotku01   2000     1    NYN   NL  79 157  22  34   7   1  6  12  1  1  14
3 abreubo01   2000     1    PHI   NL 154 576 103 182  42  10 25  79 28  8 100
4 agbaybe01   2000     1    NYN   NL 119 350  59 101  19   1 15  60  5  5  54
5 alexama02   2000     1    BOS   AL 101 194  30  41   4   3  4  19  2  0  13
6 alfoned01   2000     1    NYN   NL 150 544 109 176  40   2 25  94  3  2  95
   SO IBB HBP SH SF GIDP   pred_R
1  38   1   2  2  1    2 28.11637
2  51   2   1  0  1    2 34.75163
3 116   9   1  0  3   12 76.77491
4  68   2   7  0  3    6 54.65739
5  41   0   0  2  0    0 30.32813
6  70   1   5  0  6   12 76.77491
```

Alternatively, we can predict new observations by creating a data object (`new_data`) that we pass to the `predict()` function using the `newdata` argument. This argument allows us to make predictions using an existing model at potentially different values of our independent variables. The following example shows the predicted average number of runs (and 95% confidence intervals) for two players who hit 30 and 15 home runs. Note that you can adjust the confidence level of the interval using the `level` argument in the `predict()` function. The default level is 0.95:

```
new_data <- data.frame(R = c(NA, NA),
                       HR = c(30, 15))
predict(lm_batting_1,
        newdata = new_data,
        interval = "confidence",
        level = 0.95)
```

```
       fit      lwr      upr
1 87.83366 87.07886 88.58846
2 54.65739 54.28427 55.03052
```

The `fit` column shows the predicted values of average runs scored at 30 and 15 home runs, and `lwr` and `upr` are the lower and upper 95% confidence limits for those predictions.

The final estimated regression equation is $\hat{R} = 21.48 + 2.21 \cdot HR$. Further, the mean squared error (MSE) and R^2 values are 17.78 and 0.60, respectively.

4.7 Player Comparisons Using Runs above Average

Earlier we discussed how we might use the runs created metric to compare and evaluate players who we might want to add to our team. In this section, we will look at how much better the "average" team would be if we could add a specific player. For example, we will look at replacing an average player with Mike Trout in 2018. While Mookie Betts actually won the AL MVP in 2018, one could argue that throughout the 2010s, Mike Trout could be named MVP every year.

Suppose we decided that a model for predicting runs is based on singles, doubles, triples, home runs, and walks plus hit by pitches. Let's create a tibble that

- selects all the team-level data from 2010 to the present,
- calculates and stores the number of singles in another column, and
- calculates and stores the sum of walks and hit by pitches into yet another column.

```
df_teams <- tibble(Teams) |>
  filter(yearID >= 2010) |>
  mutate(X1B = H - X2B - X3B - HR,
         BB_HBP = BB + HBP) |>
  select(yearID, R, X1B, X2B, X3B, HR, BB_HBP)
head(df_teams)
```

```
# A tibble: 6 × 7
  yearID     R   X1B   X2B   X3B    HR BB_HBP
   <int> <int> <int> <int> <int> <int>  <int>
1   2010   713   851   301    34   180    628
2   2010   738   935   312    25   139    685
3   2010   613  1022   264    21   133    478
4   2010   818   920   358    22   211    634
5   2010   752  1006   263    21   177    546
6   2010   685   940   298    27   149    529
```

While the last `select` call in the code chunk above isn't necessary, it is good practice to subset a tibble to include only the variables that you will use in your model-building process—particularly when it comes to making predictions and updating models.

Multiple Regression

So far we have only looked at univariate regression, where we try to predict the value of a dependent variable from a single independent variable. These are perhaps more easily understood and definitely more easily visualized in two-dimensional space, but they limit our power to look at multiple independent variables at the same time. Multiple regression allows us to look at many variables simultaneously in developing a model that predicts the value of the dependent variable, and here we show how to add this to our analysis tool belt.

If we know the variables that will be used in our "final model," we can just select these variables into another data frame in order to more efficiently deal with post-model-building analysis. The model that we are fitting is

$$R = \beta_0 + \beta_1 X1B + \beta_2 X2B + \beta_3 X3B + \beta_4 HR + \beta_5\,(BB\_HBP) + \varepsilon.$$

For example, we can fit the final model using the following code. Note that the "." notation means "Include every variable from the data frame as a predictor other than the y variable," and the "-" tells R, "Do not include the `yearID` variable."

```
lm_runs <- lm(R ~ . - yearID, data = df_teams) ## Multiple regression model
summary(lm_runs)
```

```
Call:
lm(formula = R ~ . - yearID, data = df_teams)

Residuals:
    Min      1Q  Median      3Q     Max
-86.083 -18.561   2.275  20.172  90.613

Coefficients:
             Estimate Std. Error t value Pr(>|t|)
(Intercept) -13.44415    7.99534  -1.681   0.0935 .
X1B           0.17441    0.01748   9.978  < 2e-16 ***
X2B           0.70752    0.06252  11.317  < 2e-16 ***
X3B           0.81482    0.18033   4.519 8.3e-06 ***
HR            1.27516    0.04628  27.552  < 2e-16 ***
BB_HBP        0.22606    0.02376   9.513  < 2e-16 ***
---
Signif. codes:  0 '***' 0.001 '**' 0.01 '*' 0.05 '.' 0.1 ' ' 1

Residual standard error: 28.69 on 384 degrees of freedom
Multiple R-squared:  0.9569,    Adjusted R-squared:  0.9563
F-statistic:  1705 on 5 and 384 DF,  p-value: < 2.2e-16
```

The formula in the `lm_runs` definition above is equivalent to writing the model using long-form notation that we show below. Either line of code will yield the same results.

```
lm_runs <- lm(R ~ X1B + X2B + X3B + HR + BB_HBP, data = df_teams)
```

We can use the `broom` package to make the output from a linear model fit (and others) a little more presentable. The two functions that we use the most are `tidy()` and `augment()`. The former function is simply a more readable way of presenting some of the information that we've seen previously.

```
tidy(lm_runs)
```

```
# A tibble: 6 × 5
  term        estimate std.error statistic  p.value
  <chr>          <dbl>     <dbl>     <dbl>    <dbl>
1 (Intercept)  -13.4      8.00       -1.68 9.35e- 2
2 X1B            0.174    0.0175      9.98 5.33e-21
3 X2B            0.708    0.0625     11.3  8.07e-26
4 X3B            0.815    0.180       4.52 8.30e- 6
5 HR             1.28     0.0463     27.6  5.44e-93
6 BB_HBP         0.226    0.0238      9.51 2.08e-19
```

The latter, on the other hand, will create a new tibble that contains the predicted values, standard errors of the predictions, residuals, and other relevant information about the model results using the `augment()` function. We show the first six lines of the new data frame using the `head()` function here:

```
head(augment(lm_runs))
```

```
# A tibble: 6 × 13
      R yearID   X1B   X2B   X3B    HR BB_HBP .fitted .resid    .hat .sigma
  <int>  <int> <int> <int> <int> <int>  <int>   <dbl>  <dbl>   <dbl>  <dbl>
1   713   2010   851   301    34   180    628    747. -34.1  0.0131    28.7
2   738   2010   935   312    25   139    685    723.  15.2  0.0266    28.7
3   613   2010  1022   264    21   133    478    646. -33.3  0.0166    28.7
4   818   2010   920   358    22   211    634    831. -12.6  0.0282    28.7
5   752   2010  1006   263    21   177    546    714.  37.7  0.0123    28.7
6   685   2010   940   298    27   149    529    693.  -7.92 0.00760   28.7
# i 2 more variables: .cooksd <dbl>, .std.resid <dbl>
```

Model Assumptions

Note that when doing inference (e.g., testing the significance of a parameter value) in regression, several theoretical properties related to the model are assumed. These include the following:

- The true relationship between the independent and dependent variables is linear.
- The residuals (errors) are independent of each other.
- The residuals are normally distributed.
- The residuals have a constant level of variance (are homoscedastic).

It is therefore important to assess the validity of these assumptions, even though with enough data, regression can be robust to some violations of these assumptions. In R, we can create a residuals plot and a normal probability plot using the fitted `lm()` model object itself. Recall that the residuals versus the fitted (or predicted) values should appear random (no obvious patterns), and the `qq-plot` should appear linear.

```
plot(lm_runs)
```

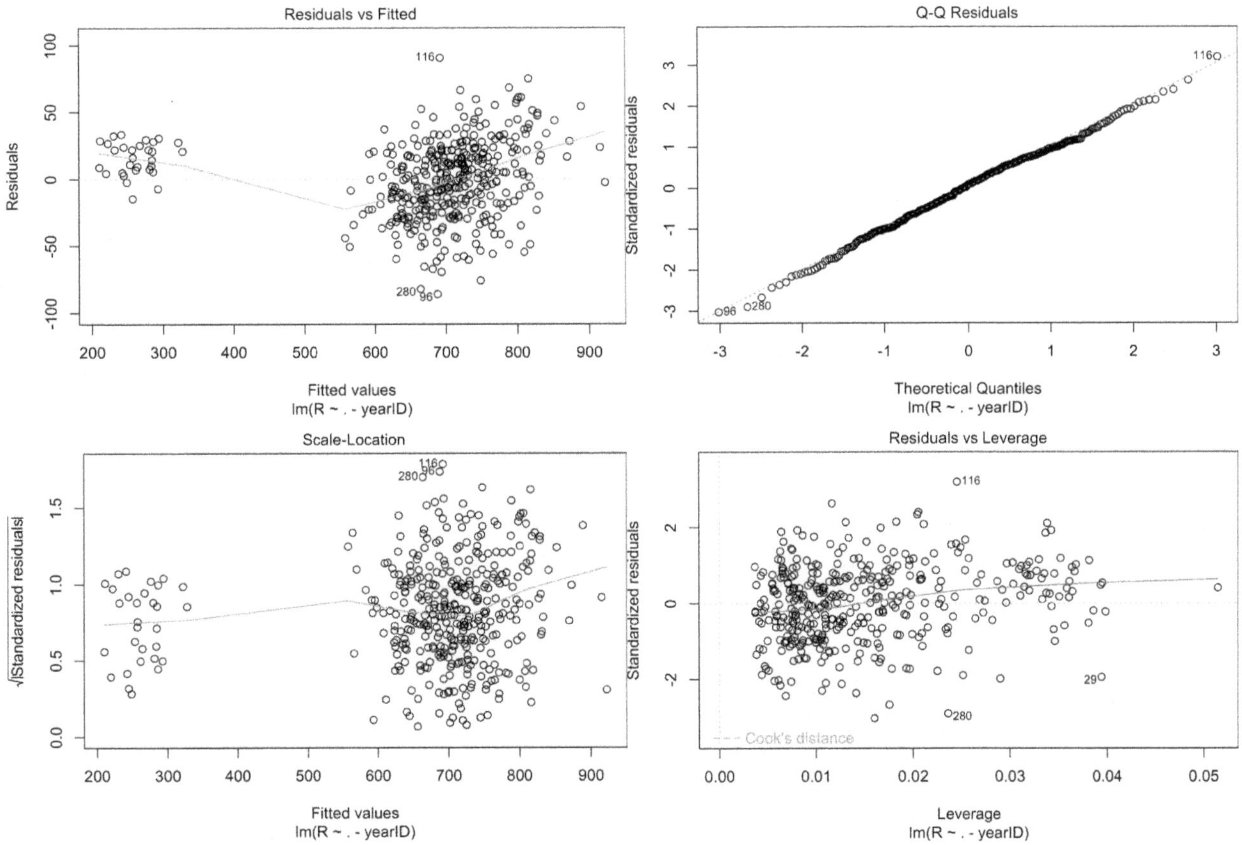

Looking at the plots above, created from the `lm_runs` model, there do not appear to be any noticeable violations.

4.8 Runs above Average: Mike Trout (2018)

Figure 4.7: Mike Trout.
Source: Keith Allison / CC BY-SA 2.0

In this example, we will show how a specific player—in this case, Mike Trout in 2018—would impact an "average" team. The comparison of Trout to an "average player" is based on two calculations:

1. Compute the average team prediction of runs using, for example, a regression model.
2. Adjust this average for Trout's impact by calculating a scaling factor.

We will need to move from looking at team-based metrics to looking at player-specific metrics. We will utilize the `Batting` table given in the Lahman database, and because we are using Mike Trout in 2018, we will filter appropriately.

First, we need to find Trout in the database. You can use the `playerInfo()` function to find Mike Trout's unique `playerID` in the Lahman database. If you issue the command `playerInfo(nameLast = "Trout")` into the console, it will return the player IDs of all players with the last name Trout. As we are interested in Mike and neither Steve nor Dizzy, our `playerID` of interest will be `troutmi01`:

```
playerInfo(nameLast = "Trout")
```

```
      playerID nameFirst nameLast
18864 troutdi01     Dizzy    Trout
18865 troutmi01      Mike    Trout
18866 troutst01     Steve    Trout
```

The following code shows Trout's information, along with a new column, `Outs`, which we will need later. Here we calculate `Outs` as at bats (`AB`) – hits (`H`), with adjustments for grounding into double plays (`GIDP`), sacrifice flies (`SF`), sacrifice hits (`SH`), and times caught stealing (`CS`). Note that we multiply `AB` by 0.982 due to the fact that approximately 0.8% of all at bats result in an error, as suggested in a similar analysis in Winston, Nestler, and Pelechrinis's *Mathletics* (`https://press.princeton.edu/books/paperback/9780691177625/mathletics`).

```
trout <- tibble(Batting) |>
  filter(playerID == "troutmi01", yearID == 2018) |>
  mutate(X1B = H - X2B - X3B - HR,
         BB_HBP = BB + IBB + HBP,
         Outs = .982*AB - H + GIDP + SF + SH + CS) |>
  select(yearID, R, X1B, X2B, X3B, HR, BB_HBP, Outs)
head(trout)
```

```
# A tibble: 1 × 8
  yearID     R   X1B   X2B   X3B    HR BB_HBP  Outs
   <int> <int> <int> <int> <int> <int>  <int> <dbl>
1   2018   101    80    24     4    39    157  327.
```

The average team in this context is defined by the average values across all statistical categories. It is found using the `summarize_all()` function within the `dplyr` package. We then find the expected runs based on the average statistics:

```
avg_team <- df_teams |>
  filter(yearID == 2018) |>
  summarize_all(.funs = mean) ## compute the mean of each column in df_teams
predict(lm_runs, newdata = avg_team) ## predict(lm_object, newdata)
```

```
       1
727.5637
```

Next, we need the average number of outs per team during the 2018 season. This is given as the `IPouts` variable in the `Teams` data frame:

```
avg_outs <- Teams |>
  filter(yearID == 2018) |>
  summarize(outs = mean(IPouts))
avg_outs
```

```
    outs
1 4348.9
```

The player-specific adjustment is based on how many outs the player (Trout) makes over the course of the season. Recall from earlier that Mike Trout was responsible for approximately 327 outs during this season. Therefore, the scaling factor for Trout is given by

$$\text{scaling factor} = 1 - \frac{327}{4349}.$$

Therefore, take the average team statistics (singles, doubles, etc.) and multiply by 0.925. Finally, we add Mike Trout's statistics (singles, doubles, etc.) to the scaled average statistics. The basic recipe is to scale the average team according to the outs made by the player of interest and then add the player's statistics to this average team:

```
trout_scale <- (avg_outs$outs - trout$Outs)/avg_outs$outs
trout_scale
```

```
[1] 0.9249185
```

```
avg_team_w_trout <- avg_team*trout_scale +
  select(trout, yearID, R, X1B, X2B, X3B, HR, BB_HBP)
avg_team_w_trout
```

```
    yearID        R      X1B      X2B      X3B      HR   BB_HBP
1 3884.486 767.8662 891.5543 278.7842 30.11353 211.189 699.8655
```

You may look at this data frame and think it is silly to calculate the average of `yearID` as part of this model. And you are right; it is silly. However, we need to keep the year in this frame to use for later calculations.

Now we can use the data frame with Mike Trout inserted into the average team and make a prediction for runs. That is, we are looking at the hypothetical of adding Trout to an average team. The runs above average (RAA) calculation for Mike Trout in 2018 is given next:

```
predict(lm_runs, newdata = avg_team_w_trout) - predict(lm_runs, newdata = avg_team)
```

```
       1
63.77877
```

Is this good? Yes, it is very good. What if we did the same for a below-average hitter? Let's compare Trout's 2018 statistics with those of Ian Desmond from the Colorado Rockies:

```
playerInfo(nameLast = "Desmond")
```

```
      playerID nameFirst nameLast
4625 desmoia01       Ian  Desmond
```

```
ian <- tibble(Batting) |>
  filter(playerID == "desmoia01", yearID == 2018) |>
  mutate(X1B = H - X2B - X3B - HR,
         BB_HBP = BB + IBB + HBP,
         Outs = .982*AB - H + GIDP + SF + SH + CS) |>
  select(yearID, R, X1B, X2B, X3B, HR, BB_HBP, Outs)
ian_scale <- (avg_outs$outs - ian$Outs)/avg_outs$outs
avg_team_w_ian <- avg_team*ian_scale +
  select(ian, yearID, R, X1B, X2B, X3B, HR, BB_HBP)
predict(lm_runs, newdata = avg_team_w_ian) - predict(lm_runs, newdata = avg_team)
```

```
       1
1.406111
```

Unfortunately for Rockies' fans, Ian Desmond did not add too much in the 2018 season.

4.9 Analyzing Defense: Pitching

So far, all of our baseball analysis has looked at offensive production, commonly referred to as "hitting." Of course, this is only part of the game. Nearly half the players on a Major League Baseball team are pitchers, whose main job, of course, is to pitch the ball in such a way that the hitting team does not score runs. We now look at some analysis of pitching.

It can be difficult to isolate the effects of pitching. Traditional metrics like wins do not tell the whole story. For example, if a pitcher happens to pitch on days when the offense scores nine runs, he can give up seven runs over five innings and earn the win even though, in reality, he pitched rather poorly. Similarly, a defense behind the pitcher that makes many throwing and catching errors can make the pitcher look artificially bad.

Fielding independent pitching (FIP) is a statistic that, according to FanGraphs, found at `https://www.fangraphs.com`, is "what a player's 'Earned Run Average' would look like over a given period of time if the pitcher were to have experienced league average results on balls in play and league average timing." The formula for FIP, found at `https://www.mlb.com/glossary/advanced-stats/fielding-independent-pitching`, is defined as

$$FIP = \frac{13 \cdot HR + 3 \cdot (BB + HBP) - (2 \cdot SO)}{IP} + constant.$$

As mentioned on MLB's site, the constant ensures that FIP is on the same scale as earned run average (ERA). The constant changes year to year but generally averages around 3.10. The explicit (annual) definition is dependent on the league averages of ERA, HR, BB, HBP, and strikeouts. The constant is found by substituting the league-average ERA for FIP above and solving for the constant.

Again working with the Lahman database, let's create a tibble that pulls in all team-level data, filters it to only include data from 1970 to the present, and appends the column FIP with its calculation according to the formula above:

```
df_team <- Teams |>
  filter(yearID >= 1970) |>
  mutate(FIP = (13*HRA + 3*BBA - 2*SOA)/IPouts + 3.10)
```

Now compare a team's FIP to its ERA using a scatterplot:

```
p <- ggplot(data = df_team,
            aes(x = FIP, y = ERA))
p + geom_point(alpha = .25) +
  theme_bw()
```

We can see that team FIP and ERA are fairly well correlated in this 50-year sample, which should give us some faith in the formula used for FIP. However, there are outliers that should reflect teams with excellent (and poor) defenses relative to league averages. We would also have more variation when evaluating certain players rather than entire teams.

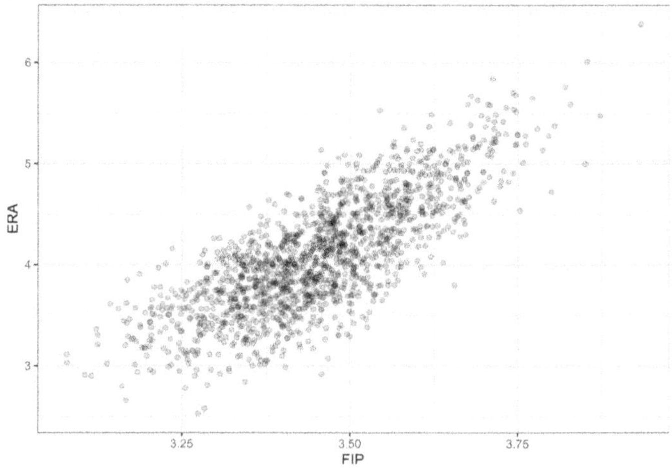

Figure 4.8: Field independent pitching (x) versus earned run average (y) for every team since 1970 in the Lahman database.

4.10 Statcast

What Is Statcast?

Statcast is Major League Baseball's ball-and-player tracking system that has been in every MLB ballpark since 2015. The current system has two components: (1) TrackMan Doppler radar tracks baseball events, and (2) ChryonHego cameras track player movements. In the first three seasons alone, 2.1 million pitches and 400,000 balls in play were tracked. In a nutshell, the location of the players and the ball is sampled multiple times per second to allow for a 3D re-creation of the game and also can be used to evaluate the optimal defensive placement of the players for particular batters or in certain game situations. The most obvious of these in the last 10 years has been the defensive shift in the infield, where three infielders might be on one side of second base and only one on the other side instead of the traditional equidistant placement of the infielders.* There are other game situations where the strategy would dictate we place defenders either very deep (relatively farther away from home plate than normal) or shallow (the opposite of deep). You can find more detailed information in the "Introducing Statcast 2023" article, found at `https://technology.mlblogs.com/introducing-statcast-2023-high-frame-rate-bat-and-biomechanics-tracking-3844890264a6` on the MLB's website.

Figure 4.9: Statcast.
Source: Stefan Stevenson / Fort Worth Star-Telegram / Tribune News Service via Getty Images

We are going to focus mostly on the ball in the following section. We will become familiar with terms such as *spin rate* and *exit velocity* throughout this section to measure the force and rotation of the ball. How do you think these might be used?

`baseballr`

We will use the `baseballr` package to query the MLB Baseball Savant (searchable Statcast) website, found at `https://baseballsavant.mlb.com`. In addition, `baseballr` can also be used to query `baseball-reference.com`, FanGraphs, and other sites as well. We will only use the Statcast functionality in this chapter, although you should explore all its functions as you work on your own analysis projects.

Players and Player IDs

Suppose we want to look up players and query the Statcast API. Let's do this in order to look at data on the Los Angeles Dodgers' designated hitter (and pitcher) Shohei Ohtani. The first function that we will use is a general function called `playerid_lookup()`. This function is not Statcast-specific in that there are a host of IDs available for additional websites, but it is slightly different from the function we used to find Mike Trout's `playerID` in the Lahman database earlier in this chapter. Note that this query may take a few seconds depending on the speed of your Internet connection:

```
ohtani_id <- playerid_lookup(last_name = "Ohtani",
                             first_name = "Shohei")
```

Figure 4.10: Shohei Ohtani.
Source: Mogami Kariya / CC BY-SA 2.0

As mentioned, this function call will return all players matching the `last_name` and `first_name` arguments, along with the IDs. In this case, only one row is returned matching Shohei Ohtani. Shohei Ohtani, the holder of the record for the largest contract in MLB history, as mentioned at the beginning of this chapter, is a special case because he is both an everyday designated hitter *and* a starting pitcher. He is the first person to do this since the legendary Babe Ruth, who was known more for his home run hitting prowess but was also a Hall of Fame–capable pitcher during his first several seasons with the Boston Red Sox. The correct ID for querying Statcast is the one listed in the `mlbam_id` field. This is 660271 for Shohei Ohtani. Now we can use that ID to get all of his information from any season of interest. We will use the `scrape_statcast_savant()` function to capture all Ohtani's data for the 2023 season and insert it into the tibble `df_ohtani_bat`. Note the Angels' (the team Ohtani played for in 2023) first game in 2023 was on March 30 and their last was on October 1:

* In 2023, the defensive shift was outlawed as a part of many rule changes designed to make the game more offensive and enjoyable while yet limiting the length of the game. The authors believe that 2012–22 may be referred to by baseball historians as the "Shift Era" in much the same way that 1900–1920 is referred to as the "Dead Ball Era."

```
df_ohtani_bat <- scrape_statcast_savant(start_date = ymd("2023-03-30"),
                                        end_date = ymd("2023-10-01"),
                                        playerid = 660271)
```

To compare, we will also look at defensive measures with Statcast. New York Yankees' pitcher Gerrit Cole won the 2023 AL Cy Young Award, an award given each year to the top pitcher in each league. Let's take a look at his pitching data from those same dates as Shohei Ohtani. Note that in the call to `scrape_statcast_savant()`, we specify `player_type = "pitcher"` because we are requesting his pitching data; otherwise, the default is to return a player's batting data:

```
cole_id <- playerid_lookup(last_name = "Cole",
                           first_name = "Gerrit")$mlbam_id
df_cole_pitch <- scrape_statcast_savant(start_date = ymd("2023-03-30"),
                                        end_date = ymd("2023-10-01"),
                                        playerid = cole_id,
                                        player_type = "pitcher")
```

Figure 4.11: Babe Ruth.
Source: Public domain

Figure 4.12: Gerrit Cole.
Source: All_Pro Reels from District of Columbia, USA / CC BY-SA 2.0

Batting

With batters, we are sometimes interested in "advanced" metrics like `launch_speed`, `launch_angle`, and `hit_distance_sc`. These metrics provide different attributes about how hard, high, and far a ball is hit in the air by the player, which give us an indication of the chances for success. Balls that are hit high and softly allow more time for the defenders to gather under the ball and catch it, while balls that are hit hard give the defense much less time to react. In addition, we may also want to pair these values with information about the ball that was thrown to the batter—for example, `pitch_type`. Let's examine this information. First, consider the type of pitches thrown to Shohei Ohtani in 2023 (figure 4.13). The abbreviations for each pitch type in Statcast are given in table 4.2.

```
p <- ggplot(df_ohtani_bat,
            aes(x = pitch_type, y = ..prop.., group = 1))
p + geom_bar() +
  labs(title = "Types of Pitches Thrown to Shohei Ohtani in 2023",
       x = "Pitch Type",
       y = "Proportion of Pitches") +
  theme_bw()
```

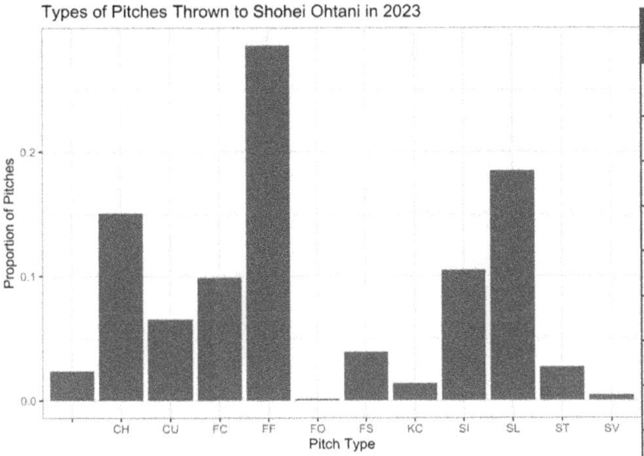

Figure 4.13: Bar chart showing the proportion of pitch types thrown to Shohei Ohtani in 2023.

Table 4.2: Pitch type abbreviations in Statcast

Abbreviation	Pitch type	Abbreviation	Pitch type
AB	Automatic ball	GY	Gyroball
AS	Automatic strike	IN	Intentional ball
CH	Changeup	KC	Knuckle curve
CU	Curveball	KN	Knuckleball
EP	Eephus	NP	No pitch
FC	Cutter	PO	Pitchout
FF	Four-seam fastball	SC	Screwball
FO	Forkball	SI	Sinker
FS	Splitter	SL	Slider
FT	Two-seam fastball	UN	Unknown

This shows us that, by far, Shohei Ohtani has more four-seam fastballs (FF) thrown to him than any other type of pitch. This is not surprising, as not every pitcher tries to throw every type of pitch, but every pitcher has some type of fastball.

While this bar chart gives us some visual information about the pitches that Ohtani sees, it is not as easy to read as it could be. For starters, how can we reorder the bars by percentage (ascending or descending)? First, let's use some slightly different code and re-create the figure given above in a different way. Next, let's re-create the tibble by ordering the data by percentage (most to least) and then plotting the data, which will order the bars in descending order:

```
df_ohtani_grouped <- df_ohtani_bat |>
  group_by(pitch_type) |>
  summarize(perc = n()/nrow(df_ohtani_bat)) |>
  arrange(desc(-perc)) |>
  mutate(pitch_type = factor(pitch_type, pitch_type))

p <- ggplot(df_ohtani_grouped,
            aes(x = pitch_type, y = perc))
p + geom_bar(stat = "identity", fill = "gray40") +
  scale_y_continuous(labels = scales::percent) +
  coord_flip() +
  labs(title = "Types of Pitches Thrown to Shohei Ohtani in 2023",
       x = "Pitch Type",
       y = "Proportion of Pitches") +
  theme_bw()
```

Ohtani's Exit Velocity

Note that the following code shows an alternative way of defining the plot object, `p`. That is, rather than defining a new dataset prior to calling the `ggplot()` function, we do some data manipulation on the data object and then pipe that data into the `ggplot()` function. We will use this style quite a bit because it allows us to do many visualizations from the same main dataset.

We are also going to filter the data by pitch type and eliminate the four least common pitches (ST, KC, SV, FO, and missing values), as each represents a very small amount of the number of pitches that Ohtani sees, and it will make our graphic much more readable.

We will also use a new type of plot, a violin plot (figure 4.15). This violin plot shows the relative density of the number of occurrences of each exit velocity for a given pitch type. The "fatter" the plot is at a particular place, the more instances of that value are in the dataset. This plot shows us that most of Shohei Ohtani's balls in play have an exit velocity between 80 and 110 mph, but different pitches have different ranges of exit velocity:

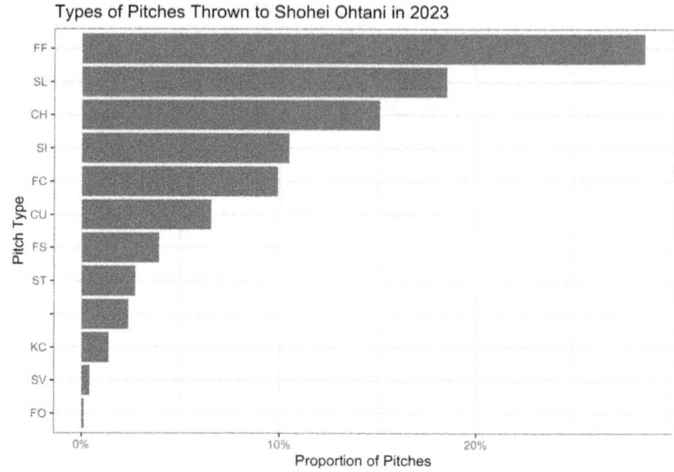

Figure 4.14: Ordered bar chart showing the proportion of pitch types thrown to Shohei Ohtani in 2023.

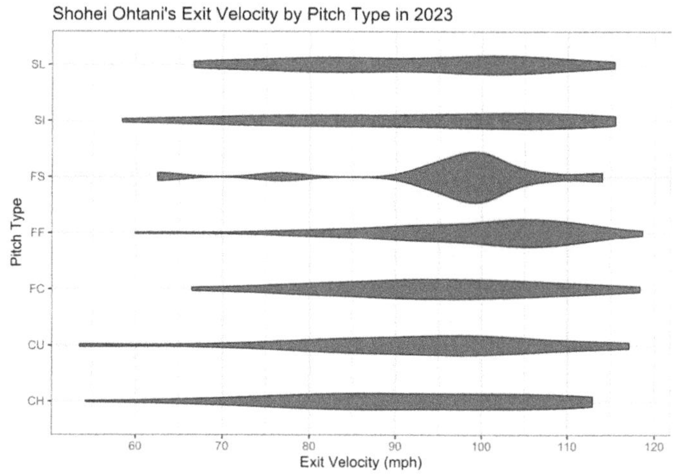

Figure 4.15: Violin plots showing Shohei Ohtani's exit velocity by pitch type thrown to him in 2023.

```
p <- df_ohtani_bat |>
  filter(pitch_type %in% c("CH", "CU", "FC", "FF", "SI", "SL", "FS"),
         type == "X") |>
  ggplot(aes(x = pitch_type, y = launch_speed))

p + geom_violin(fill = "gray40") +
  scale_fill_grey("type") +
  labs(title = "Shohei Ohtani's Exit Velocity by Pitch Type in 2023",
       x = "Pitch Type",
       y = "Exit Velocity (mph)") +
  scale_y_continuous(breaks = seq(60, 120, by = 10)) +
  coord_flip() +
  theme_bw()
```

Density Plots and Facets

We might also look at this data in a different way, through a density plot. However, we may want to view each pitch type individually though together on one page. We do that below by using a `facet_wrap()` added to the `ggplot()` function:

```
p <- df_ohtani_bat |>
  filter(pitch_type %in% c("CH", "CU", "FC", "FF", "SI", "SL", "FS"),
         type == "X") |>
  ggplot(aes(x = launch_speed))

p + geom_density(alpha = 0.5, fill = "gray40") +
  facet_wrap(. ~ pitch_type, ncol = 3) +
  labs(title = "Shohei Ohtani's Exit Velocity by Pitch Type in 2023",
       x = "Pitch Type",
       y = "Exit Velocity (mph)") +
  scale_y_continuous(breaks = seq(60, 120, by = 10)) +
  theme_bw()
```

Which visualization do you prefer? Why?

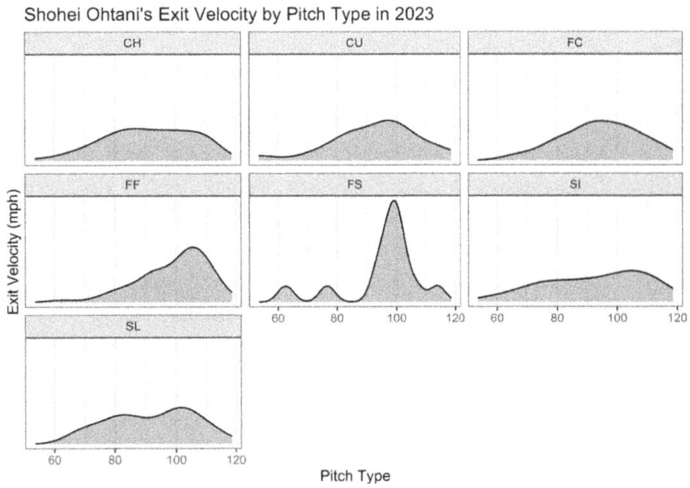

Figure 4.16: Density plots showing Shohei Ohtani's exit velocity by pitch type thrown to him in 2023.

Visualizing Pitcher Statcast Data

As mentioned above, we might look at `pitch_type` variables, but we will also want to consider variables such as `release_spin_rate` and `release_speed`. We will also consider, for both batters and pitchers, release positioning variables that we will talk about in the future.

Much like earlier where we analyzed the pitches that were thrown to Shohei Ohtani, we can now see the pitches that Gerrit Gole threw to all batters. Working with the tibble we created above for his data, we can plot these pitches. Note how we use `y = ..prop..` in the aesthetics to request proportions rather than counts in the bar chart:

```
p <- ggplot(df_cole_pitch,
            aes(x = pitch_type, y = ..prop.., group = 1))
p + geom_bar() +
  labs(title = "Types of Pitches Thrown by Gerrit Cole in 2023",
       x = "Pitch Type",
       y = "Proportion of Pitches") +
  theme_bw()
```

As the chart in figure 4.17 shows proportions, you may have a different visualization that you like. For example, you could present this as a pie chart. If you wanted to compare multiple pitchers on the same graph, you may choose to use a stacked bar chart instead.

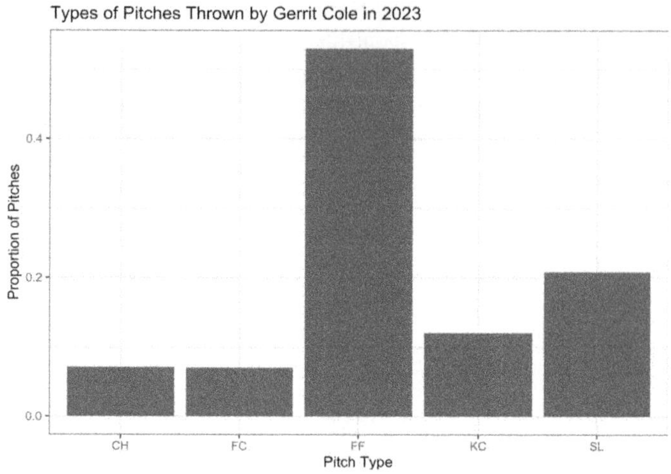

Figure 4.17: Bar chart showing the proportion of pitch types thrown by Gerrit Cole in 2023.

Cole's Spin Rate

We can not only visualize the pitch type frequency count; we can also graph the spin rate for each of those pitches thrown. To do this, we will use the violin plot to show the number of pitches at each spin rate for each type of pitch. As those more familiar with baseball might expect, Cole's knuckle curveball spins the most, and his changeup spins the least:

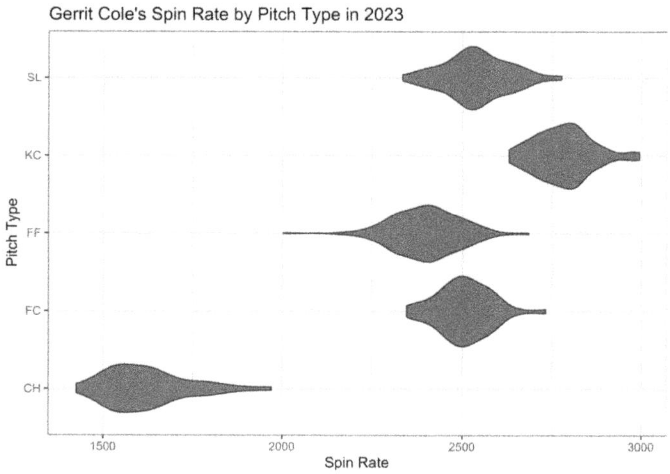

Figure 4.18: Violin plots showing the spin rate by pitch types thrown by Gerrit Cole in 2023.

```
p <-  df_cole_pitch |>
  filter(pitch_type %in% c("CH", "FC", "FF", "SL", "KC"),
         type == "X")  |>
  ggplot(aes(x = pitch_type, y = release_spin_rate))

p + geom_violin(fill = "gray40") +
  scale_fill_grey("type") +
  labs(title = "Gerrit Cole's Spin Rate by Pitch Type in 2023",
       x = "Pitch Type",
       y = "Spin Rate") +
  coord_flip() +
  theme_bw()
```

Cole's Release Speed by Month

Perhaps we are also concerned about fatigue with Gerrit Cole over a long six-month season or that batters are able to catch on to his tendencies as the season goes along, or we might even wonder if it takes him a few games into the season to get precise with his pitches. To do that, we will look at his pitch release speed, but we will group the data by month so that we see line plots in a time series. We will then plot the data for each pitch type on the same graph:

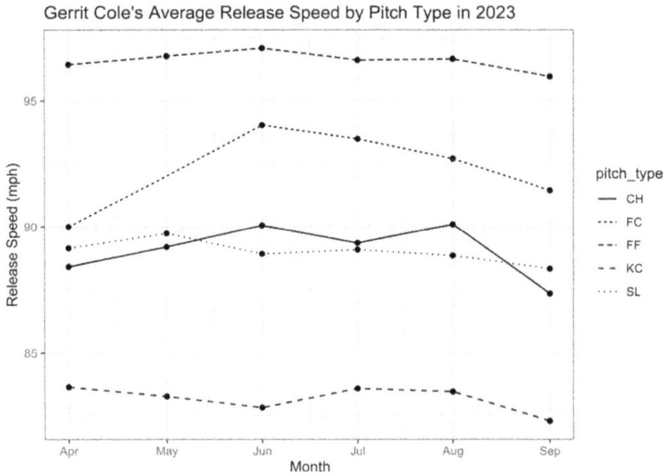

Figure 4.19: Average release speed in each month of the 2023 season by pitch types thrown by Gerrit Cole.

```
p <-  df_cole_pitch |>
  filter(pitch_type %in% c("CH", "FC", "FF", "SL", "KC"),
         type == "X",
         game_date >= ymd("2023-04-01")) |>
  group_by(month = month(game_date), pitch_type) |>
  summarize(avg_sp = mean(release_speed)) |>
  ggplot(aes(x = month, y = avg_sp, linetype = pitch_type))

p + geom_line() +
  geom_point() +
  scale_color_brewer("type", palette = "Dark2") +
  scale_x_continuous(labels = c("Mar", "Apr", "May", "Jun",
                                "Jul", "Aug", "Sep"),
                     breaks = 3:9) +
  labs(title = "Gerrit Cole's Average Release Speed by Pitch Type in 2023",
       x = "Month",
       y = "Release Speed (mph)") +
  theme_bw()
```

What inferences can you draw about Gerrit Cole over the course of the 2023 season?

4.11 Research Block: Did the Houston Astros Cheat Their Way to the 2017 World Series Title?

The Houston Astros were viewed as a test case in analytics during the 2010s. In the early part of the decade, the team was a perennial loser, but it seemed as though they were developing a strategy to field a championship team later in the decade. *Sports Illustrated* now famously predicted on the cover of their June 30, 2014, issue that the Houston Astros would be the 2017 World Series champions, despite them holding a record of 36–48 at the time. They hired mathematicians and scientists to run their decision sciences department and to be their analysts, forsook spending money on free agents to just sell tickets, and instead keyed all their efforts and contracts on winning in the future. Indeed, their strategy worked, and *Sports Illustrated* editors seemed like time travelers 3.5 years later when the Astros were crowned 2017 champions. Their new use of analytics seemed like a recipe for success for other teams, but perhaps their success had an unfair advantage.

By 2019, stories began to swirl that Astros' hitters may have been unfairly tipped off as to what pitch the pitcher was preparing to throw. This has happened since the beginning of baseball in a process known as "stealing signs," or having players on one team intercept the hand signals that coaches and players on the opposite team deliver to their teammates so that they are all aware of the action that is about to follow. What made this accusation different is that in this case, it was alleged that the Astros were using high-tech cameras to observe the signs when playing games in Houston and then were relaying the information to the Astros' hitters. While a player stealing a sign by observing it and relaying it to their teammates might fall into a gray zone and be dealt with by a pitcher throwing a ball up near the batter's head, the use of this technology was expressly against MLB rules. There were even accusations that players wore electronic devices under their uniforms to receive the signals, and others suggested that players beat trash can lids in the dugout to signal to the batter what type of pitch was coming. Proving that this happened several years later is difficult to do, but this is where analytics come in.

Sports Illustrated cover, June 30, 2014, issue.
Source: Andrew Urbaczewski

In their paper in the *American Statistician*, "Bang the Can Slowly: An Investigation into the 2017 Houston Astros," found at `https://www.tandfonline.com/doi/full/10.1080/00031305.2021.1902391`, Elmore and Matthews studied whether the team's actions (i.e., stealing the opposing pitching signs) affected the team's on-field performance. In particular, the authors investigated three key areas, and the results follow. First, the odds of swinging at a pitch decreased when a sign was stolen. Second, the odds of making contact with the baseball increased when the Astros' player swung the bat after a stolen sign. Lastly, the exit velocity increased significantly when the player made contact. In other words, the sign-stealing scheme certainly affected the on-field performance.

Regardless of academic study, MLB concluded that something nefarious had indeed happened in Astros' home games in 2017. While they were allowed to keep their World Series title, manager A. J. Hinch and general manager Jeff Lunhow were suspended for one year, a $5 million fine was paid, and certain star players from that team that were identified as potentially benefiting from unauthorized assistance, such as José Altuve, were ostracized within the league.

4.12 Strike Zones

As is the case with a lot of topics within sports analytics, we sometimes have to make a few simplifying assumptions. When looking at strike zones, or the XYZ space in which a pitch is declared to be a strike, it will vary by batter (height) and, to some extent, even by the tendencies of the umpire. However, we can use an "average" zone as the basis for our figures. In Statcast, the `plate_x` and `plate_z` fields contain the location of pitches from the center of the strike zone.

Creating the Strike Zone in R

A reasonable definition of a strike zone is found in the text *Analyzing Baseball Data with R (3e)*, found at `https://beanumber.github.io/abdwr3e/`, by Albert, Marchi, and Baumer. It states the bottom of the strike zone (on average) as 1.5 feet above the ground and the top as 3.6 feet above the ground. Given that home plate is 17 inches wide, and Albert, Marchi, and Baumer mention that "only a part of the ball need pass over home plate in order for the pitch to be called a strike," they define the strike zone width to be $17 + 2 \times (9/\pi)$ inches:

```
plate_width <- 17 + 2 * (9/pi)
```

Now we can use this zone as an outline on a graph where we will plot all of the pitches delivered to Shohei Ohtani:

```
p <- ggplot(df_ohtani_bat,
            aes(x = plate_x,
                y = plate_z))
p + geom_point(alpha = 0.2) +
  geom_rect(xmin = -(plate_width/2)/12,
            xmax = (plate_width/2)/12,
            ymin = 1.5,
            ymax = 3.6,
            alpha = 0,
            lwd = .7,
            col = "red") +
  labs(x = "Horizontal Location (ft)",
       y = "Vertical Location (ft)") +
  xlim(-4, 4) +
  coord_fixed() +
  theme_bw()
```

You may notice that several pitches are shown as having a negative vertical location. Of course, it is impossible for pitches to burrow into the ground. The authors do not know why this happens, although we suspect that these pitches bounced before they reached home plate, or possibly that there was some measurement error from the camera. It is up to you in your analyses how you treat these locations. We have left them here, but perhaps you would like to filter out any pitch that has a `plate_z` value of less than zero.

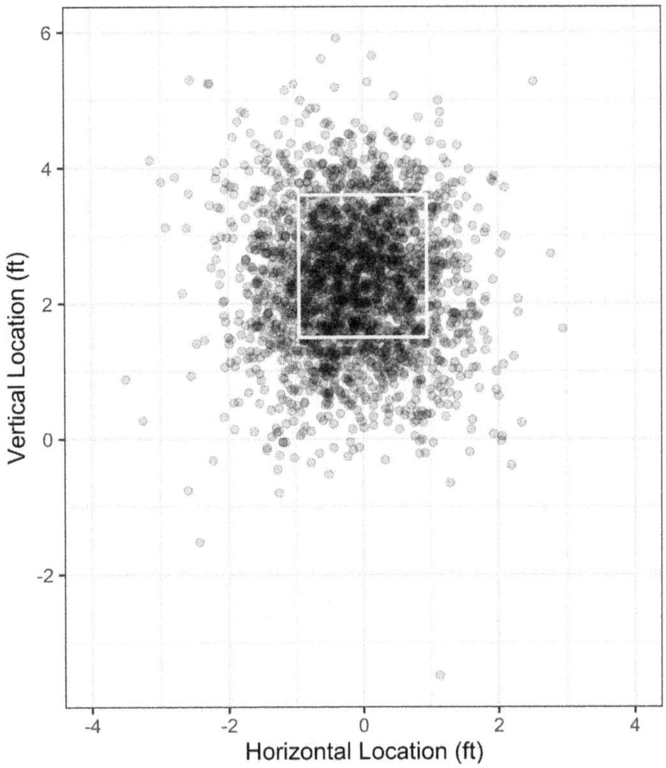

Figure 4.20: All pitch locations to Shohei Ohtani during the 2023 season.

Good Eye, Shohei?

Next we can identify which pitches delivered to Ohtani caused him to swing or not swing. To do this, we will use the `ifelse()` function to segregate all the pitches that he did not swing at from the ones where he swung. Then we will plot them using different colors to denote swings and takes:

```
df_ohtani_bat <- df_ohtani_bat |>
  mutate(swing = ifelse(description %in% c("ball", "blocked_ball",
                                          "automatic_ball", "called_strike",
                                          "hit_by_pitch"), 0 , 1))
p <- ggplot(df_ohtani_bat,
            aes(x = plate_x, y = plate_z, col = as.factor(swing)))
```

```
p + geom_point(alpha = 0.5) +
  scale_color_brewer("swing", palette = "Set1", labels = c("No", "Yes")) +
  geom_rect(xmin = -(plate_width/2)/12,
            xmax = (plate_width/2)/12,
            ymin = 1.5,
            ymax = 3.6,
            alpha = 0,
            lwd = .7,
            col = "black") +
  labs(x = "Horizontal Location (ft)",
       y = "Vertical Location (ft)") +
  xlim(-4, 4) +
  coord_fixed() +
  theme_bw()
```

A (potentially) more useful plot could be to just look at the pitches that did not result in Ohtani swinging the bat and whether or not a strike was called. How could we achieve this result?

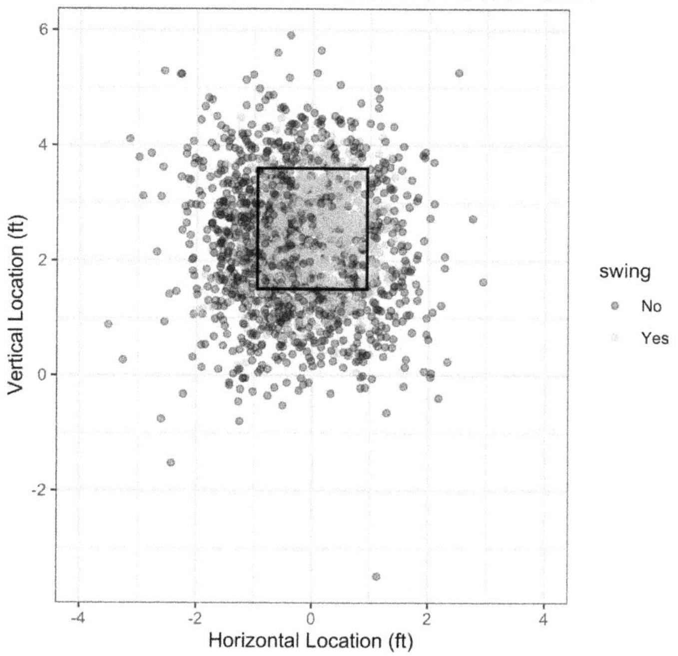

Figure 4.21: All pitch locations to Shohei Ohtani during the 2023 season shaded by whether (1) or not (0) he swung.

```
p <- df_ohtani_bat |>
  filter(swing == 0, type != "X") |>
  ggplot(aes(x = plate_x, y = plate_z, col = type))

p + geom_point(alpha = 0.5) +
  scale_color_brewer("call", palette = "Set1") +
  geom_rect(xmin = -(plate_width/2)/12,
            xmax = (plate_width/2)/12,
            ymin = 1.5,
            ymax = 3.6,
            alpha = 0,
            lwd = .7,
            col = "black") +
  labs(x = "Horizontal Location (ft)",
       y = "Vertical Location (ft)") +
  xlim(-4, 4) +
  coord_fixed() +
  theme_bw()
```

We can see that Ohtani is more likely to swing at pitches close to his body (inside) and take pitches that are outside and/or low (we will show how we know this later). We can also see that Ohtani is given the benefit of the doubt more often than not when he does not swing, as there are many more pitches inside the strike zone that were called balls than outside of the strike zone that were called strikes. This could be an unconscious bias from umpires, who may feel that Ohtani is so good, if a pitch is close and he does not swing, it must be a ball.

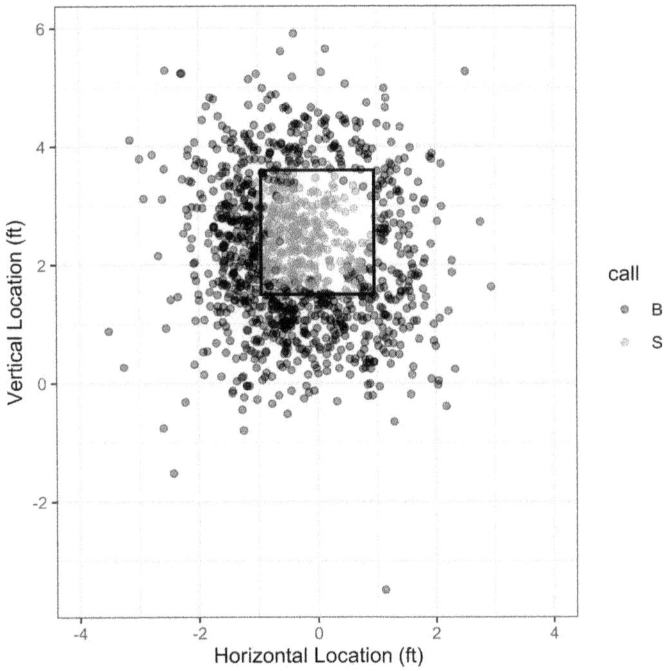

Figure 4.22: All pitch locations to Shohei Ohtani in which he did not swing during the 2023 season shaded by the pitch being called a ball or strike by the umpire.

4.13 Estimating Probabilities

While both authors are big fans of Shohei Ohtani, there are other players in the league. Let's examine the data from one of his 2023 teammates, Mike Trout.

Managers of baseball teams have to make many in-game decisions to implement their strategy and have the best chance of success. These involve deciding when to substitute a player, choosing to try to steal a base or not, and on defense, determining whether to intentionally walk a batter or where to defensively position players. Probabilities are what drive these decisions, and managers doing this are often referred to as "playing the numbers."

What are obvious events that we might want to look at in terms of probabilities? Hitting? Getting an out? HR? Let's consider the first one, hits. In Statcast, how do we know if a player got a hit? We will have to combine a few columns. In the Statcast data, `type = X` is an indicator that the ball was put in play, and the `events` field will tell you the type of hit. For example, here are the first six rows from the tibble where Trout has put balls into play:

```
trout_id <- playerid_lookup(last_name = "Trout",
                            first_name = "Mike")$mlbam_id
df_trout_bat <- scrape_statcast_savant(start_date = ymd("2023-03-30"),
                                       end_date = ymd("2023-10-01"),
                                       playerid = trout_id)
df_trout_bat |>
  filter(type == 'X') |>
  select(type, events, launch_angle, launch_speed) |>
  head()
```

```
# A tibble: 6 × 4
  type  events                    launch_angle launch_speed
  <chr> <chr>                            <dbl>        <dbl>
1 X     grounded_into_double_play           12         57.6
2 X     single                               3         78.7
```

```
3 X     field_out                                63          86.4
4 X     single                                   10         111.
5 X     single                                   14          75.1
6 X     home_run                                 34         108.
```

Launch Angle

Using the above dataset, we can create a density plot showing the launch angle for all balls Trout put into play in 2023:

```
p <- ggplot(data = df_trout_bat |>
              filter(type == 'X') |>
              select(type, events, launch_angle, pitch_type),
            aes(x = launch_angle))
p + geom_density() +
  theme_bw()
```

You may also be wondering, What is a negative launch angle? It means that he hit the ball toward the ground in a downward motion rather than in the air. The graphic in figure 4.23 tells us the frequency of launch angles for Trout, but it does nothing to tell us whether the event was a success (i.e., a hit). Suppose we want to know the probability of a hit given the launch angle. Maybe we can find an optimal launch angle for Trout. Let's first see the distinct values for all events:

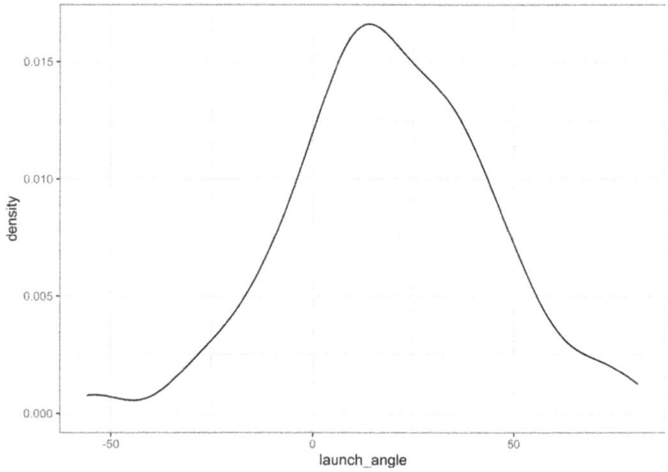

Figure 4.23: Density plot for launch angle for Mike Trout's balls that were put into play during the 2023 season.

```
df_trout_bat |>
  filter(type == "X") |>
  distinct(events)
```

```
# A tibble: 9 × 1
  events
  <chr>
1 grounded_into_double_play
2 single
3 field_out
4 home_run
5 fielders_choice
6 double
7 triple
8 force_out
9 sac_fly
```

We see that single, double, triple, and home run are good, and most everything else is bad. Maybe a sacrifice fly isn't bad, but let's ignore that for now as we are concentrating on hits. So we will create a column, `hit`, that we will set to 1 if the event is a single, double, triple, or home run, and 0 if it is anything else. We will also exclude any events that do not include launch angle by telling it to include everything that has a value for launch angle. Actually, we are telling it to include things that do not have nothing for the launch angle by using the `!` to mean "not" and `is.na()` to mean "has nothing there." "Not nothing" is a bit of a double negative equals a positive, but it works:

```
df_trout_hits <- df_trout_bat |>
  filter(type == "X", !is.na(launch_angle)) |>
  mutate(hit = ifelse(events %in% c("single", "double",
                                    "triple", "home_run"),
                      1, 0))
```

We will then start by creating a basic plot with points. Hit or not a hit will be on the y-axis, and launch angle will be on the x-axis. We can estimate a smooth function (a loess curve) and its associated pointwise confidence interval using `geom_smooth()`:

```
p <- ggplot(data = df_trout_hits,
            aes(x = launch_angle, y = hit))
p + geom_point(alpha = .15) +
  scale_x_continuous(breaks = seq(-60, 80, by = 20)) +
  labs(x = "Launch Angle",
       y = "Hit") +
  geom_smooth(col = "black") +
  theme_bw()
```

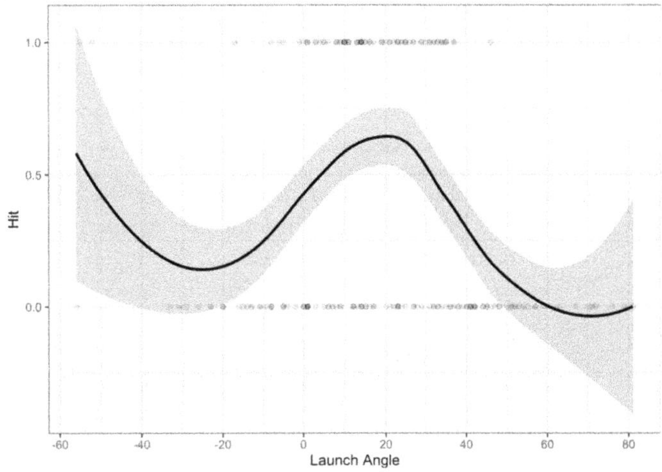

Figure 4.24: Mike Trout's hits (1) or not (0) along with their launch angle during the 2023 season.

What does figure 4.24 tell us in terms of the probability of getting a hit for a given launch angle? Does the smooth curve seem to make sense?

It tells us that his highest probability of getting a hit is with a launch angle of about 20 degrees. Does your baseball knowledge seem to confirm that or contrast with that? No matter your answer, a good analyst will confirm any findings through multiple analyses and potentially multiple methodologies. For example, you may see a few extreme outliers (balls with -50- to -60-degree launch angles) that are confounding the smooth function. You may also see that between 60- and 80-degree launch angles, the probability of a hit is actually less than zero—an impossibility. The smooth function helps us get an idea of the data, but it never should be taken as the absolute truth by itself.

Launch angle is only one variable related to balls put in play. Statcast also captures exit velocity as `launch_speed`. We can do the same analysis as above for exit velocity by starting with a basic plot of the points using exit velocity on the x-axis:

```
p <- ggplot(data = df_trout_hits,
            aes(x = launch_speed, y = hit))
p + geom_point(alpha = .15) +
  labs(x = "Launch Speed",
       y = "Hit") +
  geom_smooth(col = "black") +
  theme_bw()
```

Ignoring a few outliers on the low end, it seems that hit probability remains fairly constant when exit velocity is between about 65 and 90 mph, and it accelerates continuously above 95 mph. "Hit it harder" seems like good advice! Of course, that is easier said than done.

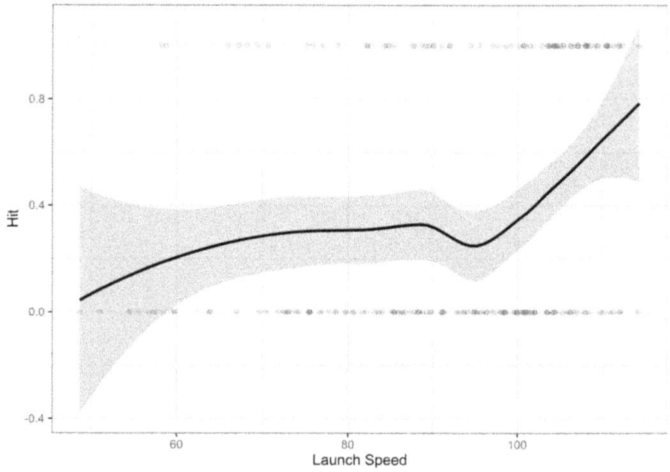

Figure 4.25: Mike Trout's hits (1) or not (0) along with their launch speed during the 2023 season.

4.14 Logistic Regression Model

One method (among many) for modeling the probability of an event with two outcomes is to use logistic regression. We will not get into the details when it comes to the theoretical nuances of logistic regression, but understand that in linear regression, the dependent variable is continuous (like ERA, for example). We use logistic regression more as a classification model, as we are trying to classify an output as one of two possibilities (in this case, a hit or not a hit). Its implementation is similar to a standard linear model. This is a technique that we will use throughout the book.

For example, suppose we want to predict the probability of a hit based on launch angle. We would then use the `glm()` function to run a generalized linear model with `family = "binomial"`, which will account for logistic regression:

```
glm_trout <- glm(hit ~ launch_angle,
                 data = df_trout_hits,
                 family = "binomial")
summary(glm_trout)
```

```
Call:
glm(formula = hit ~ launch_angle, family = "binomial", data = df_trout_hits)

Coefficients:
              Estimate Std. Error z value Pr(>|z|)
(Intercept)  -0.220927   0.178561  -1.237   0.2160
launch_angle -0.011485   0.005915  -1.942   0.0522 .
---
Signif. codes:  0 '***' 0.001 '**' 0.01 '*' 0.05 '.' 0.1 ' ' 1

(Dispersion parameter for binomial family taken to be 1)

    Null deviance: 276.11  on 205  degrees of freedom
Residual deviance: 272.22  on 204  degrees of freedom
AIC: 276.22

Number of Fisher Scoring iterations: 4
```

Note that the interpretation of the coefficients is not as straightforward as that in a simple linear regression model. Just know that if the coefficient related to a predictor variable (in this case, launch angle) is greater than zero, then the probability of `Y=1` increases as the predictor variable increases and decreases if the coefficient is less than zero. How do we visualize this fit?

```
p <- ggplot(data = df_trout_hits,
            aes(x = launch_angle, y = hit))
p + geom_point(alpha = .15) +
  scale_x_continuous(breaks = seq(-60, 80, by = 20)) +
  geom_smooth(col = "black",
              method = "glm", formula = y ~ x,
              method.args = list(family = "binomial")) +
  labs(y = "P(hit)",
       x = "Launch Angle") +
  theme_bw()
```

Does this model seem like a good fit? We don't think so. We think that this probability increases as launch angle increases and then starts to decrease, whereas the logistic model in figure 4.26 is showing a fairly constant decrease as launch angle increases. How could we fit a curve that allows for an increase (decrease) followed by a decrease (increase) as launch angle increases? The easiest way to do this is to include a quadratic term in the launch angle. In R, we can fit a logistic regression with a quadratic term by specifying the launch angle in a polynomial form. In this case, we represent `launch_angle` as a quadratic effect using `poly(launch_angle, 2)`, where 2 represents a quadratic term:

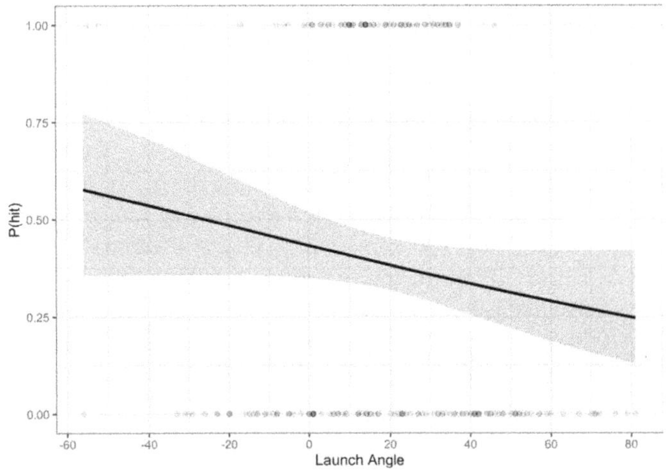

Figure 4.26: Estimated probability of Mike Trout getting a hit (1) or not (0) as a function of launch angle during the 2023 season. We estimate the probability using a simple logistic regression model with launch angle as a predictor variable.

```
glm_trout_2 <- glm(hit ~ poly(launch_angle, 2),
                   data = df_trout_hits,
                   family = "binomial")
summary(glm_trout_2)
```

```
Call:
glm(formula = hit ~ poly(launch_angle, 2), family = "binomial",
    data = df_trout_hits)

Coefficients:
                       Estimate Std. Error z value Pr(>|z|)
(Intercept)             -0.6833     0.1860  -3.673 0.000240 ***
poly(launch_angle, 2)1  -6.9496     3.0697  -2.264 0.023579 *
poly(launch_angle, 2)2 -17.7605     4.7639  -3.728 0.000193 ***
---
Signif. codes:  0 '***' 0.001 '**' 0.01 '*' 0.05 '.' 0.1 ' ' 1

(Dispersion parameter for binomial family taken to be 1)

    Null deviance: 276.11  on 205  degrees of freedom
Residual deviance: 246.10  on 203  degrees of freedom
```

```
AIC: 252.1

Number of Fisher Scoring iterations: 5
```

Note that the asterisks indicate that a quadratic term is highly significant as a predictor of a hit. As a model-building principle, we must keep the linear term in the model, regardless of its significance, if the quadratic term is significant. We can visualize the model in the following way, and we think this makes more sense than our linear model:

```
p <- ggplot(data = df_trout_hits,
            aes(x = launch_angle, y = hit))
p + geom_point(alpha = .15) +
  scale_x_continuous(breaks = seq(-60, 80, by = 20)) +
  geom_smooth(col = "black",
              method = "glm", formula = y ~ poly(x, 2),
              method.args = list(family = "binomial")) +
  labs(y = "P(Hit = 1)",
       x = "Launch Angle") +
  theme_bw()
```

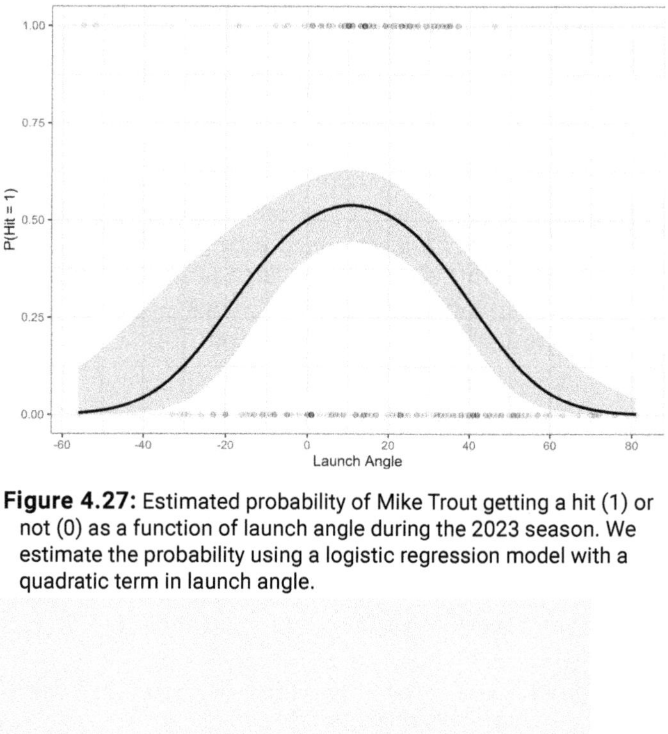

Figure 4.27: Estimated probability of Mike Trout getting a hit (1) or not (0) as a function of launch angle during the 2023 season. We estimate the probability using a logistic regression model with a quadratic term in launch angle.

Catcher or Pitcher Perspective?

From looking at the data, we may not know whether we are seeing the data from the catcher's perspective or the pitcher's perspective. One way you could tell is that if you know which side of the plate the batter hits from, you can examine just the pitches in which the batter was hit by the pitch. The following plot shows the pitches that hit Mike Trout, a right-handed hitter. Are the data displayed from the pitcher's or the catcher's perspective?

```
p <- df_trout_bat |>
  filter(description == "hit_by_pitch") |>
  ggplot(aes(x = plate_x, y = plate_z))

p + geom_point() +
  geom_rect(xmin = -(plate_width/2)/12,
            xmax = (plate_width/2)/12,
            ymin = 1.5,
            ymax = 3.6,
            alpha = 0,
            lwd = .7,
            col = "black") +
  labs(x = "horizontal location (ft)",
       y = "vertical location (ft)") +
  xlim(-4, 4) +
  ylim(0, 5) +
  coord_fixed() +
  theme_bw()
```

Trout is a right-handed batter, so figure 4.28 is clearly from the catcher's (or plate umpire's) perspective. That's a few too many pitches up by his head for any manager's liking!

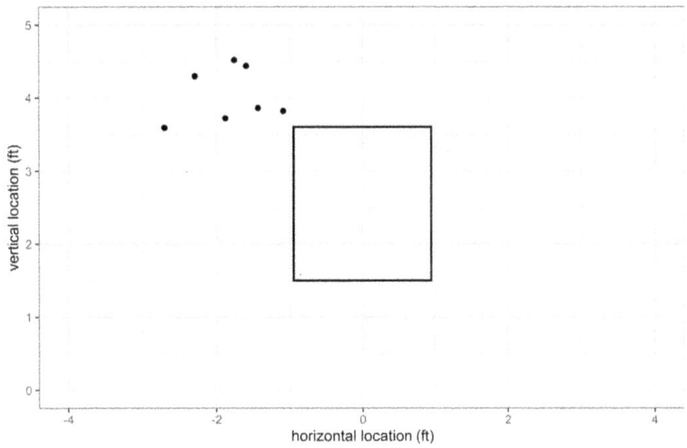

Figure 4.28: Pitch locations for pitches that hit Mike Trout in 2023.

4.15 Swing Probability

Next we will tie together our previous work on pitch location, swings, and so on with some of the logistic regression models in order to compute probability heat maps. We will start with a heat map on the swing plot given in figure 4.21 and model the probability of swinging based on location alone. This, again, is a simplification of a more complicated process, but it's still useful.

First, we will fit a nonparametric regression model. The specific nonparametric model is a logistic regression variant of a generalized additive model, or GAM, using the `gam()` function from the `mgcv` package. This formulation is particularly useful when the underlying functional form is unknown and you wish to model probabilities. We will illustrate this concept using data from Shohei Ohtani's 2023 season:

```
swing_gam <- gam(swing ~ s(plate_x) + s(plate_z),
                 family = binomial,
                 data = df_ohtani_bat)
swing_predict_data <- expand.grid(plate_x = seq(-1.5, 1.5, length = 50),
                                  plate_z = seq(0.5, 5, length = 50))
# Get the predicted values from the model and convert to probability values:
swing_preds <- predict(swing_gam,
                       newdata = swing_predict_data,
                       type = "response")
swing_predict_data <- swing_predict_data |>
  mutate(swing_prob = swing_preds)
p <- ggplot(data = swing_predict_data,
            aes(x = plate_x, y = plate_z))

p + geom_tile(aes(fill = swing_prob)) +
  scale_fill_distiller("P(Swing)", palette = "Spectral",
                       direction = -1,
                       limit = c(0,1)) +
  geom_rect(xmin = -(plate_width/2)/12,
            xmax = (plate_width/2)/12,
            ymin = 1.5,
            ymax = 3.6,
            alpha = 0,
            lwd = .7,
            col = "black") +
  coord_fixed() +
  labs(x = "Horizontal Location (ft)",
       y = "Vertical Location (ft)",
       title = "When Does Shohei Ohtani Swing?") +
  theme_bw()
```

What does this figure tell you about his swinging? He likes to swing at pitches on the inside of the plate!

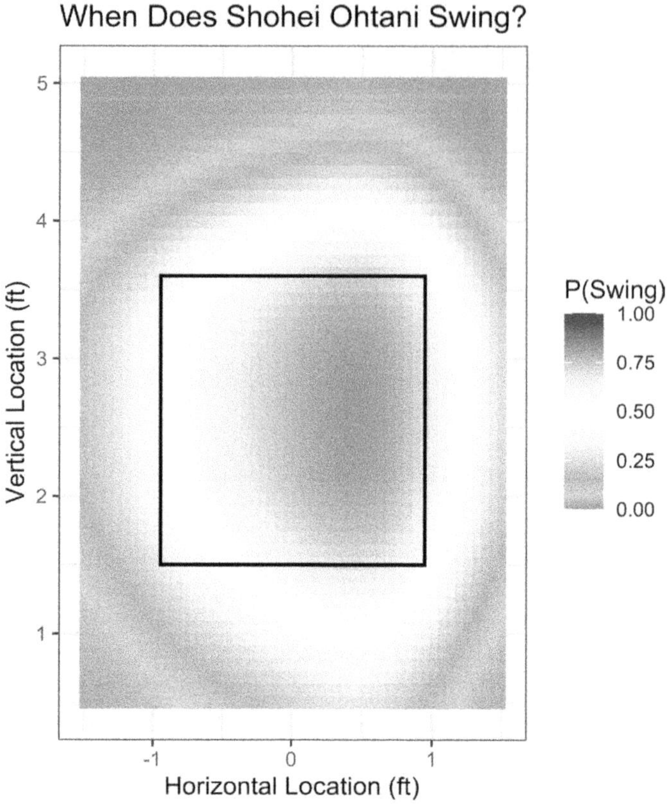

4.16 Conclusion

In the century and a half that professional baseball has been played in the United States, there have been tons of data generated. Yet this will only continue to grow as much more data are collected every day. Camera systems in major-league ballparks now record the positions of every player and the ball 30 times per second. We have only begun to scratch the surface of what we can do with data and baseball. In fact, we could have done the entire book on just baseball. If you are more interested in baseball and want to do a deeper dive than we can provide here, we recommend the text *Analyzing Baseball Data with R*, available at `https://beanumber.github.io/abdwr3e/`.

Fortunately for those of us who do not work for Major League Baseball teams, the volume of this data that is available to the public for free allows us to do our own analysis. We used the Lahman database to gather information about both teams and players, and we used it to not only see what has happened in the past, such as when Shohei Ohtani or Mike Trout liked to swing at pitches, but also predict the future in terms of how many runs a team will score and then how many games they will win. Of course, this is nowhere near all of the data that are collected, nor is it the summation of everything that can be done with that data. We hope this chapter not only introduces you to baseball analytics and improves your R programming skills but also inspires you to create your own analysis!

4.17 Lab: Calculating Baseball Metrics

Earlier in the chapter, we went through the details of calculating runs created. As a reminder, here is the code we used:

```
team_df <- tibble(Teams) |>
  filter(yearID >= 1970)
rc_df <- team_df |>
  mutate(HBP = ifelse(is.na(HBP), 0, as.numeric(HBP)),
```

```
         X1B = H - X2B - X3B - HR,
         TB = X1B + 2*X2B + 3*X3B + 4*HR,
         RC = (H + BB + HBP)*TB/(AB + BB + HBP))
```

Now we can go through a similar methodology to calculate some of the other metrics we will use in baseball analysis. We will start with on base percentage (OBP), slugging percentage (SLG), and on base percentage plus slugging (OPS), or the ability to get on base and hit for power. Note that the equation for OBP is

$$OBP = \frac{(H+BB+HBP)}{(AB+BB+HBP)},$$

and

$$SLG = (1B + 2 \cdot 2B + 3 \cdot 3B + 4 \cdot HR) \,/\, AB,$$

and that $OPS = OBP + SLG$.

1. Add `OBP`, `SLG`, and `OPS` to the `rc_df` object we defined previously:

```
rc_df <- rc_df |>
  mutate(OBP = (H + BB + HBP)/(AB + BB + HBP),
         SLG = (X1B + 2*X2B + 3*X3B + 4*HR)/AB,
         OPS = OBP + SLG)
```

2. Compute a correlation matrix for `R`, `RC`, `AB`, `H`, `HR`, `OBP`, `SLG`, and `OPS` and plot the results using `ggcorrplot()`. Which pairs of variables appear to be the most correlated?

```
cor_mat <- cor(select(rc_df, R, RC, AB, H, HR, OBP, SLG, OPS))
ggcorrplot(cor_mat, method = "circle",
           colors = c( "#2c7bb6", "#ffffbf", "#d7191c"))
```

3. Perhaps we want to consider a different metric than `RC` when looking at the ability of a player to generate runs. An alternative to `RC` created by David Smythe is base runs (`BsR`). `BsR` was created in order to provide a better model for the run-scoring process. The formula is defined by

$$BsR = \frac{A \cdot B}{B+C} + D,$$

   where

$$A = H + BB - HR,$$
$$B = (1.4 \cdot TB - 0.6 \cdot H - 3 \cdot HR + 0.1 \cdot BB) \cdot 1.02,$$
$$C = AB - H, \text{ and}$$
$$D = HR.$$

   So next, add `BsR` to the `rc_df` object:

```
rc_df <- rc_df |>
  mutate(A = H + BB - HR,
         B = (1.4*TB - .6*H - 3*HR + .1*BB)*1.02,
         C = AB - H,
         BsR = (A*B)/(B + C) + HR)
```

4. Compute the correlation matrix and plot for `R`, `RC`, `AB`, `H`, `HR`, `OBP`, `SLG`, `OPS`, and `BsR`:

```
cor_mat <- cor(select(rc_df, R, RC, AB, H, HR, OBP, SLG, OPS, BsR))
ggcorrplot(cor_mat, method = "circle",
           colors = c( "#2c7bb6", "#ffffbf", "#d7191c"))
```

5. Compare simple linear regressions of R on each of RC and BsR individually. Which of RC and BsR seems to give the best fit (and why)?

```
rc_r_lm <- lm(R ~ RC, data = rc_df)
summary(rc_r_lm)
```

6. Now let's look at some more outstanding players. Compare Ronald Acuña Jr.'s 2023 season to Mookie Betts's 2023 season in terms of runs above the average player. Use the Teams dataset from 2010 to the present as the baseline model. Note that Acuña and Betts were the NL MVP and runner-up in 2023, respectively. Exclude the 2020 COVID year:

```
df_teams <- Teams |>
  filter(yearID >= 2010, yearID != 2020) |>
  mutate(X1B = H - X2B - X3B - HR,
         BB_HBP = BB + HBP) |>
  select(R, X1B, X2B, X3B, HR, BB_HBP)
lm_runs <- lm(R ~ ., data = df_teams)
summary(lm_runs)
playerInfo(nameLast = "Acuna")
acuna <- Batting |>
  filter(playerID == "acunaro01",
         yearID == 2023) |>
  mutate(X1B = H - X2B - X3B - HR,
         BB_HBP = BB + IBB + HBP,
         Outs = .982*AB - H + GIDP + SF + SH + CS)
select(acuna, R, X1B, X2B, X3B, HR, BB_HBP)
#playerInfo(nameLast = "Betts")

betts <- Batting |>
  filter(playerID == "bettsmo01",
         yearID == 2023) |>
  mutate(X1B = H - X2B - X3B - HR,
         BB_HBP = BB + IBB + HBP,
         Outs = .982*AB - H + GIDP + SF + SH + CS)
select(betts, R, X1B, X2B, X3B, HR, BB_HBP)
avg_player <- df_teams |>
  summarize_all(.funs = mean)
predict(lm_runs, newdata = avg_player)
avg_outs <- Teams |>
  filter(yearID >= 2010, yearID != 2020) |>
  summarize(outs = mean(IPouts))
avg_outs
acuna_scale <- (avg_outs$outs - acuna$Outs)/avg_outs$outs
w_acuna <- avg_player*acuna_scale +
  select(acuna, R, X1B, X2B, X3B, HR, BB_HBP)
betts_scale <- (avg_outs$outs - betts$Outs)/avg_outs$outs
w_betts <- avg_player*betts_scale +
  select(betts, R, X1B, X2B, X3B, HR, BB_HBP)
predict(lm_runs, newdata = w_acuna) -
  predict(lm_runs, newdata = avg_player)
predict(lm_runs, newdata = w_betts) -
  predict(lm_runs, newdata = avg_player)
```

7. Using the Teams data from 1970 to the present, predict (using regression) RA (runs against) from HRA (home runs allowed), BBA (walks allowed), and SOA (strikeouts against). Print out the summary of the regression using either the summary() or tidy() function:

```
df_team_ra <- Teams |>
  filter(yearID >= 1970)
lm_ra <- lm(RA ~ HRA + BBA + SOA,
```

```
            data = df_team_ra)
tidy(lm_ra)
```

8. Add the predicted values from the regression in problem 7 to your data matrix and call these values FIP_new. Add a column for FIP as well. Construct the correlation matrix (and correlation plot) for RA, FIP, FIP_new, HRA, BBA, and SOA:

```
df_team_ra <- df_team_ra |>
  mutate(FIP = (13*HRA + 3*BBA - 2*SOA)/IPouts + 3.10,
         FIP_new = predict(lm_ra))
cor(select(df_team_ra, RA, FIP, FIP_new, HRA, BBA, SOA))
ggcorrplot(cor(select(df_team_ra, RA, FIP, FIP_new, HRA, BBA, SOA)))
```

9. Using the Batting dataset from the years 2010 to the present, fit a regression model to predict the runs (R) variable based on the following independent variables: BB_HBP, singles, doubles, triples, and home runs. You will need to create a new variable, call it BB_HBP, that is walks plus hit by pitches:

```
df_batting <- Batting |>
  filter(yearID >= 2010) |>
  mutate(X1B = H - X2B - X3B - HR,
         BB_HBP = BB + HBP)
lm_a <- lm(R ~ X1B + X2B + X3B + HR + BB_HBP,
            data = df_batting)
tidy(lm_a)
```

10. Speaking of outstanding players, in 2022, Aaron Judge (New York Yankees) set the AL record for home runs. Use this model to predict runs for Aaron Judge in the 2022 season:

```
judge_pred <- filter(df_batting,
                     playerID == playerInfo(nameLast = "Judge")$playerID)
judge_pred <- judge_pred |>
  mutate(preds = predict(lm_a, newdata = judge_pred)) |>
  select(playerID, yearID, R, preds)
judge_pred
```

11. Should you use this model to predict Barry Bonds's 2003 runs? Why or why not?

4.18 Case Study: Adjusting to Baseball in Colorado

When Major League Baseball expanded to Colorado in 1993, it was a live experiment in how the game would change. It was long known that objects tend to travel farther for a given level of force when the altitude level increases. For example, a golf ball hit in Mexico City, with an altitude of 7,800 feet above sea level, tends to travel about 15% farther than the same golf ball hit with the same force at a golf course at sea level in Miami. This is due to a variety of factors, but primarily, it is because of the decreasing amount of wind resistance as the air becomes less dense at higher altitudes. Before the league expansion in 1993, the MLB ballpark with the highest altitude was Atlanta's Fulton County Stadium at approximately 1,100 feet, and even it was known as "The Launching Pad" due to the travel of baseballs in that stadium. How would baseball change with a ballpark in Denver, the "Mile High City," which is almost five times higher than Atlanta?

As predicted, in its first few years, home runs were hit at prodigious levels in Colorado. The Montreal Expos, on their first trip to Denver to play in the first MLB games there, famously used all of the baseballs they brought for four days of batting practice on their first day. A game that was 11–3 entering the ninth inning would normally be considered all but over, but not in Denver. Coors Field was given the nickname "Coors Canaveral," and the players were known as the Blake Street Bombers.

The challenges to baseball in thin air were varied. While an obvious answer to reducing home runs might be to just make the fences farther away from the batter—and indeed, Coors Field is known as a relatively large ballpark (for readers less familiar with baseball, each MLB stadium has different dimensions, unlike a soccer pitch or basketball court of standard sizing)—but that did not reduce the offense. Why? The same three outfielders now have more ground to cover as the size of the field has increased, and there is much more room for a hitter to land the ball inside the park and also between the outfielders for a (extra) base hit.

Figure 4.29: Coors Field and the famous row of purple seats at one mile above sea level.
Source: Justin Edmonds / Contributor / Getty Images Sport via Getty Images

In 2002, Coors Field installed a humidor where the baseballs would be kept prior to games. They were stored at a constant 70 degrees and 50% humidity, making the baseballs slightly heavier and easier for the pitchers to grip (and spin) than in the normal 10%–20% humidity found at the higher altitudes of Denver. This alleviated the issue of baseballs leaving the stadium at abnormal rates and reduced the number of home runs hit in the stadium from a major-league record 307 in 1999 to 185 in 2007, only the 10th most of any stadium that year—and perhaps coincidentally, the only year that the Colorado Rockies won the National League and played in the World Series. In 2018, the Arizona Diamondbacks also installed a humidor in their stadium, which at 1,100 feet of altitude and also low desert humidity experienced some of the same effects (though much less pronounced) as those in Denver. By 2021, nine MLB ballparks had installed humidors to standardize the baseball across parks.

Despite all of these improvements, pitchers still complain that the baseball spins less from the pitcher's hand to home plate in Denver. This means that balls that may normally curve sharply at sea level will not curve as much at Coors Field, and an average curveball at sea level may be a "hanging curve" in Denver, which batters are able to hit with ease. The batters may delight in the easier hitting conditions, but it becomes more difficult for the Rockies' hitters to adjust to the road conditions. This leads to a weird dichotomy: Colorado batters and pitchers who play 81 games per year in Denver are used to this effect at home and, as such, routinely have one of the best records in the major leagues at home. However, they also routinely have one of the worst records away from Coors Field, as they are constantly having to adjust away from Denver to more sea level–like conditions. For example, in the 2023 baseball season, the Rockies were 37–44 at home but 22–59 on the road.

This effect has become frustrating to both hitters and pitchers as they struggle to adjust every time they leave Coors Field. Analytics could be used to address the problem; we have measurements for spin rates and other ballpark effects, and these data are available for each pitch at the Statcast source mentioned earlier in the chapter.

Answer the following using data from the hitters or the pitchers:

1. How would you measure the effect of spin rate? Does it analytically differ in Coors Field from other parks?
2. If you were the manager, general manager, or pitching coach of the Colorado Rockies, how would you propose addressing the issues?
3. Based on your answers to the question above, how would you measure success?

4.19 Exercises

1. Choose two teams from the `Pitching` table in the Lahman database. Define a new data frame by filtering the original data frame to include only those two teams. How many rows are in the new data frame?
2. Using the teams from problem 1, compute the total earned runs (ER) given up for each team by year. Plot your results using points and lines for 1970 through 2018 colored by `teamID`.
3. Create a new data frame using the `Batting` data from Lahman and filter based on the Colorado Rockies. Call this new data frame `col_df`. Add two new columns to this data frame for total bases and slugging percentage and pipe this result into the `na.omit()` function.
4. Plot the average `SLG` per year for the Rockies from 1993 to the present.
5. Note that this solution looks a bit wacky in comparison to what is given on MLB's website or `baseball-reference.com`. This is because we asked for the average `SLG` and not the team `SLG`. Remember, there are a lot of pitchers included in this average, and they generally are not great hitters.

6. Using Statcast data, find the `mlbam_id` for the following players: Shohei Ohtani, Ronald Acuña Jr., Gerrit Cole, and Blake Snell. Note that Ohtani and Acuña won the 2023 AL and NL MVP award (respectively), and Cole and Snell won the 2023 AL and NL Cy Young Award, respectively. Note that you will need to use the tilde on the *n* in Acuña.
7. Download the data for each player from the 2023 regular season (March 30, 2023, through October 1, 2023).
8. Compute a two-by-three facet plot of Ronald Acuña Jr.'s exit velocity for the six most common types of pitches that he saw in 2023. Do the same for Shohei Ohtani and compare your results.
9. Create a bar chart showing the proportion of pitch types thrown by Blake Snell in 2023. Sort the bars in either decreasing or increasing order.
10. Compute two-by-two facet plots showing Blake Snell's spin rate by month for his four most common types of pitches (ignore null).
11. Construct a strike zone map for pitches by either Snell or Cole.
12. Do the same as in 11 but facet by the handedness of the batter facing the pitcher. This is contained in the `stand` variable. You will need to change the `stand` variable to a factor using `as.factor()`.
13. Can you determine the perspective on these pitch figures? In other words, is this view from the catcher's or the pitcher's perspective?
14. It looks like two common pitches by both pitchers are the four-seam fastball (`FF`) and the changeup (`CH`). Compute two-by-two faceted strike zone plots showing the location of pitches for `FF` and `CH` pitch types when facing R and L batters (`stand`).
15. What locations of pitches cause the hitters to swing and miss based on the two pitch types mentioned in 14? Create a new figure similar to problem 14 and color the points based on whether the pitch resulted in a strike given that the batter swung and then missed. You'll have to create a new column based on the `description == "swinging_strike"` and filter for swings.
16. We will compute the probability of a swing and a miss heat map for Snell's changeup versus right-handed hitters (based on location).
17. Do the same as in problem 16 but look at the map for Cole's four-seam fastball when facing right-handed hitters.

Chapter 5

Basketball

> It was the first time someone was speaking my language in basketball. . . . It wasn't just [about] heart and grit.
>
> —Former NBA player Shane Battier upon joining the Houston Rockets in 2006 and working with analytics-minded general manager Daryl Morey
>
> When I was on the Rockets, Hakeem would tell me, "Play simple." And I would tell him, "I am; all I do is give you the ball!" He said, "Yes, and when I get the ball, I either score, get fouled, or you get an open three." That is analytics, and they have been around forever.
>
> —Scott Brooks sharing an anecdote at the 2016 Sloan Sports Analytics Conference about playing with Hakeem Olajuwon
>
> Everybody pulls for David; nobody roots for Goliath.
>
> —Wilt Chamberlain

5.1 R Packages

We will use the following R packages in this chapter that we have used in previous chapters:

```
library(ggplot2)
library(dplyr)
library(ISAR)
library(lubridate)
library(mgcv)
```

We will also introduce the following R packages in this chapter:

```
library(gganimate) # works with ggplot2 to create animations
library(nbastatR) # access NBA data through the league's official API
library(sportyR) # ggplot-scaled representations of sports fields/courts
library(gifski) # converts images to GIF animations
library(wehoop) # access women's basketball play-by-play data
library(tidyr) # pivots and nests data
library(teamcolors) # the color palettes for pro sports teams
```

If you do not remember how to install new packages in R or RStudio, refer to chapter 2, where there is a detailed discussion.

The textbook's `ISAR` package contains three datasets that are used extensively throughout this chapter: `nba_games_2023`, `nba_adv_team_2023`, and `nba_ff_team_2023`. The first dataset contains the game log information for each regular season game in the 2022–23 NBA season. The latter two are the advanced and four-factor team statistics for each of the 2022–23 regular season games, respectively. In both cases, we use the `hoopR` package to obtain the data, and all are in the book's R package `ISAR`.

We will also be using multiple regression as an analysis technique. If you do not remember that from previous chapters, see the more complete description in the baseball chapter.

5.2 If You Don't Know Anything about Basketball

Basketball is a simple enough game that older adults and young children can play it using exactly the same parameters as those who play it at the highest levels. The court is still 94 feet long, the basket is still 10 feet in the air, and the ball is the same size, albeit women's competitions use a 28.5-inch ball instead of the 29.5-inch ball that the men use. The real difference, of course, is in the skill of the players.

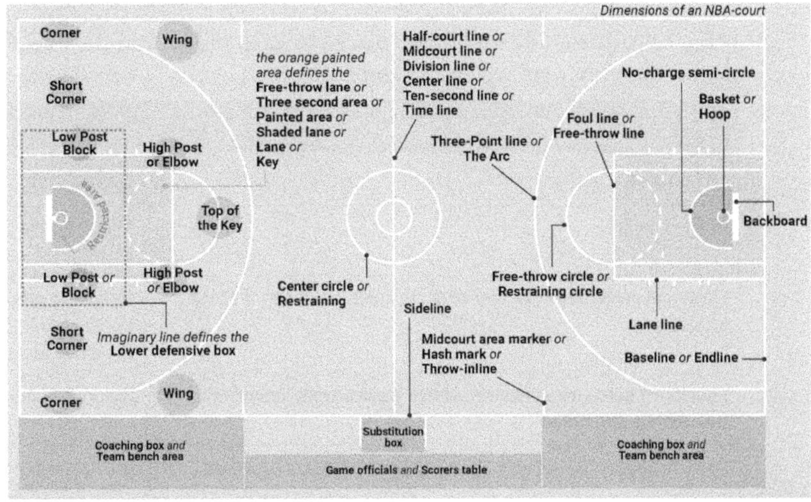

Figure 5.1: Diagram of an NBA basketball court.

In its simplest form, two teams of five players each try to score more points than the other team over either two halves or four quarters. In the NBA, the game is played through four 12-minute quarters. Points are scored by throwing the ball (shooting) into the basket, which is perched generally 10 feet (3.05 meters) over the floor, one at each end of the court representing the goal for each team. Two points are awarded for a made basket, and if the shot was taken from a long way away, behind an arc approximately 23 feet (7 meters) from the basket, three points are awarded. The defense tries to disrupt the players from making the baskets by standing close to them and trying to take the ball away (steal) from them or knock the ball away as it leaves the shooter's hands (block). If the defense were to knock the player's arms or legs or push them while they are shooting, a foul is called on the defender, and the shooter will get two attempts to make an unimpeded shot (free throws) from a line 15 feet (4.57 meters) directly in front of the basket. Each free throw is worth one point. If a player commits five or six fouls (depending on the league) during the course of a game, that player is disqualified for the rest of the game. When the game is played on the playground, it is often played as the first team to reach a certain number of baskets (usually 15) with shots behind the three-point line counting double.

There are, of course, many more nuances to the game, but this gives you the basics of how to play basketball. You can see much more information at `https://www.rookieroad.com/basketball/` on the play of the game and strategies at different levels.

Basketball has grown to perhaps the second most popular sport globally, behind only soccer. While it is the one major team sport played in America that is likely uniquely and authentically American, there have been many efforts to grow the game around the world. The USA still dominates the men's Olympic basketball tournament, having won the gold medal in 16 of the 19 Olympics in which it has participated, but hotbeds of basketball are developing around the world. China, Western Europe, Australia, the Baltic Republics, and the Adriatic countries are large markets for basketball and send many players to play in professional and amateur leagues in the United States.

For the purposes of this book, we will be using the dimensions of an NBA court and games played under NBA rules. The international court is slightly smaller, and the three-point line is also slightly closer under international rules, and there are other more subtle differences, but NBA players usually have no trouble adjusting when going back and forth between NBA games and international competitions such as the Olympic Games. FIBA, the governing body for basketball globally, has continually made the court and the rules more similar to NBA rules over the years.

5.3 Basic Basketball Metrics

Unlike baseball, which we examined in the prior chapter, basketball is free-flowing and is not a collection of discrete events that can be studied individually or on the whole. That is, there are not defined breaks between pitches or balls in play in basketball. It can be divided somewhat accurately into possessions, and certainly, we can track things like shots and rebounds (though both of those with a bit of a margin for error when balls are being tipped around), fouls, time played by each player, and the like. With this in mind, we will apply analytics a bit differently than we do in baseball.

Table 5.1: Early metrics used in basketball analytics

Offensive	Defensive
Points scored	Minutes played: amount of game time a player is one of the five people active on the court
Field goal percentage: number of shots made / number of shots attempted	Defensive rebounds: catching the ball as it bounces off the rim after an opponent's missed shot (Offensive rebounds, when the rebounder is on the same team as the shooter, could be considered an offensive metric.)
Free throw percentage: number of free throws made / number of free throws attempted	Blocks: swatting the ball away as it leaves the opponent's hand
Assists: passes that directly result in a teammate scoring a field goal	Steals: taking the ball away from a player without committing a foul
Three-point shots: shots made from behind the three-point line	Fouls: breaking the rules of permissible conduct on the floor as it relates to interacting with an opponent (Usually this is physical contact with a player in the act of shooting.)
Turnovers: committing an act (other than a foul or a missed shot) that causes the other team to gain possession of the ball (This can often be throwing the ball out of bounds on a bad pass.)	Plus/minus: the number of points your team scored while you were in the game less the number of points your team allowed while you were in the game

5.4 Four Factors

The notion of the "four factors" was developed by Dean Oliver and is explained in his book *Basketball on Paper*, available at `http://basketballonpaper.com`. His original formulation assigned the following weight to wins: shooting (40%), turnovers (25%), rebounding (20%), and free throws (15%). There has been a lot of debate about the appropriateness of the weighting of these factors, and we will look at some aspects of weighting in this chapter. Most people still agree, however, that the four factors are extremely important to a team's success. Note, too, that while these four factors describe a team's offensive efficiency, they can also be used to describe the efficiency of a team's defense (i.e., What is our opponent's effective field goal percentage?). The factors are as follows:

1. Effective field goal percentage
2. Turnovers committed per possession
3. Offensive rebounding percentage
4. Free throw rate

Effective Field Goal Percentage

Effective field goal (EFG) percentage is a means of resolving the difference between two-point and three-point field goals. It gives more weight to three-pointers relative to two-pointers. How much more weight? It adds 50% more to a three-pointer because they are worth 50% more points. The exact formula is

$$EFG = \frac{fg2m + 1.5 * fg3m}{fga},$$

where fg2m and fg3m are the number of two-point baskets made, respectively, and fga is the number of overall shots attempted.

Upon examining the nba_games_2023 data frame (which you will find in the ISAR package), we note that we can mutate this data frame to calculate EFG, or we could also just look at the advanced box score for each game. Let's examine these and compare the figures from both tables:

```
games <- nba_games_2023 |>
  mutate(fg2m = fgm - fg3m, #explicitly separate 2 and 3 point baskets
         efg = (fg2m + 1.5*fg3m)/(fga))
df_merge <- dplyr::left_join(games, nba_adv_team_2023,
                              by = c("team_id", "team_abbreviation", "game_id", "min"))
p <- ggplot(data = df_merge,
            aes(x = efg, y = efg_pct))
p + geom_point(alpha = .5) +
  labs(title = "Comparing our calculated EFG to NBA.com's EFG",
       x = "EFG (Our Calculation)",
       y = "EFG (From NBA.com)") +
  theme_bw()
```

We find that these are the same in both sets, which is good news for our calculations!

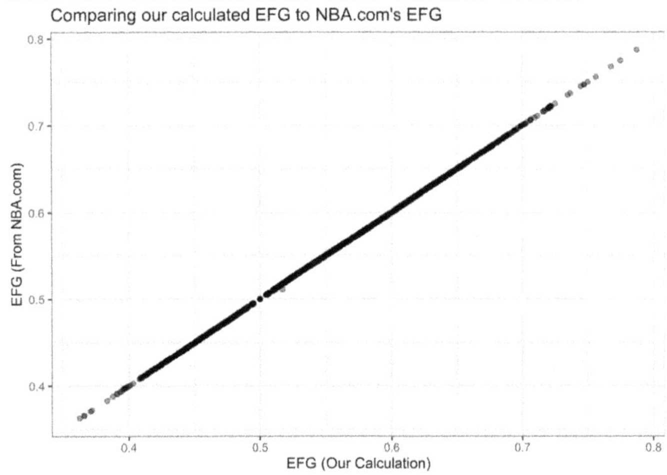

Figure 5.2: The effective field goal percentage from our calculations (x) versus what is reported on NBA.com (y).

Turnovers Committed per Possession

As the name suggests, turnovers committed per possession (TPP) is the number of turnovers committed relative to the number of possessions the team had during the game. Turnovers (tov) and possessions (poss) are given in the nba_games_2023 and nba_adv_team_2023 tibbles, respectively:

```
df_merge <- df_merge |>
  mutate(tpp = tov/poss)
```

Offensive Rebounding Percentage

Roughly, offensive rebounding percentage (ORP) is the ratio of the total number of offensive rebounds to the number of offensive rebound possibilities. Note that both offensive and defensive rebounds are given in the nba_games_2023 tibble, and the actual rates are given in the nba_ff_team_2023 and nba_games_2023 tibbles. A team's ORP for a given game is simply

$$ORP = \frac{\text{team offensive rebounds}}{\text{team offensive rebounds} + \text{opponent defensive rebounds}}.$$

Free Throw Rate

Free throw rate (FTR) is the ratio of free throw attempts (`fta`) to field goal attempts (`fga`). Both statistics are given in the `nba_games_2023` tibble, and FTR is given in `nba_ff_team_2023`. Let's look below at manually calculating the FTR in the `nba_games_2023` tibble and compare it to what is reported in the `nba_ff_team_2023` table. We will print the first few rows to the console as a proof of concept:

```
left_join(nba_games_2023, nba_ff_team_2023,
                    by = c("team_id", "team_abbreviation", "game_id", "min")) |>
  mutate(ftr = fta/fga) |>
  select(fta_rate, ftr) |>
  head()
```

```
# A tibble: 6 × 2
  fta_rate   ftr
     <dbl> <dbl>
1    0.35  0.35
2    0.341 0.341
3    0.232 0.232
4    0.266 0.266
5    0.221 0.221
6    0.261 0.261
```

These four factors are Oliver's representations of the areas where teams need to excel. Earlier, we showed how to obtain the data to calculate these metrics. We will continue to explore the four factors throughout the rest of the chapter.

5.5 Densities, Percentiles, and Z-Scores

In the last section, we saw how to calculate and retrieve values for the four factors, but we did not discuss their usefulness. So how can we use the four factors? We could examine the distribution of values for a single (or multiple) season(s). Let's first look at these values for each team in the 2022–23 NBA season. We will do this with a density plot (`geom_density`), which shows us the distribution of EFG across all teams in this season.

Density

```
p <- ggplot(data = nba_adv_team_2023,
            aes(x = efg_pct))
p + geom_density() +
  labs(title = "2023 NBA EFG",
       x = "Effective Field Goal Percentage") +
  theme_bw()
```

We can see that the highest density of team EFG is somewhere between 50% and 55%, but what is the average in this sample, and can we add a reference line to this previous plot to represent it? Certainly we can:

- We will use `mean()` to calculate the mean.
- We will use `geom_vline()` to add the vertical line.
  - We will see the x-intercept of that line to the value of the mean.
  - We will make the line dashed so that it stands out from the grid lines.

Note that we do not need to redefine the initial plot object, `p`, as we created it above. We are merely adding new layers to that plot object:

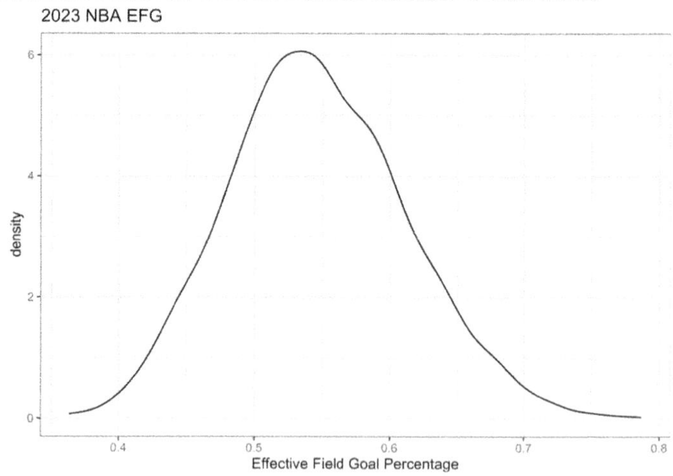

Figure 5.3: A density plot of effective field goal percentage.

```
mean(nba_adv_team_2023$efg_pct, na.rm = T)
```

```
[1] 0.5468923
```

```
p + geom_density() +
  geom_vline(xintercept = mean(nba_adv_team_2023$efg_pct, na.rm = T),
             linetype = "dashed") +
  labs(x = "Effective Field Goal Percentage") +
  theme_bw()
```

One way to view the graphical results is to plot the four factors all at the same time. We can do this by creating a faceted plot. To do this, we have to introduce a new function from the `tidyr` package, `pivot_longer`. First, we merge our previous dataset with the four factors data (`nba_ff_team_2023`). Next, we define a `win` variable to `TRUE` if the game was a win, calculated by whether the variable `plus_minus` is greater than zero (meaning that the team scored more points than they allowed), and otherwise set it to `FALSE`, meaning the game was a loss. Finally, we reformat the dataset to a long format from the traditional wide format. The long format denormalizes the data so that we can print the plots as facets, as we can't facet the data if a variable is split across multiple columns. Let's look at the entire dataset visually first before getting into wins and losses:

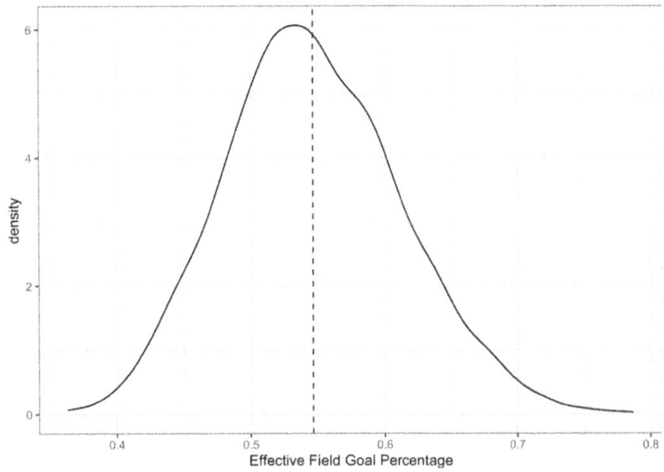

Figure 5.4: A density plot of effective field goal percentage along with the mean reference line.

```
df_pivot <- df_merge |>
  left_join(nba_ff_team_2023,
            by = c("team_id", "team_abbreviation", "game_id", "min")) |>
  mutate(win = ifelse(plus_minus > 0, TRUE, FALSE),
         efg_pct = efg_pct.x,
         tov_pct = tm_tov_pct.x/100,
         oreb_pct = oreb_pct.x) |>
  select(efg_pct, oreb_pct, tov_pct, fta_rate, win) |>
  pivot_longer(cols = 1:4)
p <- ggplot(data = df_pivot,
            aes(x = value))
p + geom_density() +
  facet_wrap(~ name, ncol = 2) +
  labs(x = "NBA Four Factors (2023 Season)") +
  theme_bw()
```

Now let's see how the results of the four factors compare in games that were wins and games that were losses. We can do this now by changing the aesthetics (`aes`) to plot the values of each of the four factors on the x-axis (`x = value`) by each of the values for the win variable (`TRUE` and `FALSE` as we calculated earlier). Note that we use the `scale_fill_brewer()` to distinguish between the two cases, wins and losses:

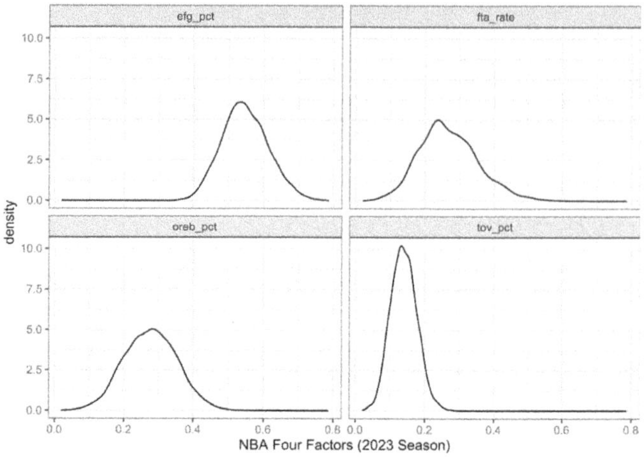

Figure 5.5: Density plots of the four factors for the 2023 season.

```
p <- ggplot(data = df_pivot,
            aes(x = value, fill = win))
p + geom_density(alpha = .25) +
  facet_wrap(~ name, ncol = 2) +
  scale_fill_brewer(palette = "Set1") +
  theme_bw()
```

Mostly, it seems that there is a lot of overlap, with the biggest difference being in EFG. EFG being different makes sense on its face, as games are graded not on rebounds or turnovers but rather on points, and a higher EFG should yield higher points scored, which should create more wins. But why do you think there is not a large difference in the other statistics?

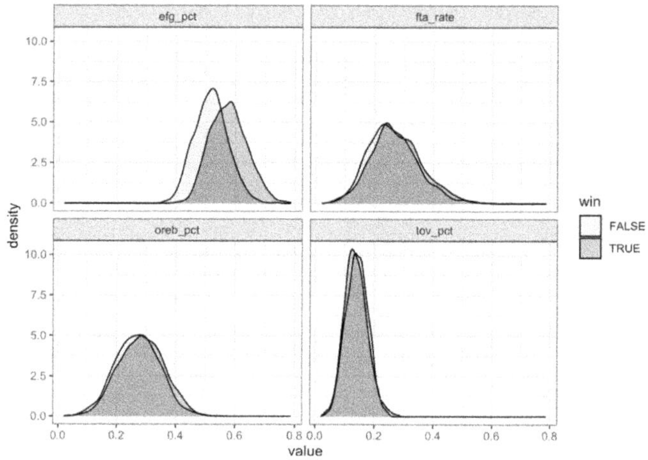

Figure 5.6: Density plots of the four factors by wins and losses for the 2023 season.

5.6 Specific Game Evaluation

In 2023, the Denver Nuggets defeated the Los Angeles Lakers for the NBA Western Conference Championship. But how did they play against each other in the 2022–23 regular season? We can turn our attention to the Denver Nuggets at Los Angeles Lakers game on December 6, 2022. The Lakers won this game 126 to 108, but the question remains: Did they play a good game? Similarly, did the Nuggets necessarily play a bad game given that they lost? One could simply point to the scoreboard and say that this is all that is needed to evaluate the results; however, given that we are interested in sports analytics and seek to remove the anomalous results from our overall evaluation, we can do deeper dives into the data. To do this, we need to filter for the appropriate game in the `nba_games_2023` table, get the game ID, and then use that to filter the `nbagames_2023` table:

December 16, 2022, Denver Nuggets at LA Lakers, final score.
Source: `www.basketball-reference.com/boxscores/202212160LAL.html`

```
den_lal_id <- nba_games_2023 |>
  dplyr::filter(game_date == ymd("2022-12-16"),
                team_abbreviation %in% c("LAL", "DEN")) |>
  dplyr::pull(game_id)

den_lal_adv <- nba_adv_team_2023 |>
  dplyr::filter(game_id == den_lal_id[1])
```

Now let's create some lines to show how both the Nuggets and the Lakers performed on this night with respect to EFG. This will show the performances for this one game as opposed to all the games from the 2023 season. How would you interpret these results?

```
p <- ggplot(data = nba_adv_team_2023,
            aes(x = efg_pct))
p + geom_density() +
  geom_vline(data = den_lal_adv,
             aes(xintercept = efg_pct, col = team_abbreviation)) +
  guides(col = guide_legend("team")) +
  scale_color_manual(values = c("#4D90CD", "#FDB927")) +
  labs(title = "Nuggets @ Lakers 12/6/2022 EFG vs 2022-23 NBA Averages",
       x = "Effective Field Goal Percentage") +
  theme_bw()
```

It seems that the Nuggets had a fairly average night, and the Lakers were better than average relative to EFG. Let's take the same logic and apply it to ORP. What is your interpretation of this plot?

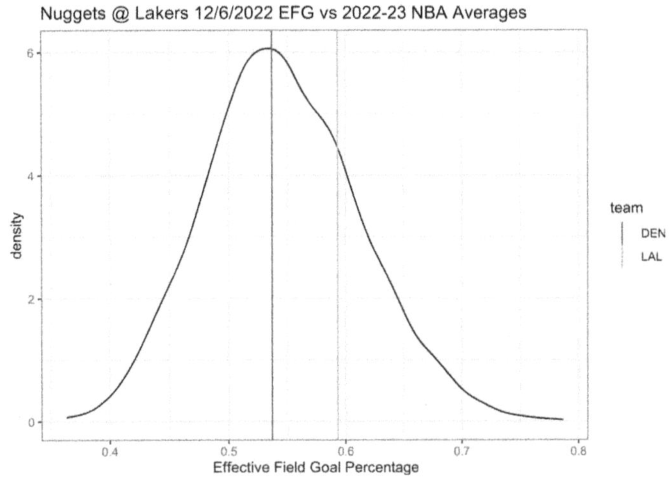

Figure 5.7: Effective field goal percentage density plot from the 2023 season along with the specific values from the Denver Nuggets at Los Angeles Lakers game on December 6, 2022.

```
p <- ggplot(data = nba_adv_team_2023,
            aes(x = oreb_pct))

p + geom_density() +
  geom_vline(data = den_lal_adv,
             aes(xintercept = oreb_pct, col = team_abbreviation)) +
  guides(col = guide_legend("team")) +
  scale_color_manual(values = c("#4D90CD", "#FDB927")) +
  labs(title = "Nuggets @ Lakers 12/6/2022 OREB vs 2022-23 NBA Averages",
       x = "Offensive Rebound Percentage") +
  theme_bw()
```

The OREB shows that Denver performed less well than the overall season average (across all teams) and that Los Angeles performed quite well. This matches up with the EFG in the previous figure. So one argument could be that the Nuggets did not do the little things well—guarding Lakers players and following their shots to the rim to create putback opportunities in the cases of missed shots.

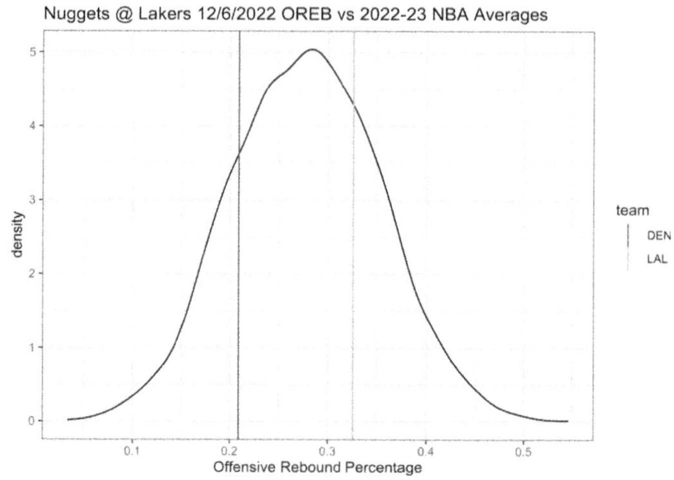

Figure 5.8: Offensive rebounding percentage density plot from the 2023 season along with the specific values from the Denver Nuggets at Los Angeles Lakers game on December 6, 2022.

5.7 Computing Estimated Probabilities

We still need to answer the question of whether the teams played particularly well on this night. To do this, we can look at the EFG percentage that we calculated earlier and compare it to the probability of the events happening. We will use the `ecdf()` function to find where in the cumulative distribution the points for Denver's and Los Angeles's EFG appear given all the games in the 2020–23 season:

```
ecdf(nba_adv_team_2023$efg_pct)(den_lal_adv$efg_pct)
```

```
[1] 0.7674797 0.4585366
```

This is saying that about 77% and 46% of the teams in this dataset (all 2023 games) had effective field goal percentages less than the Lakers and Nuggets, respectively, in this game.

5.8 Z-Scores

You may also remember z-scores from statistics as a calculation of the number of standard deviations that an observation is from the mean. We can calculate the z-score for the offensive rebounding percentages that we examined earlier in the chapter. Recall that the formula for a z-score is

$$z = \frac{\text{observed value} - \text{mean}}{\text{standard deviation}}.$$

The code below shows the z-scores for Los Angeles and Denver in terms of offensive rebounding percentage. Note that Los Angeles had a little more than a one-half standard deviation better than average night in offensive rebounding. On the other hand, Denver's night was one to forget in that their offensive rebounding percentage was approximately almost one standard deviation *less* than average:

```
(den_lal_adv$oreb_pct - mean(nba_adv_team_2023$oreb_pct)) /
  sd(nba_adv_team_2023$oreb_pct)
```

```
[1]  0.6412986 -0.9171681
```

We can compute percentiles assuming a normal distribution by using the `pnorm()` formula. We use the z-scores computed above as the input into the `pnorm()` function:

```
z_vals <- pnorm((den_lal_adv$oreb_pct -
                 mean(nba_adv_team_2023$oreb_pct)) /
                sd(nba_adv_team_2023$oreb_pct))
names(z_vals) <- den_lal_adv$team_abbreviation
z_vals
```

```
      LAL       DEN
0.7393357 0.1795273
```

5.9 Using the Four Factors to Predict Wins and Losses

Another way we could use the four factors is to predict their effects on whether a team wins a game. To do this, we will use logistic regression. We touched on this in the chapter on baseball, and we will use it again here.

In this case, we will use the generalized linear model (`glm`) function, with `win` as the dependent variable. We define a new data frame, `df_reg`, that we essentially created earlier but did not store. Note that we must remove the variable `plus_minus`, because `win` is directly derived from `plus_minus`. To fit the model, we write that the logit of `win` is a linear function of (~) by all the other variables in the data frame (`.`) except for the `plus_minus` variable (`- plus_minus`). We also tell `glm` that the dependent variable is binary (`family = "binomial"`), as it is either a win or a loss. We then print the output of the `glm` function:

```
df_reg <- df_merge |>
  dplyr::left_join(nba_ff_team_2023,
                   by = c("team_id", "team_abbreviation", "game_id", "min")) |>
  dplyr::mutate(win = ifelse(plus_minus > 0, TRUE, FALSE),
                efg_pct = efg_pct.x,
                tov_pct = tm_tov_pct.x/100,
                oreb_pct = oreb_pct.x) |>
  dplyr::select(efg_pct, oreb_pct, tov_pct, fta_rate, win)

adv_glm <- glm(win ~ .,
               data = df_reg,
               family = "binomial")
summary(adv_glm)
```

```
Call:
glm(formula = win ~ ., family = "binomial", data = df_reg)

Coefficients:
            Estimate Std. Error z value Pr(>|z|)
(Intercept) -12.1854     0.6120 -19.910  < 2e-16 ***
efg_pct      20.2032     0.9476  21.319  < 2e-16 ***
oreb_pct      7.0847     0.6837  10.362  < 2e-16 ***
tov_pct     -11.4324     1.3246  -8.631  < 2e-16 ***
fta_rate      2.8803     0.5604   5.139 2.75e-07 ***
---
Signif. codes:  0 '***' 0.001 '**' 0.01 '*' 0.05 '.' 0.1 ' ' 1

(Dispersion parameter for binomial family taken to be 1)

    Null deviance: 3410.3  on 2459  degrees of freedom
Residual deviance: 2680.2  on 2455  degrees of freedom
AIC: 2690.2

Number of Fisher Scoring iterations: 4
```

You may look at this output and not remember what all this means, or maybe chapter 4 was the first time you saw it. Or both. As we discussed there, the important thing to note is the last column, more commonly known as a p-value. P-values are the probability that the component is contributing to the model purely by chance and not because it has real predictive power. You will see that the probabilities associated with the coefficients, in order of presentation, are 2e-16, 2e-16, 2e-16, and 2.75e-07. All of these values are extremely small numbers, which for our purposes are virtually 0. This means that there is an approximately 0% chance that these variables do not contribute to the model's prediction of the win variable. Generally speaking, whenever the p-value is less than .05, we want to consider that variable as an important predictor in our model.

Also important with the coefficients is their sign. EFG, ORP, and FTA all have positive signs, which means that as their value increases, the probability of a win will also increase. Conversely, the sign of the TPP coefficient is negative, and hence, the probability of a win will decrease as TPP increases. This should make sense, as we would expect high levels of EFG, ORP, and FTA to correlate with wins and high levels of TPP to correlate with losses.

An alternative formulation of the adv_glm object assignment is to explicitly write out the independent variables that are contained in the model. The following code chunk shows the longhand version of the previous model specification:

```
adv_glm <- glm(win ~ efg_pct + oreb_pct + tov_pct + fta_rate,
               data = df_reg,
               family = "binomial")
```

5.10 Research Block: Is the Season Over after 20 Games in the NBA?

In the United States, Thanksgiving Day is a holiday celebrated on the fourth Thursday in November. While known as a time for giving thanks and celebrating with family and friends over a large dinner feast, it is also synonymous with NFL football on TV. It is similar to Boxing Day cricket in Australia or, with the NBA, Christmas Day. However, Thanksgiving is also a day on the calendar that in 2023 marks approximately 20 games played for NBA teams. This is only about one-fourth of the way through an 82-game season but yet is important for other reasons, as it is often viewed as a predictor of which 20 out of 30 teams will make the playoffs (and which 8 of those teams will have to play an additional round of games).

Author Ryan Elmore, in his paper "Predicting Which Teams Will Make the NBA Playoffs," published in the *Italian Journal of Applied Statistics*, available at https://www.sa-ijas.org/ojs/index.php/sa-ijas/article/view/30-9, considered data from the 2002–15 NBA seasons to investigate this problem. Using factors such as whether the team made the prior year's playoffs and the number of away games, among others, Elmore fit a series of generalized linear models to predict if a team made the playoffs in their current season based on the covariates at any point in the season. The research suggests that you can predict the teams that will make the playoffs with about 80% accuracy after only 20 games.

So the answer to the question "Are you who you are (overall) after 20 games?" appears to be yes. So what does that matter for the teams involved? Teams can then position themselves for the future through player acquisition or salary dumping, preparing for future draft selections, or deciding whether to try to win this year or in future years. Yet as they make these decisions, each team still has approximately 31 home games to sell for the current year. Current decisions can affect media coverage, ticket and merchandise sales, and the overall perception of the franchise. Even potential players may decide to join a team based on whether this team is viewed as a win maximizer or a profit maximizer.

5.11 Shot Charts

While we have in the previous section examined the four factors and calculated their effectiveness in predicting wins and losses, one area we have left unexplored is individual performance. EFG considers all two-point shots to be equivalent, no matter where on the court they happen between the three-point arc and the basket, and it also considers all three-point shots to be equivalent no matter where beyond the arc they occur. We can use additional visualizations and analysis to create shot charts for players or teams to show greater detail on shot selection and success rates.

Coaches use shot charts to identify where players are shooting the ball and where they are making shots. Basketball analytics has changed much about shot selection for players and teams. For example, a layup from 1 foot away from the basket counts for the same two points as a jump shot from 19 feet away from the hoop, and the success rate on the layup is much greater than that of the midrange jumper. Moreover, the power of the three-point shot has been noted as coaches look at points per possession and recognize that a 35% three-point success rate is better in points per possession (1.05) than a 50% two-point shot success rate (1.00). So if players are going to shoot the ball inside the three-point arc, they should probably work to get a shot from as close to the basket as possible. Similarly, not all three-point shots are created equally, as the shot from 25 feet counts the same as one from 75 feet away. All-Star players like Steph Curry and Damian Lillard are uncommonly accurate from 30 feet or more away from the basket, and neither are afraid to shoot from that distance. Being accurate from a longer range forces opposing coaches to stretch out the defenses farther away from the basket, which creates more opportunities for passing or dribbling all the way to the hoop unmolested for an easy layup attempt.

In order to construct NBA shot charts, we first need to get data from the NBA Stats API using the `nbastatR` package employing the `teams_shots()` function. The following code will download every shot by the Dallas Mavericks during the 2022–23 season. If you tried to execute it without increasing the connection buffer, you would find it doesn't work at all. So we need to include the `Sys.setenv()` function to enable the data to download correctly, but it will still take quite a while:

```
Sys.setenv("VROOM_CONNECTION_SIZE" = 131072 * 2)
nba_mavs_shots <- teams_shots(teams = "Dallas Mavericks", seasons = 2023)
```

The `ISAR` package contains a data file, `nba_nuggets_shots`, that contains every Nuggets' shot from the 2014–15 through 2022–23 seasons, and we will use it rather than redownloading data from the NBA Stats API every time we want to run code examples for this chapter. The following code shows how to display all of Nikola Jokić's shots from his 2022–23 NBA MVP season. The package `sportyR` includes many different backgrounds, such as basketball courts and hockey rinks, that we can then use as layers for our plots. Here we use an NBA court through the `geom_basketball()` function with `NBA` as the argument so that it shows the court used in NBA games. While many of the graphing techniques are the same, note how many options there are for displaying the NBA court—for example, its various colors:

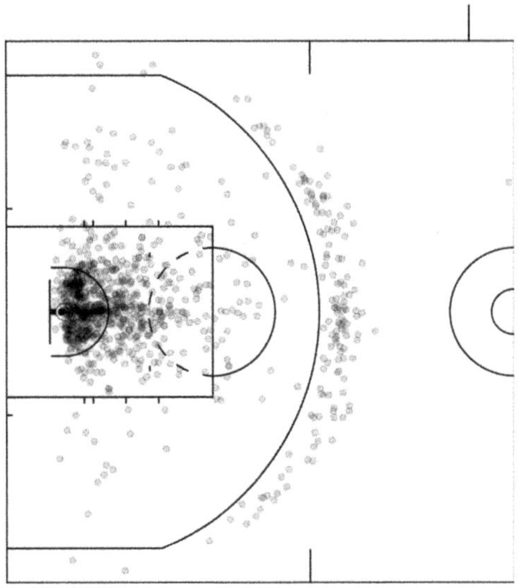

Figure 5.9: Shot chart for the Denver Nuggets center Nikola Jokić.

```
player_name <- "Nikola Jokic"
p <- geom_basketball(league = "NBA",
                     display_range = "defense",
                     color_updates = list(
                     defensive_half_court = "white",
                     offensive_half_court = "white",
                     court_apron = "white",
                     center_circle_fill = "white",
                     two_point_range = "white",
                     painted_area = "white",
                     free_throw_circle_fill = "white",
                     basket_ring = "black"))
p + geom_point(data = nba_nuggets_shots |>
               filter(namePlayer == player_name,
                      yearSeason == 2023,
```

```
                        zoneBasic != "Backcourt"),
                aes(y = locationX/10,
                    x = (locationY - 420)/10),
                alpha = .25) +
                labs(title = "2022-23 Shot Attempts for Nikola Jokic")
player_name <- "Nikola Jokic"
p <- geom_basketball(league = "NBA",
                     display_range = "defense",
                     color_updates = list(
                     defensive_half_court = "white",
                     offensive_half_court = "white",
                     court_apron = "white",
                     center_circle_fill = "white",
                     two_point_range = "white",
                     painted_area = "white",
                     free_throw_circle_fill = "white",
                     basket_ring = "black"))
p + geom_point(data = nba_nuggets_shots |>
                   filter(namePlayer == player_name,
                          yearSeason == 2023,
                          zoneBasic != "Backcourt"),
                aes(y = locationX/10,
                    x = (locationY - 420)/10,
                    col = zoneBasic),
                alpha = .25) +
                labs(title = "2022-23 Shot Attempts for Nikola Jokic by Zone", shape = "")
```

While we have shown how to create shot charts for the NBA players, we can also do this for any league where we have data. The WNBA provides much of this same data through an API, and we can access that API through the `wehoop` package. Two useful functions in the `wehoop` package are `load_wnba_pbp` for play-by-play data and `load_wnba_player_box` for box score data. The first code block shows us downloading the Seattle Storm play-by-play data, and we plot their two- and three-point shots in the subsequent code block. In this analysis, we also need to eliminate free throws, or else we will have those clouding our shot chart. To do that, we use the `grepl()` function to identify shots of type "Free," and we exclude them by using the exclamation point before the function. Note that this time, when we display the court, we use the WNBA court, which has slightly different dimensions than an NBA court:

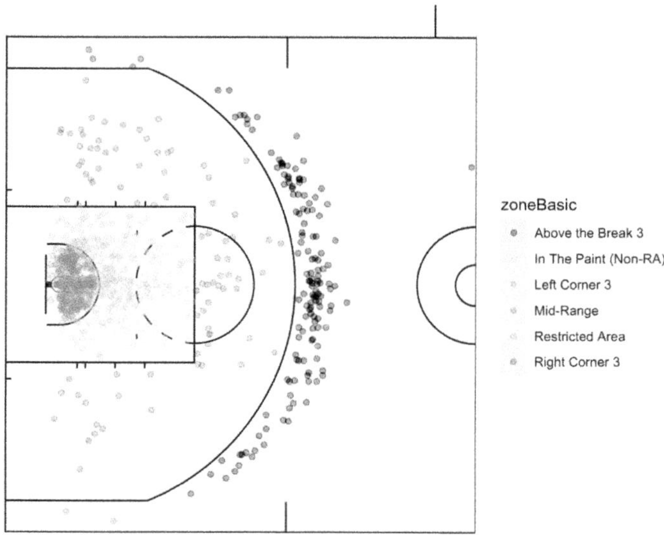

Figure 5.10: Shot chart for the Denver Nuggets center Nikola Jokić. Here we specify different shades of gray based on the zone in which the shot was taken.

```
df <- load_wnba_pbp(2022) |>
  filter((home_team_name == "Seattle" |
           away_team_name == "Seattle"),
         shooting_play == "TRUE",
         !grepl("Free", type_text),
         coordinate_y < 45)
p <- geom_basketball(league = "WNBA",
                     display_range = "defense",
                     color_updates = list(
```

```
                        defensive_half_court = "white",
                        offensive_half_court = "white",
                        court_apron = "white",
                        center_circle_fill = "white",
                        two_point_range = "white",
                        painted_area = "white",
                        free_throw_circle_fill = "white",
                        basket_ring = "black"))
p + geom_point(data = df,
               aes(x = coordinate_x, y = coordinate_y,
                   col = as.factor(scoring_play)),
               alpha = .15) +
  labs(title = "2022 Seattle Storm shot chart",
       color = "Made Shot?") +
  scale_color_brewer(palette = "Set1")
```

Suppose we want to compare shots from two players: Sue Bird and Breanna Stewart. We can facet by the `athlete_display_name` column:

Figure 5.11: Shot chart for the Seattle Storm. Here we specify different shades based on either a make or a miss.

```
df_box <- load_wnba_player_box(2022)

df_player <- df_box |>
  filter(team_short_display_name == "Storm") |>
  select(athlete_display_name, athlete_id, team_short_display_name) |>
  distinct()

df_storm <- left_join(df,
                      df_player,
                      by = c("athlete_id_1" = "athlete_id"))

p + geom_point(data = df_storm |>
                 filter(athlete_display_name %in%
                          c("Sue Bird", "Breanna Stewart")),
               aes(x = coordinate_x, y = coordinate_y),
               alpha = .15) +
  facet_wrap(~ athlete_display_name, ncol = 2) +
  labs(caption = "",
       title = "Shot charts for Breanna Stewart and Sue Bird in 2022") +
  theme(legend.position = "bottom")
```

We illustrate the use of `load_wnba_player_box` scores to display the average points scored per game for each team. In this case, we show the average points per game for each player on the New York Liberty. Note the `NaN` associated with Kaila Charles, given that she only signed a two-day contract and never actually played for the team in a game:

Shot charts for Breanna Stewart and Sue Bird in 2022

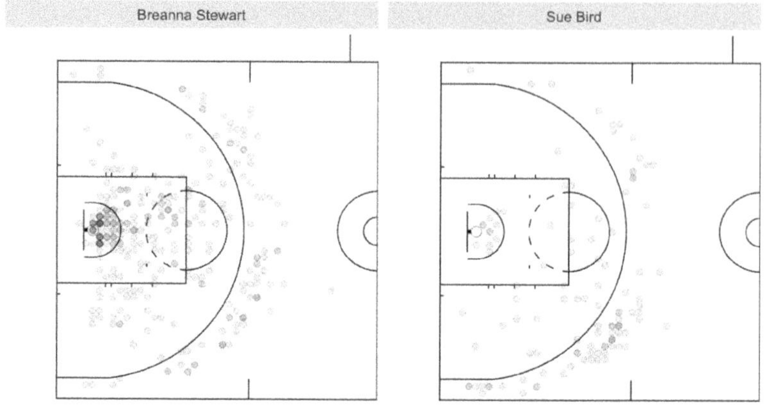

Figure 5.12: Shot charts for Breanna Stewart and Sue Bird during the 2022 season.

```
df_liberty <- df_box |>
  group_by(team_name, athlete_display_name) |>
  summarize(ppg = mean(points, na.rm = T)) |>
  filter(team_name == "Liberty") |>
  arrange(desc(ppg))
df_liberty
```

```
# A tibble: 15 × 3
# Groups:   team_name [1]
   team_name athlete_display_name     ppg
   <chr>     <chr>                  <dbl>
 1 Liberty   Sabrina Ionescu       17.2
 2 Liberty   Natasha Howard        15.1
 3 Liberty   Betnijah Laney        11.2
 4 Liberty   Marine Johannes        9.56
 5 Liberty   Han Xu                 8.26
 6 Liberty   Stefanie Dolson        7.92
 7 Liberty   Rebecca Allen          6.68
 8 Liberty   Sami Whitcomb          6.26
 9 Liberty   Crystal Dangerfield    5.12
10 Liberty   Michaela Onyenwere     4.68
11 Liberty   Jocelyn Willoughby     2.69
12 Liberty   DiDi Richards          2.5
13 Liberty   AD Durr                1.4
14 Liberty   Lorela Cubaj           0.727
15 Liberty   Kaila Charles        NaN
```

5.12 Lab: NBA Shots and Animation

One question that you might have after looking at several of the previous figures is "How can we look at these figures as an animation?" For example, you might be interested in looking at a particular player's shots year after year or comparing individual players within the same season. Fortunately, the `gganimate` package makes turning a series of figures into a `gif` animation relatively easy.

Figure 5.13: The core of the 2022–23 Denver Nuggets. *Left to right:* Jamal Murray, Nikola Jokić, Aaron Gorden, and Michael Porter Jr.
Source: AAron Ontiveroz / Contributor/ Denver Post via Getty Images

Consider the four shot takers from the Denver Nuggets during the 2022–23 season: Jamal Murray, Nikola Jokić, Michael Porter Jr., and Aaron Gordon. Take the following code and see how it lays out the mechanics of how to create an animated shot chart for these players. For obvious reasons, this output does not appear in the printed edition of the text:

```
players <- c("Jamal Murray", "Nikola Jokic",
             "Michael Porter Jr.", "Aaron Gordon")
df <- nba_nuggets_shots |>
  filter(yearSeason == 2023 &
           namePlayer %in% players &
           zoneBasic != "Backcourt") #eliminate desperation end of period shots

geom_basketball(league = "NBA",
                display_range = "defense",
                color_updates = list(
                  defensive_half_court = "white",
                  offensive_half_court = "white",
                  court_apron = "white",
                  center_circle_fill = "white",
                  two_point_range = "white",
                  painted_area = "white",
                  free_throw_circle_fill = "white",
                  basket_ring = "black")) +
  geom_point(data = df,
             aes(y = locationX/10,
                 x = (locationY - 420)/10,
                 shape = zoneBasic),
             alpha = .25) +
  transition_manual(namePlayer) + ### Here is where the animation starts
  labs(title = '2022-23 Shots for Player: {current_frame}', shape = "")
```

The previous figure cycles through plots by creating individual plots for each player and then piecing them together using the `transition_manual()` argument. An alternative animation is creating a sequence of plots by interpolating between the individual plots:

```
geom_basketball(league = "NBA",
                display_range = "defense",
                color_updates = list(
                  defensive_half_court = "white",
                  offensive_half_court = "white",
                  court_apron = "white",
                  center_circle_fill = "white",
                  two_point_range = "white",
                  painted_area = "white",
                  free_throw_circle_fill = "white",
                  basket_ring = "black")) +
  geom_point(data = df,
             aes(y = locationX/10,
                 x = (locationY - 420)/10,
                 shape = zoneBasic),
             alpha = .25) +
  transition_states(namePlayer) + ### Here is where the animation starts
  labs(title = '2022-23 Shots for Player: {closest_state}', shape = "")
```

Compare the `transition_manual()` to `transition_states()`. How do they differ?

1. Pick a team and create an animation showing how the team's shots evolved over the nine years in the `nba_nuggets_shots` dataset. What do you observe to have happened over the years?

```
df <- nba_nuggets_shots |>
  filter(zoneBasic != "Backcourt")

geom_basketball(league = "NBA",
                display_range = "defense",
                color_updates = list(
                  defensive_half_court = "white",
                  offensive_half_court = "white",
                  court_apron = "white",
                  center_circle_fill = "white",
                  two_point_range = "white",
                  painted_area = "white",
                  free_throw_circle_fill = "white",
                  basket_ring = "black")) +
  geom_point(data = df,
             aes(y = locationX/10,
                 x = (locationY - 420)/10,
                 shape = zoneBasic),
             alpha = .25) +
  transition_manual(yearSeason) + ### Here is where the animation starts
  labs(title = 'Season: {current_frame}', shape = "")
```

2. Construct an animated bar chart showing the count of each type of shot and whether or not it was made (`typeEvent`) over each season. The bars should represent each zone (`zoneBasic`) for each season.
3. Predict the probability of make/miss based on shot distance for Nikola Jokić during the 2022–23 season using a generalized linear model. Filter the data to use only shots less than or equal to 30 feet.

5.13 Case Study: Should We Trust the Process? Evaluating Talent in the NBA before They Arrive

Sam Hinkie, 76ers former general manager.
Source: Mitchell Leff / Contributor / Getty Images Sport via Getty Images

One of the side effects of the analytics revolution in sports has been the discovery of the value of draft picks. In general in major North American professional team sports, once per year, professional teams get to select the rights to players, or "draft" them onto their teams from amateur or overseas professional leagues. There are, of course, many other side deals and negotiations that go on, but as the US/Canadian leagues are generally thought of as the top leagues in most team sports, with the top competition and the highest salaries (soccer and women's professional basketball are the most notable exceptions), there is no shortage of players wishing to come to play in those leagues.

The selection order for teams in the draft is in general inversely related to the order in which they finished the previous year. For example, in the 2023 NFL Draft, the Chicago Bears were awarded the first pick (which they subsequently traded to Carolina), as at 3–14, they held the worst record among NFL teams in 2022–23. In that same NFL draft, the Kansas City Chiefs selected last, as they won the Super Bowl and were the champions of the 2022–23 NFL season. As the draft has seven rounds of selections, the teams select in that order seven times. So this meant the Bears were scheduled to select 1st, 33rd (the first pick of the second round), 65th, 97th, and so on. This is a bit of a simplification, as the NFL rules allow this to change a bit, but the point remains the same.*

* The leagues invented and refined this selection process to promote equality among the teams. That is, the worst teams are given the best chance to get better by getting to select new players first. This is just another way to promote equality in competition, much like salary caps and revenue sharing. It is interesting to the authors that these teams, whose owners have succeeded by and large in capitalism, here find it in their best interests to behave like socialists.

As the regular seasons in these sports come to a close, approximately 30%–50% of teams (depending on the league) will qualify for the playoffs and have a chance to win the championship. Teams who see that they will not make the playoffs may find it in their best interest to stop trying to win games in the current year in order to improve their position in the draft. This strategy is commonly known as tanking. One of the authors of this text discovered through research that as early as 25% of the way through the NBA season, playoff teams are already well determined (see the research block earlier in this paper). As clubs try to improve their position more and more, they may begin to tank their games. The players themselves will not try to intentionally miss shots or lose games, as that would not be in their best interest in showing their value in the free agent market, but coaches and general managers may do subtle things to give themselves less of a chance of winning a game on any given night. This could include resting star players, not making optimal substitutions for situations, and not seeking more talented players to supplement the team in case of injuries.

76ers player 21, Joel Embiid.
Source: Keith Allison / CC BY-SA 2.0

This, of course, is a delicate balance. No league or team wants to be known for not trying to win, and fans who are still asked to pay premium dollars for tickets, parking, and beer become upset when the local team is subpremium. This is true especially in basketball, where one player can influence the team more than in any other sport, as there are only five players on the court. Holding that good player out of the game can hurt the team, but the promise of getting that collegiate or foreign superstar onto the team the following year can be tempting. In fact, leagues have put in measures to prevent tanking, such as going to a weighted lottery process to determine the exact draft order, and in 2023–24, the NBA implemented new rules about how many games star players must play to qualify for statistical titles and games on national TV.

Such is the story of the Philadelphia 76ers and their analytics-minded general manager Sam Hinkie. Hinkie took over the team in 2013, and the 76ers had not been good for quite a long time. In the previous year, they missed the playoffs by one spot, and in the two years before that, they were among the last two teams to qualify for the playoffs. This put them in quite a perceived quandary: they were not good enough to really challenge for a championship, and yet they were not bad enough to get one of the best two or three players available in the next draft. Hinkie used a strategy to trade current players to another team in return for the use of their spot in the next draft. He viewed this not as tanking but as prioritizing wins in the long term over those in the short term. He informed people that it would get worse before it got better but that they needed to "trust the process."

In the 2013–14 season, the 76ers finished 29th out of 30 teams in the NBA, ahead of only the 2021 NBA champion Milwaukee Bucks. In 2014–15, they had a virtually identical record, finishing one game ahead of the New York Knicks and two games ahead of the Minnesota Timberwolves. In 2015–16, they finished in last place, winning only 10 out of 82 games and nearly matching the record for the worst NBA team ever (the 9–73 76ers of 1972–73). With each loss, "trust the process" became the rallying cry, a cry that was getting harder and harder to believe amid years of misery with only a faint memory of their last trip to the NBA Finals in 2001. Before the season ended, Hinkie resigned from the team.

Was the plug pulled on Hinkie and the process too soon? In 2016–17, they won 17 more games than the previous year but still finished 27th out of 30. In the following two years, the team finished 52–30 and 51–31 and returned to the playoffs for the first time since 2011–12. They had a similar winning percentage in the COVID-19-interrupted season of 2019–20 at 43–30, and after that season, they hired Hinkie's mentor, Daryl Morey, as the president of basketball operations. In the COVID-19-shortened 2020–21 season, the 76ers finished first in the Eastern Conference and third overall, with a 49–23 record, but lost to Atlanta in the second round of the playoffs. The years 2021–22 and 2022–23 saw similar results: second-place finishes in the Atlantic Division and losses in the second round of the playoffs.

This has happened in other sports as well—a stockpiling of draft picks and young talent who will likely lose currently but are believed to have a good chance of winning in the future. Recall from the research block in the baseball chapter on the strategy the Astros used to build a championship team. Indeed, they won the

World Series in 2017, though not without the other controversy mentioned in that research block. Answer the following questions:

1. How would you use analytics to verify if this is a good long-term strategy?
2. What are the issues with using data to evaluate players who are not currently playing in the league / at the level in which top-flight league administrators aspire for them to compete?
3. How do you communicate this to the fan base?

5.14 Exercises

Use datasets provided in the `ISAR` package to answer the following questions:

1. Mutate the `nba_games_2023` table to include a column for free throw rate (FTR). You will need to use the `fga` and `fta` columns in the table. Plot your new variable against `fta_rate` from the `nba_ff_team_2023` table.
2. The NBA defines pace as the number of possessions per 48 minutes for a team or a player, and this is denoted as pace in the advanced statistics table. Compute the average pace for the Denver Nuggets when they play at home and when they play away from Denver. The data are in the `nba_adv_team_2023` table, and you will need to join this with the `game_summary` object defined in the code block below.

```
game_summary <- nba_games_2023 |>
  mutate(location = ifelse(grepl("@", matchup), "away", "home")) |>
  select(game_date, game_id, team_id, matchup, location,
         wl, plus_minus)
```

3. Construct a new data frame (call it `df_ff`) that has `game_id`, `game_date`, `team_name`, the four factors (from `nba_ff_team_2023`), offensive rating (`ortg`), defensive rating (`drtg`), win/loss (`wl`), location (`location`), and plus/minus (`plus_minus`). Create an `is_win` variable to be true if it was a win and false if it was a loss.
4. Use the `nba_games_2023` and `nba_adv_team_2021` datasets to obtain the advanced statistics for both teams in the December 6, 2022, game between the Denver Nuggets and the Dallas Mavericks. Compute the z-scores for offensive and defensive ratings for both teams relative to the league distributions.
5. Using the `df_ff` dataset, run a multiple regression model using the four factors and offensive rating to predict `plus_minus`. What are the predicted values of `plus_minus` for both teams from problem 4?
6. Use the data related to the Nuggets shots from 2015 through 2023 and create a bar chart showing the total number of observations by season. Show the zone (`zoneBasic`) as a color within each bar. Filter out backcourt shots.
7. Who took the most shots in each season for the Nuggets?
8. Compute and plot the shot chart for Denver's 2022–23 season. Use points colored by the zone.
9. Add a layer to the previous figure showing points shaped by `typeEvent` (make or miss the shot).
10. Compare Michael Porter Jr.'s shots from the 2021–22 and 2022–23 seasons. Create a two-by-two facet plot (like the plots showing the four factors earlier in this chapter) showing his makes/misses by zone for both years.
11. Download the shot charts for the 2022–23 Golden State Warriors and construct a heat map showing the probability of Stephen Curry making shots.

Chapter 6

Football

> I'm sure we got killed on going for it on fourth down, but that's analytics. We believe in our players, and it doesn't work all the time. When it works or it doesn't work and you follow the book, it doesn't look good. Also, that's why it's analytics, not just doing whatever you want to do because you can easily get a punt blocked . . . you can give up a punt return for [a] net of nothing and be exactly the same. Disappointing, but it's one game. That never defines a season.
>
> —University of Mississippi head coach Lane Kiffin
> following their loss to Alabama on October 2, 2021

> It's nice to look at the numbers and how they go through the flow of the game, but the analytics change based on the opponent, based on who you have available for the game, and [based on] how the flow of the game is going too. You can look at a stat sheet all you want. I promise you if Excel was going to win football games, Bill Gates would be killing it right now. You got [to] take those numbers as a tool, and then you've got to go and factor in how your team is playing at the time and what [players] the opponent has as well. You've got to measure your strengths and weaknesses against the opponent every time, and then also in terms of [the] flow of the game.
>
> —New York Giants head coach Joe Judge
> following his team's 2021 0–3 start
> (Consequently, he was fired after the season.)

> Sometimes coaches'll say, "In this zone, 6% of the time, they run this trick play." But what are you going to do with 6%? They're going to beat you with all the stuff they do 94% of the time. There's a point to where you have to respond to their best pitch.
>
> —Mississippi State head coach Mike Leach (1961–2022)

6.1 R Packages

We will again in this chapter use the following R packages that we have used in previous chapters:

```
library(ggplot2)
library(dplyr)
library(lubridate)
library(ISAR)
library(tidyr)
library(mgcv)
library(teamcolors)
```

We will also introduce the following packages that we have not used so far:

```
library(nflfastR) #functions to access NFL play-by-play data
library(NFLSimulatoR) #used to simulate plays or drives in NFL games
```

If you do not remember how to install new packages in R or RStudio, refer to chapter 2, where there is a detailed discussion.

6.2 If You Don't Know Anything about Football

For the purposes of this book, *football* will refer to the game known as "football" in the United States and "American football" in the rest of the world.

Football is the most popular sport in the United States. It has effectively come to define a day of the week (Sunday) in the American calendar. Though a version of it has been played professionally in Canada since 1875, and professional leagues have existed at various times and capacities in Europe since the latter half of the 20th century, it is a game that can be said to be truly American.

Football has some of its roots in other sports, most predominantly soccer and rugby. In football, a team of 11 players tries to run or throw the ball down a 100-yard field to score a touchdown (TD) for six points while a team of 11 defenders tries to prevent this. If they are successful in scoring a TD, they will then have the option to try to kick the ball between a set of posts (uprights) for one additional point or try to move the ball two yards in one play for two additional points. Also at any time, a team can attempt to kick the ball off the ground through the uprights for three points, usually if they believe they cannot score a touchdown in the given situation.

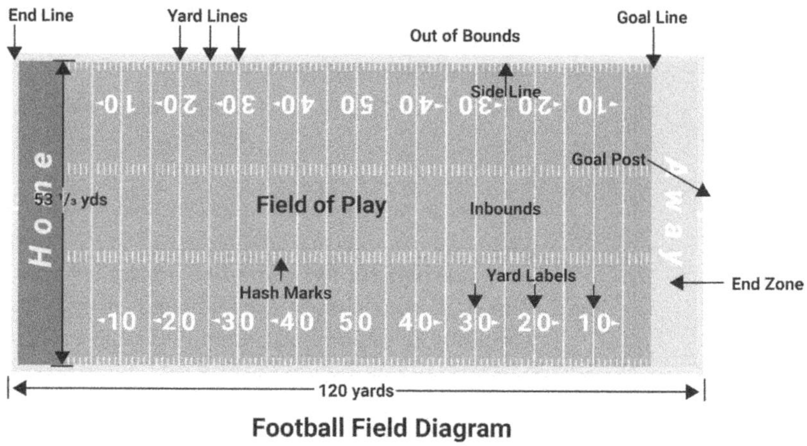

Figure 6.1: Diagram of an NFL field.

Ironically enough given the name, the use of the foot and kicking the ball is not a primary part of the game. However, it can be the part with the most strategic consequences, and much of this chapter will deal with kicking plays, as analytics can play a big role here.

If you are not familiar with football, you can get a quick primer at `https://www.rookieroad.com/football/101/`. Unlike soccer and rugby, the gameplay of football breaks itself into discrete events, called plays. This can make the analysis seem more like what is used in baseball and, in fact, may seem similar to that sport at times during our analyses.

6.3 Why Football Analytics?

Football is a game that lends itself to almost continuous decision-making. In an average NFL game, a team has about 135 plays per game between offensive, defensive, and kicking plays. Each one of those plays presents a new opportunity for an offense to make the best possible decision toward scoring more points and keeping the ball away from the other team and, similarly, for the defense to make the best decision to stop the offense from moving the ball down the field to score points and return the ball to their offense. Because these plays, like pitches in baseball, are all discrete events, the game lends itself to fans second-guessing the decisions of coaches, but this also provides opportunities for deep analysis.

One insight that has been gained from football analytics has been a strategy for an NFL team that is down 14 points in the fourth quarter and then scores a touchdown. The conventional wisdom had been to kick an extra point, try to score another touchdown, and then kick another extra point and tie the game. As you may recall, the team scoring a touchdown also has the option to try for a 2-point conversion from the two-yard line. The league average on successful 2-point conversions since 2015 is about 48%, while the success rate on extra-point kicks is approximately double that at about 94%, also since 2015, when the length of the extra point was extended to its current distance.

With analytics, many teams have decided after scoring that first touchdown (cutting the deficit to eight) to attempt a two-point conversion (cutting the deficit to six). If they are successful, if they score another touchdown, then they will kick the extra point and take a one-point lead. If they miss the initial two-point conversion, after the second touchdown, they still have a chance to try a two-point conversion again and tie the game.

Analytics has revealed that in the above situation, about 46% of the time, a team will win the game by one point; about 25% of the time, the game will be tied; and about 29% of the time, the team will still be behind. This compares with a team that always kicks the extra point. This team will never be leading, will be tied about 88% of the time, and will still be behind 12% of the time. This is just one example of how so much of what we see in football analytics directly relates to decisions that have been made or are about to be made, and this is how the rest of this chapter will be organized.

6.4 The Coach's Dilemma: What to Do on Fourth Down?

In football, when the team possesses the ball, they get four plays (downs) to advance the ball a net of at least 10 yards (inclusive of negative plays and penalties, which would cause them to move backward). If they advance it at least 10 yards, the down counter resets to one, and the process begins again until the team reaches the offensive goal line and scores a touchdown (six points), is pushed backward to the defensive end of the field and the defensive team scores a safety (two points for the opposing team), or turns the ball over to the other team by having a forward pass caught by the defense (interception). The ball might also be dropped by an offensive player and picked up by the defense. If the offensive team does not advance the total of 10 yards, the defensive team gets to take over the ball at the spot where the fourth-down play ended.

(a) (b) (c)

Three different kinds of kicking plays: (a) kickoff, (b) punt, and (c) placekick.

Sources: (a) iStockphoto.com/razihusin; (b) © BrokenSphere / Wikimedia Commons / CC BY-SA 3.0; (c) iStockphoto/YinYang

Because of this change of possession, coaches can try three different strategies on their fourth-down plays:

1. They can try to get the necessary yardage for the first down, and if they are unsuccessful, the opponents will possess the ball where the play ends.
2. They can try to kick a field goal (FG), which is an offensive play where the team will snap the ball back about 8 yards to a player who will hold the ball on the ground with a finger while another player attempts to kick it between upright posts at the end of the field and over a crossbar joining them that is 10 feet above the ground. If the FG attempt is successful, the offensive team gets three points. If it is unsuccessful, the defense is awarded possession at the spot where the ball was placed on the ground to kick or the 20-yard line, whatever is more beneficial to the nonkicking team. Defensive players can also try to block the kick in the air with their arms or other body parts to keep it from going through the uprights.*

* In 1991, University of Tennessee cornerback Jeremy Lincoln famously preserved a one-point win over Notre Dame by blocking a field goal with his rear end.

3. They can punt the ball, which is an offensive play where the team will snap the ball back about 15 yards to a player who will then drop the ball onto his foot and kick the ball down the field. At the moment the ball is kicked, the offensive team surrenders possession of the ball to the defensive team wherever the kick lands after flying through the air and coming to a stop. The receiving team can elect to catch the punt in the air or field the ball on the ground and run with the ball until the player is tackled by the kicking team or the returning player goes out of bounds or reaches the end of the field and scores a touchdown.

As you may have ascertained, the aggressive strategy is to not kick the ball (option 1), whereas the conservative strategy is to punt the ball (option 3) or attempt a FG (option 2) if you are close enough, meaning generally that the offense has moved the ball to 35 yards or closer from the goal line (depending on a variety of factors, such as weather, game situation, and kicker leg strength).

Head coaches must make decisions about what to do on fourth down several times per game. Some decisions are more obvious than others. Here are a few possible situations:

1. Fourth down with 30 seconds to play, down by 5 points and 1 yard from a touchdown—this is an obvious option 1.
2. Fourth down with 10 seconds to play, down by 1 point on your opponent's 10-yard line—this is an obvious option 2.
3. Fourth down with 2 minutes to play, down by 11 points and 30 yards to go for a first down—this is an obvious option 3.

But others are less clear, such as fourth down and 3 at the 41-yard line while up 4 points and 2 minutes to play. One could make legitimate arguments for all three options in this case, depending on the personnel and the weather, of course. This is where we start to look for analytics to help us in decision-making.

6.5 Expected Points

To help with decision-making on whether it makes sense to kick the ball on fourth down or attempt to continue the drive, we need to have a variable we can measure against. In football, the team with the most points at the end of the game is the winner, and assuming that our objective is to win games, we want to make decisions that are going to increase the likelihood that we will score more points than our opponents.* The metric expected points was developed to establish the number of points a team can expect to score in a given situation when it possesses the football. Many different analysts have constructed their own means of calculating expected points, but the one we will use is derived by `OpenSourceFootball.com` and represented in the R package `nflfastR`. It uses the time remaining in the game, the down and distance and location of the football, whether the team possessing the ball is home or away, whether the game is indoors or outdoors (or outdoors but has a retractable roof), the number of time-outs remaining, and a corrector for the era in which the game is being played. At a high level, expected points is then derived using the expected value from a discrete set of possible events given the aforementioned conditions. Let's walk through some examples of how we can obtain the play-by-play data, visualize the data, and finally, use them to help us in the decision-making process.

* There are some situations in football, as in all sports with a clock, where the chances of winning increase more by executing strategies that run the clock down closer to zero rather than by trying to score more points. We will ignore those possibilities for simplicity's sake in these examples.

6.6 Play-by-Play Data

Data on every play in the NFL going back to 1999 can be obtained using the `nflfastR` package. It is a very handy package for doing play-by-play analysis with multiple built-in functions. We will rely on the last 10 seasons of data (2013–22 seasons) in this chapter, and the following code shows how to obtain them. There are 372 variables (each of which is defined at `https://nflreadr.nflverse.com/articles/dictionary_pbp.html`) related to every single play in the NFL. This amounts to approximately 50,000 plays and almost 20 million data points per season! Let's explore this subset of data by loading it into a data frame:

```
df <- load_pbp(seasons = 2013:2022)
```

Field Goals

The `play_type` in `nflfastR` data tells you the current type of play. Suppose we wanted to just look at situations when field goals were attempted during the game. How do we know whether the FG was successful? Let's create a `field_goals` data frame with just the plays that were field goal attempts during the regular season. To do this, we subset the full play-by-play dataset by filtering on the `play_type` and `season_type` variables and selecting a host of relevant variables. Furthermore, we can define `success` and `fg_distance` variables to denote the result of the field goal attempt and official field goal distance, respectively:

```
field_goals <- df |>
  filter(play_type == "field_goal", season_type == "REG") |>
  select(game_date, time, down, yrdln, ydstogo, yardline_100, posteam,
         defteam, field_goal_result, field_goal_attempt,
         game_seconds_remaining, ep, contains("prob"), game_id) |>
  mutate(success = ifelse(field_goal_result == "made", 1, 0),
         fg_distance = yardline_100 + 17) |>
  na.omit()
```

First Downs

In addition, let us filter the play-by-play data to only include first-down plays with 10 yards to go. We will use this to illustrate basic expected value–based decision-making. If we do not filter out the plays where there are 10 yards to go, we will see our data weighted more by goal line situations or scenarios where penalties have influenced the decision-making. We will also filter out situations where expected points is zero, such as kneel-down plays at the end of a half or game:

```
first_downs <- df |>
  filter(down == 1, ydstogo == 10, ep != 0)
```

6.7 Field Goal Success versus Distance

We know instinctively that the farther away the ball is from the uprights, the less likely it is that the kicker will be successful in his field goal attempt. Let's plot all of the field goals in this dataset, and then let's create a density plot (figure 6.2) to view successes:

```
p <- ggplot(data = field_goals,
            aes(x = fg_distance, fill = as.factor(success)))
p + geom_density(alpha = .75) +
  scale_fill_brewer("success", palette = "Set1") +
  labs(title = "Made vs Missed NFL Field Goal Attempts, 2013-2022",
       x = "distance") +
  theme_bw()
```

This shows us that the most attempted field goals that are missed are between 45 and 50 yards in length. We see this number drastically drop off after about 48 yards, because coaches will not even try field goals this long in the normal course of a game. Beyond 60 yards is usually when the team has very little to lose from a miss, such as it occurring on the last play of the half or the game. The NFL record for a successful field goal is 66 yards, set by Baltimore's Justin Tucker in September 2021. No 65-yard field goals have ever been successful, and only one 64-yard field goal has ever been made.

If we want to look at field goal success as a function of distance only, we have several models from which to choose. We can use the regression models that we have utilized in other chapters, employing logistic regression by referencing the binomial family of the general linear model to see how good our model is. Let's take a look using the code below:

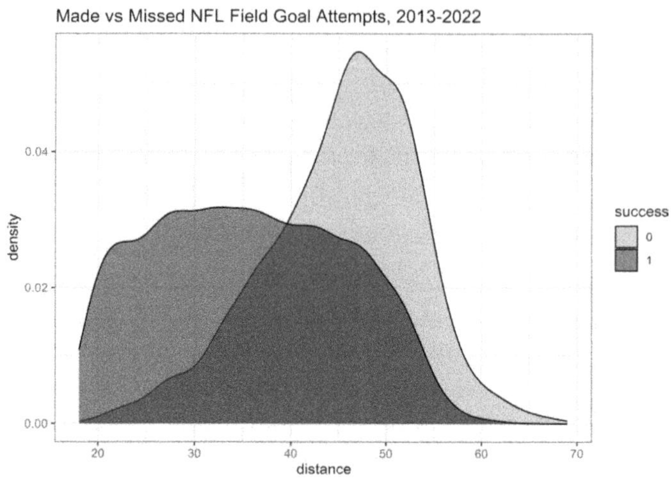

Figure 6.2: The density estimates for field goal distance for made versus missed field goals.

```
fg_glm <- glm(success ~ fg_distance,
              family = "binomial",
              data = field_goals)
summary(fg_glm)
```

```
Call:
glm(formula = success ~ fg_distance, family = "binomial", data = field_goals)

Coefficients:
             Estimate Std. Error z value Pr(>|z|)
(Intercept) 6.095833   0.156318   39.00   <2e-16 ***
fg_distance -0.107898   0.003507  -30.77   <2e-16 ***
---
Signif. codes:  0 '***' 0.001 '**' 0.01 '*' 0.05 '.' 0.1 ' ' 1

(Dispersion parameter for binomial family taken to be 1)

    Null deviance: 8620.6  on 9984  degrees of freedom
Residual deviance: 7387.0  on 9983  degrees of freedom
AIC: 7391

Number of Fisher Scoring iterations: 5
```

How do we interpret the `slope` parameter? Recall that if $\beta_1 < 0$, then the probability of success (i.e., the field goal attempt is good) decreases as distance (x) increases. What is the magnitude of this increase? Figure 6.3 shows the estimated relationship of the probability of making a kick as a function of kick distance.

```
p <- ggplot(data = field_goals,
            aes(x = fg_distance, y = success))
p + geom_point(alpha = .1) +
  geom_smooth(method = "glm", method.args = list(family = "binomial")) +
  labs(title = "Probability of a Successful FG Attempt, NFL 2013-2022",
       x = "distance",
       y = "probability of successful field goal") +
  theme_bw()
```

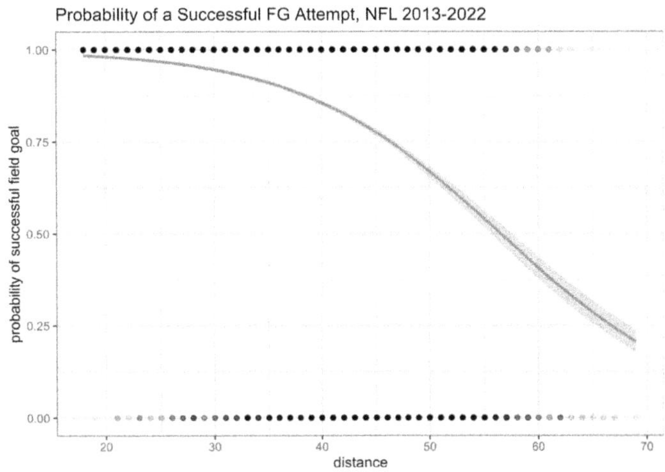

Figure 6.3: The estimated probability of making a field goal as a function of distance in the National Football League.

Nonparametric Model

You may recall in the baseball chapter when we examined swing probability that we also discussed nonparametric models. We used the generalized additive model (GAM) as a means of fitting a model to data when we would like to relax the underlying assumptions related to the distribution of the data and/or the functional form between our response and covariates. Here is how we could use GAM to predict FG success as a function of field goal distance:

```
fg_gam <- gam(success ~ s(fg_distance),
              family = "binomial",
              data = field_goals)
summary(fg_gam)
```

```
Family: binomial
Link function: logit

Formula:
success ~ s(fg_distance)

Parametric coefficients:
            Estimate Std. Error z value Pr(>|z|)
(Intercept)  2.16612    0.04645   46.64   <2e-16 ***
---
Signif. codes:  0 '***' 0.001 '**' 0.01 '*' 0.05 '.' 0.1 ' ' 1

Approximate significance of smooth terms:
                 edf Ref.df Chi.sq p-value
s(fg_distance) 4.569  5.583  836.4  <2e-16 ***
---
Signif. codes:  0 '***' 0.001 '**' 0.01 '*' 0.05 '.' 0.1 ' ' 1

R-sq.(adj) =  0.123   Deviance explained = 14.6%
UBRE = -0.26194  Scale est. = 1         n = 9985
```

How does this model compare to the probabilities given in `nflfastR`, where the dataset contains a variable `fg_prob`? To compare, we plot the estimated probabilities from all three models: the generalized linear model (GLM), the generalized additive model (GAM), and the model from `nflfastR` team:

```
field_goals <- mutate(field_goals,
                      glm_pred = predict(fg_glm, type = "response"),
                      gam_pred = predict(fg_gam, type = "response"))
p <- ggplot(data = field_goals,
            aes(x = fg_distance, y = fg_prob))
p + geom_smooth(col = "black", se = F) +
  geom_line(aes(x = fg_distance, y = glm_pred),
            linetype = "dashed", col = "black") +
  geom_line(aes(x = fg_distance, y = gam_pred),
            linetype = "dotted", col = "black") +
  labs(x = "distance",
       y = "probability") +
  theme_bw()
```

All three models are fairly similar in their predictions. The divergence in their predictions doesn't really occur until the distance is beyond 60 yards, where there are too few data points available to create robust models. So which one should you use? Our recommendation in this case is to use the model that you are most comfortable with and that you can most easily explain in terms of how it comes to its predictions.

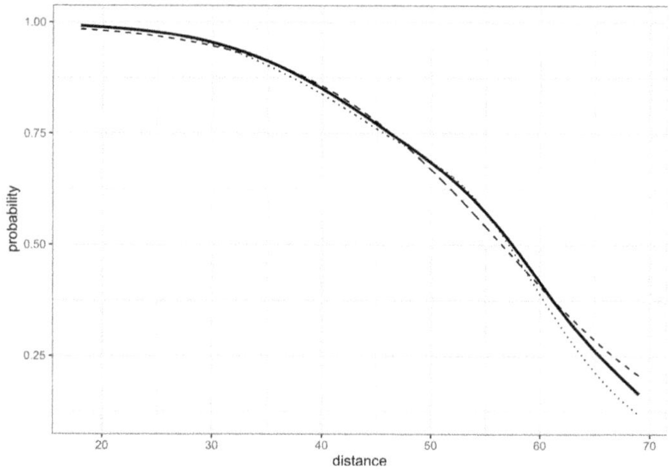

Figure 6.4: The estimated probabilities of making a field goal as a function of distance in the National Football League. The solid line represents the estimate based on the `nflfastR` model, the dashed line is the GLM model fit, and the dotted line is the GAM model fit.

6.8 Decision-Making and Expected Points

Suppose we are faced with fourth down and 2 yards to go from the opponent's 33-yard line. Should we kick the field goal?

We need to ascertain the distance of the kick (roughly 50 yards) and the probability of making the kick for that distance. We can feed that distance into each of the two models we created above and get the following results:

```
predict(fg_glm, newdata = data.frame(fg_distance = 50),
        type = "response")
```

```
        1
0.6683914
```

```
predict(fg_gam, newdata = data.frame(fg_distance = 50),
        type = "response")
```

```
        1
0.6874337
```

If we take the average of these two results, we get a probability of about 0.67. A crude estimate of the expected points of this action is 0.67 × 3 (points awarded for a successful FG) = 2.01. Another estimate is to use the result given in `nflfastR`, and that gives us 1.40 as the expected points from a 50-yard FG attempt:

```
filter(field_goals, fg_distance == 50) |>
  summarize(m = mean(ep))
```

```
# A tibble: 1 × 1
      m
  <dbl>
1  1.41
```

Why is there a discrepancy between the two values? The former calculation ignores every other outcome that could happen with positive probability—for example, a blocked field goal returned for a touchdown—and that the field position the defense will get after a missed field goal is likely to be much better than the field position following a made field goal. The `nflfastR` dataset, however, includes probabilities for all of these ancillary outcomes.

Alternatively, suppose our team decides to try to extend the drive and gains 2 yards for the first down. Now we have first and 10 at the 31-yard line. What is the expected points value for that outcome?

```
filter(first_downs, yardline_100 == 31) |>
  summarize(mean(ep))
```

```
# A tibble: 1 × 1
  `mean(ep)`
       <dbl>
1       3.72
```

What if our team does not get a first down? Say we only gain 1 yard and therefore turn the ball over to our opponent at their 32-yard line. In this case, our expected points is the negative of our opponent's expected points—that is, the expected points when starting first down and 10 from the 32-yard line. This calculation is given next:

```
filter(first_downs, yardline_100 == 68) |>
  summarize(mean(ep))
```

```
# A tibble: 1 × 1
  `mean(ep)`
       <dbl>
1       1.52
```

If p denotes the probability of a play being successful, the overall expected points in this scenario equals $(3.72 \times p) - (1.52 \times (1 - p))$. We would need to find a play that satisfies the following inequality in order to "go for it":

$$3.72 \times p - 1.52 \times (1 - p) \geq 0.$$

What is p? If $p \geq 0.29$, meaning that we have identified a play that we believe has a greater than 29% probability of gaining two yards, then we should go for it!

6.9 Simulation

Another technique in the analyst's tool belt is simulation. You may have heard of simulation in areas like warfare, space travel, or economic decision-making. We use simulation to help inform the decision-maker in contexts where performing practice rounds of the actual task is either impossible or prohibitively resource intensive or both. For example, we use simulation to test nuclear weapons as opposed to actually launching a missile. You may have seen a broadcast of an NFL game that showed the win probability of a particular team at a given point in the game. This is a result of tens of thousands of simulated games being played by a computer from that point in the game and recording the outcomes. Figure 6.5 shows a graph of the outcome of simulations being run after every play in the October 2023 game between the Indianapolis Colts and the Cleveland Browns and recording the winning percentage of each team.

Simulation is particularly helpful when we want to work with the entire distribution of possible outcomes for a given course of action we might wish to undertake rather than simply a mean and standard deviation. It helps us demonstrate the probability of an outcome as opposed to predicting that, "on average," a particular outcome will happen. Having an entire range of outcomes is useful for visualization, when we might want to view the outcome of a decision hundreds or thousands of times. We will next show how to do simulation in R for football, as we use the outcomes of past plays in similar situations to help inform our decision-making when choosing plays and strategies. We will illustrate this concept using the play-by-play data available in `nflfastR`.

Figure 6.5: Win probability chart for the Cleveland Browns at Indianapolis Colts game on October 22, 2023.
Source: `www.espn.com/nfl/game/_/gameId/401547484/browns-colts`

Simulating NFL Plays

Rules changes take place almost every year in the NFL. These are often done as a response to issues with player safety, competitive balance, or even increasing the likelihood that the game will finish in the three-hour window allotted by television to show the game. A competition committee reviews proposed rule changes, and if they are approved by the committee, they can be voted on by all the teams in the league.

Going back to the previous section where we discussed kicking, we will examine the effect of a possible rule change using simulation. To help inform this, refer to "Estimating NFL Drive Outcomes under Rules That Don't Exist," available at `https://statsbylopez.netlify.app/post/resampling-nfl-drives/`, a blog post by Dr. Michael Lopez, who was featured in chapter 1 as the director of data and analytics in the NFL.

Imagine that we took the "foot" out of football and outlawed the possibility of punting or kicking field goals. Football would be a very different game, and many purists would argue that it would be a better game if we didn't allow kickers to be a part of it. But how would we gain more insights into what the effects of this rule change might be without actually playing games? We might start by trying to simulate games by mining a database of plays that were not kicking plays. The following code shows how to simulate a large number of plays and drives in which punting or kicking a field goal is not an option. The code itself is advanced for where we are so far in this textbook, and we would not expect students to be able to produce this code themselves, but hopefully as you read the code, you can follow along and get some understanding of what Lopez has done.

We start this process by modeling our code on the example given in Lopez's blog, and we create three functions in order to simulate drives according to the rules outlined in the blog: `sample_play`, `sample_play_needs_td`, and `sample_drive`. The `sample_play` function will sample a random play from a corpus of plays (`play_by_play_data` argument) in the NFL given a specific down, yards to go, and yard line. Note that these plays only include passes and rushes, given that we will never kick the football. Next, the `sample_play_needs_td` is essentially a bookkeeping function that updates the conditions in the game according to the sampled play. Finally, `sample_drive` samples a series of plays in order to construct a drive where the team needs a touchdown to prolong or win the game—that is, the team cannot punt or attempt a field goal. This is the scenario outlined in the blog linked above:

```
sample_play <- function(down,
                        yards_to_go,
                        yard_line,
                        play_by_play_data){
  tmp <- filter(play_by_play_data,
```

```
                play_type %in% c("pass", "run"),
                down == down,
                ydstogo == yards_to_go,
                yardline_100 == yard_line) |>
    sample_n(size = 1)
  return(tmp)
}

sample_play_needs_td <- function(down,
                                 yards_to_go,
                                 yard_line,
                                 play_by_play_data){
  down_original <- down
  if (yard_line >= 95){yard_line <- 95}
  if (down == 4 & yards_to_go >= 3){down <- 3}
  if (yards_to_go >= 20){yards_to_go <- 20}

  sim_play <- sample_play(down = down,
                          yards_to_go = yards_to_go,
                          yard_line = yard_line,
                          play_by_play_data = play_by_play_data)

  yards_gained <- sim_play$yards_gained
  new_yard_line <- yard_line - yards_gained
  new_down <- ifelse(yards_gained >= yards_to_go, 1, down_original + 1)
  new_distance <- ifelse(yards_gained >= yards_to_go & new_yard_line >= 10,
                         10,
                         ifelse(yards_gained >= yards_to_go &
                                  new_yard_line < 10,
                                new_yard_line,
                                yards_to_go - yards_gained))
  if(new_distance <= 0){new_distance <- 1}
  if(new_yard_line < 0){new_yard_line <- 1}
  return(data.frame(down_original,
                    yards_to_go,
                    yard_line,
                    yards_gained,
                    new_yard_line = yard_line - yards_gained,
                    new_down,
                    new_distance,
                    turnover = sim_play$turnover,
                    td_offense = sim_play$td_offense,
                    end_drive = new_down > 4 |
                      sim_play$turnover | sim_play$td_offense,
                    play = sim_play$desc))
}

sample_drive <- function(yard_line,
                         play_by_play_data){

  drive_store <- NULL
  new_down <- 1
  new_distance <- 10
  new_yard_line <- yard_line
  end_of_drive <- FALSE
  play_num <- 1

  while(!end_of_drive){
    run_play <- sample_play_needs_td(down = new_down,
                                     yards_to_go = new_distance,
                                     yard_line = new_yard_line,
```

```
                                    play_by_play_data = play_by_play_data)
    run_play$play_num <- play_num
    drive_store <- bind_rows(drive_store, run_play)
    new_down <- run_play$new_down
    new_distance <- run_play$new_distance
    new_yard_line <- run_play$new_yard_line
    end_of_drive <- run_play$end_drive
    play_num <- play_num + 1
  }
  return(drive_store)
}
```

How do we use these functions? First, load in the last season of NFL play-by-play data and then prepare the data for use in the functions just defined. Next, we will simulate 100 sample drives starting at a team's 25-yard line. The 25-yard line is the starting position after a touchback, the most common result of a kickoff:

```
nfl_pbp <- load_pbp(seasons = 2021:2022)
nfl_pbp_df <- mutate(nfl_pbp,
                     is_fumble = !is.na(fumble_recovery_1_team),
                     turnover = grepl("INTERCEPTED", desc) |
                       (is_fumble & fumble_recovery_1_team != posteam),
                     td_offense = rush_touchdown | pass_touchdown) %>%
  filter(!is.na(yards_gained))
set.seed(2023)
nSim <- 100
yard_line_start <- 75

for (i in 1:nSim){
  if(i %% 20 == 0){
    cat(sprintf('Drive: %s at %s\n', i, Sys.time()))
  }
  tmp_result <- suppressWarnings(sample_drive(yard_line_start, nfl_pbp_df))
  tmp_result$sim <- i
  if(exists("results")){
    results <- suppressWarnings(bind_rows(results, tmp_result))
  }
  else(results <- tmp_result)
}
```

```
Drive: 20 at 2023-12-24 13:28:27.194181
Drive: 40 at 2023-12-24 13:28:28.350047
Drive: 60 at 2023-12-24 13:28:29.451475
Drive: 80 at 2023-12-24 13:28:30.476557
Drive: 100 at 2023-12-24 13:28:31.787157
```

So we've now simulated 100 NFL drives and written them to `results`. Let's examine the data a bit. To help answer our original question, let's first compute the percentage of drives that resulted in a turnover. Similarly, what is the percentage of drives that resulted in a touchdown? The remainder of the drives will end in failing to make a first down on fourth down, called a turnover on downs but not classified as a turnover in the statistics:

```
results |>
  filter(end_drive == TRUE) |>
  summarize(tos_pct = sum(turnover)/nSim,
            td_pct = sum(td_offense)/nSim) |>
  mutate(to_downs_pct = 1 - tos_pct - td_pct)
```

```
  tos_pct td_pct to_downs_pct
1    0.22   0.24         0.54
```

We can then also find the average number of plays per drive. To do this, we will filter the data to give us only the plays that are the last play of the drive, and then we will take an average of the play number for those plays. At the same time, we can create a histogram to see the total number of plays for all of the drives in our simulation:

```
results |>
  filter(end_drive == TRUE) |>
  summarize(ppd = mean(play_num))
```

```
   ppd
1 7.75
```

```
p <- results |>
  filter(end_drive == TRUE) |>
  ggplot(aes(x = play_num))
p + geom_histogram() +
  labs(title = "Mean plays per NFL drive, without kicking, simulated 100 times",
       x = "number of plays on drive") +
  theme_bw()
```

We can also then compare the number of plays in a drive that resulted in a touchdown to all of the other drives by using that same filter in the above example, grouping the results by the value of the `td_offense` field and then taking the mean:

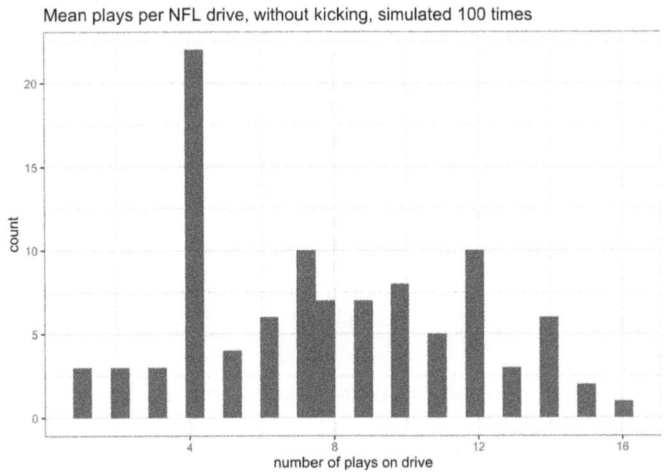

Figure 6.6: Histogram showing the distribution for the number of plays per drive in the simulated dataset.

```
results |>
  filter(end_drive == TRUE) |>
  group_by(td_offense) |>
  summarize(ppd = mean(play_num))
```

```
# A tibble: 2 × 2
  td_offense   ppd
  <lgl>      <dbl>
1 FALSE       7.14
2 TRUE        9.67
```

We can then create a histogram as we did above, but this time, we will color it by whether the offense scored a touchdown on that drive:

```
p <- ggplot(data = filter(results, end_drive == TRUE),
            aes(x = play_num, fill = td_offense))
p + geom_histogram() +
  scale_fill_brewer("TD?", palette = "Set1") +
  labs(title = "Mean plays per NFL drive, without kicking, simulated 100 times",
       x = "number of plays on drive") +
  theme_bw()
```

Other options include creating two histograms and viewing them side by side or creating a facet grid based on the value of td_offense:

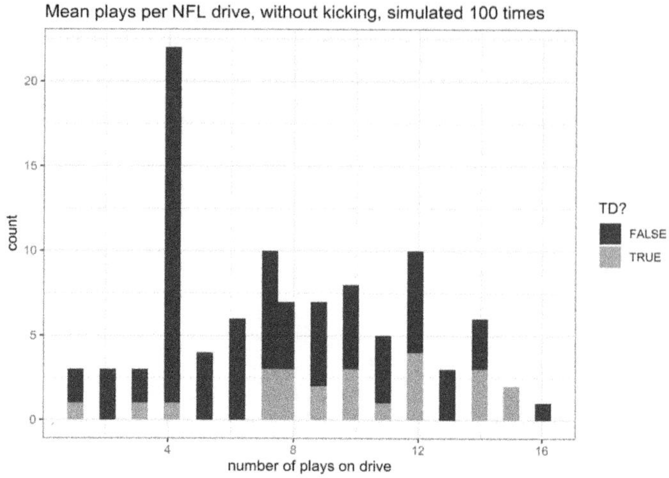

Figure 6.7: Histogram showing the distribution for the number of plays per drive in the simulated dataset. The bars are shaded by whether the drive ended in a touchdown.

```
p <- ggplot(data = filter(results, end_drive == TRUE),
            aes(x = play_num))
p + geom_histogram() +
  facet_grid(~ td_offense) +
  guides(fill = "none") +
  labs(title = "Mean plays per NFL drive, without kicking, simulated 100 times",
       x = "number of plays on drive") +
  theme_bw()
```

Why would we need to know this information about the number of plays in a drive? As mentioned at the beginning of this section, we could use this information to model the effects of potential injuries, competitive balance, or even game timing.

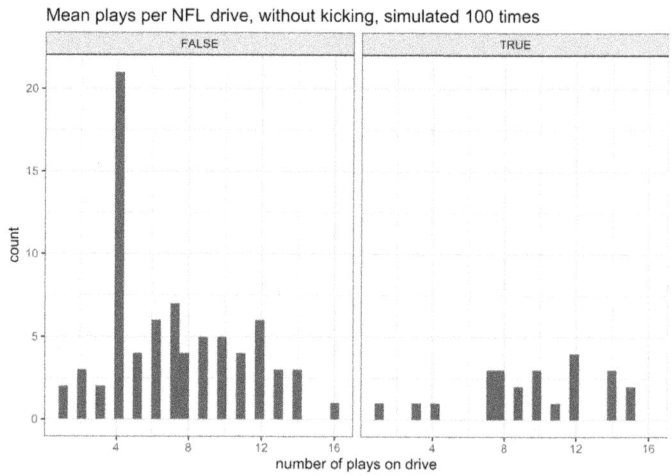

Figure 6.8: Histograms showing the distribution for the number of plays per drive in the simulated dataset facetted by whether or not the drive ended in a touchdown.

6.10 Research Block: Using Analytics for Evaluating Defensive Players

We have seen many statistics in this chapter, generally concerning offensive production. These are the statistics that are easiest to measure—touchdowns scored, passes completed, yards gained, and average yards per carry are just a few examples. Statistics covering defensive players are much more limited. Most recently, we are able to count quarterback sacks, interceptions, passes defended, and tackles made, but these are somewhat limiting in evaluating the effectiveness of a particular player. As a result, analytics on the defensive side of the field are behind those on the offensive side.

Much like the Statcast that we discussed in the baseball chapter, football has also begun using player tracking. Through a partnership with Amazon Web Services, those watching telecasts of NFL games are shown AWS Next Gen Stats on a variety of different game situations, but with player tracking, they can gain insights into individual player performances as well.

A notable example of player tracking was in the 2020 season in a game between the Arizona Cardinals and the Seattle Seahawks. While very close to scoring a touchdown, Seattle quarterback Russell Wilson had his pass intercepted by Arizona safety Budda Baker, a known speedster, who then began to run the length of the field for an apparent touchdown. Seattle receiver DK Metcalf was able to chase down Baker and tackle him at the 10-yard line. While Baker made a great play to catch the ball, much of the conversation was on Metcalf as an offensive player turned defender after the interception who was able to tackle Baker. With the player tracking, it was determined that Metcalf traveled 114.8 yards and reached a top speed of 22.64 mph in tracking down Baker, who had a top speed of 21.27 mph on his 90-yard interception return. You can see an animation of the play courtesy of Net Gen Stats at `https://twitter.com/NextGenStats/status/1320537210475683840`.

Authors Rishav Dutta, Ronald Yurko, and Samuel Ventura, in their paper "Unsupervised Methods for Identifying Pass Coverage among Defensive Backs with NFL Player Tracking Data," available at `https://arxiv.org/pdf/1906.11373v1.pdf` and published in the *Journal of Quantitative Analysis of Sports*, show how machine learning can be used to calculate and quantify how each pass defender actually influences the play in different pass coverages. They are also able to distinguish the players' effectiveness when the defenders are assigned to cover an individual receiver (man-to-man, or "man" defense) as opposed to when the defenders have the responsibility to cover a specific area of the field (zone defense). While they gain great insights by developing a model, they desire even more data, such as the orientation angle of the defender relative to the receiver and the ball. There is always more to be gained with more research opportunities!

6.11 Win Probability

Win probability is a statistic that shows, after each play, the likelihood that a particular team will win that game. This is often used to show the flow of a game or the momentum a team seems to have after a particular play or a drive. We showed an example earlier from a game between the Cleveland Browns and the Indianapolis Colts. But how would we construct this graphic?

In our play-by-play dataset, there are several columns showing win probability (`home_wp`, `away_wp`, etc.) Those two variables should sum to 1.

Let's look at an AFC playoff game between the Houston Texans and the Kansas City Chiefs from the 2019 season. The Chiefs were the higher seed and the betting favorite and playing at home, but Houston started quite strongly and took a 24–0 lead early in the second quarter. Kansas City dominated the game after that point and came back to win the game 51–31. Based on past data, teams very rarely come back to win after a 24-point deficit. Using past performance data and the relative strength of each team, the situational factors of the game are considered and win probabilities are computed as the game evolves and are given in the `wp` field of the play-by-play data. Kansas City's win probability is given in figure 6.9.

```
nfl_playoffs_pbp <- load_pbp(seasons = 2019) |>
  filter(season_type == "POST", home_team == "KC", away_team == "HOU") |>
  select(game_seconds_remaining, away_wp, away_wp_post, home_wp,
         home_wp_post, wp, desc, home_team, away_team)
p <- ggplot(data = nfl_playoffs_pbp,
            aes(x = 3600 - game_seconds_remaining,
                y = home_wp))
p + geom_line() +
  geom_point() +
  labs(title="KC win probability, Chiefs vs. Texans, Jan 12 2020",
       x = "game time (seconds)",
       y = "Kansas City win probability") +
  theme_bw()
```

This is helpful for a visualization, but we can do better and provide more information to the viewer by changing our color scheme. By using the `teamcolors` R package (created by Greg Matthews and Ben Baumer, which references Jim Nielsen's team colors website), we can change the simple black dots to points using the official team colors—in this case, a red for Kansas City and a lighter black for Houston. To do this, we will load `teamcolors` into a data frame and then filter it to only get the colors for Houston and Kansas City. To make it easier to join the information for our official team colors to our data, we will then create a variable, `team`, that is `HOU` or `KC` to reference the teams.

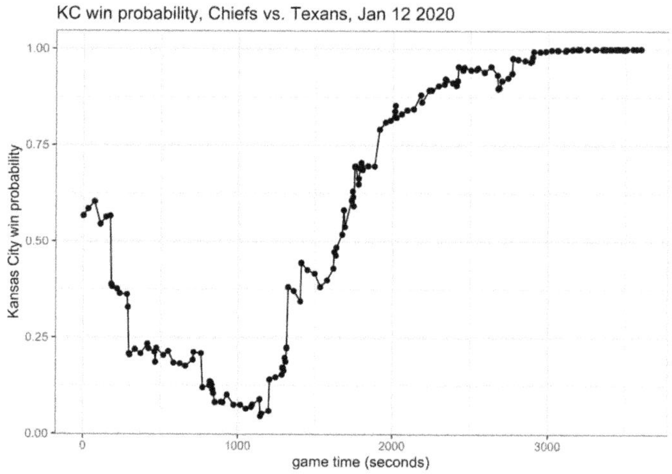

Figure 6.9: Kansas City Chiefs win probability versus the Houston Texans from the 2019–20 season playoffs.

Next we will get the data from the NFL play-by-play dataset for only this game through filtering, assign it to the data frame `g1`, and then select the fields we need for the analysis. We will then add a column, `team`, to the `g1` data frame; set it equal to whichever team has the best chance of winning at any given time; and join it to the team colors (`tc`) data frame by the value of the `team` field so that we have the official team colors available to us in our `g1` data frame.

We can then make the plot more friendly in other ways. We can change the scale of the x-axis from the number of seconds in the game to the ends of each of the quarters of play by creating breaks every 900 seconds and labeling them Q1, Q2, Q3, and Q4 to denote the beginning of each quarter and FT to mark the end of the game. We can also label the axes as "KC win probability" and "time left in game."

The following code shows how we could use the `teamcolors` package to add a little color to the win probability graph:

```
tc <- teamcolors |>
  filter(name %in% c("Kansas City Chiefs", "Houston Texans")) |>
  mutate(team = c("HOU", "KC"))
## Note the single = because this is an assignment and not a logical comparison
##  as in a filter or select.

g1 <- nfl_playoffs_pbp |>
  filter(home_team == "KC", away_team == "HOU") |>
  select(game_seconds_remaining, away_wp, away_wp_post, home_wp,
         home_wp_post, wp, desc) |>
  mutate(team = ifelse(home_wp < .5, "HOU", "KC")) |>
  left_join(tc, by = "team") |>
```

```
  na.omit()

p <- ggplot(data = g1,
            aes(x = 3600 - game_seconds_remaining,
                y = home_wp,
                col = name))
p + geom_line(col = "darkgrey", linetype = 2) +
  geom_point() +
  scale_color_teams(name = "name") +
  scale_y_continuous(limits = c(0, 1)) +
  scale_x_continuous(limits = c(0, 3600),
                     breaks = seq(0, 3600, by = 900),
                     labels = c("Q1", "Q2", "Q3", "Q4", "FT")) +
  labs(
    title="KC win probability, Chiefs vs. Texans, Jan 12 2020",
    x = "time in game",
    y = "Kansas City win probability"
  ) +
  guides(col = "none") +
  theme_bw()
```

If you want to pull this information in for another game, it requires a bit more code. While each team will only play another team one time in the playoffs, they may play multiple times in the regular season. One way to focus on a particular game would be to know what week it occurred in the schedule, use the `fast_scraper_schedules()` function in `nflfastR` to get the games for that particular week, and then search for the two teams from that week and proceed as before. Alternatively, you can just pull in a single game as follows in this example, a 2022 contest between the Kansas City Chiefs and the Los Angeles Chargers:

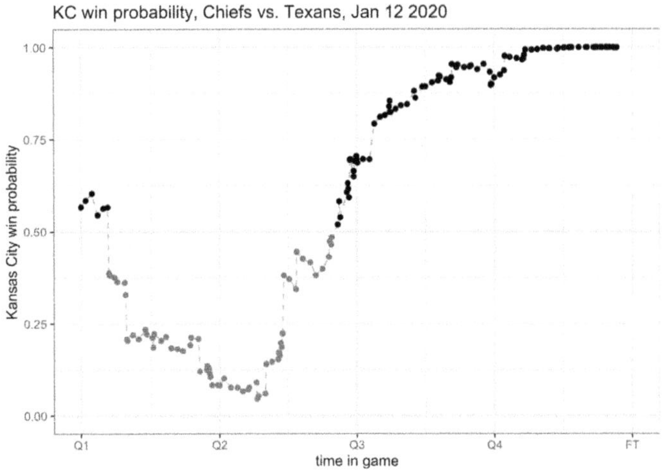

Figure 6.10: Kansas City Chiefs win probability versus the Houston Texans from the 2019–20 season playoffs. The points above and below 0.5 are shaded according to Kansas City's (light) and Houston's (dark) primary team colors.

```
week_11_ids <- fast_scraper_schedules(2022) |>
  filter(week == 11)
tc <- teamcolors |>
  filter(name %in% c("Kansas City Chiefs", "Los Angeles Chargers")) |>
  mutate(team = ifelse(name == "Kansas City Chiefs", "KC", "LAC"))

kc_at_lac_pbp <- week_11_ids |>
  filter(home_team == "LAC") |>
  pull(game_id) |>
  fast_scraper()
kc_at_lac_pbp_tc <- kc_at_lac_pbp |>
  mutate(team = ifelse(home_wp < .5, "KC", "LAC")) |>
  left_join(tc, by = "team") |>
  filter(!is.na(team))

p <- ggplot(data = kc_at_lac_pbp_tc,
```

```
            aes(x = 3600 - game_seconds_remaining,
                y = home_wp,
                col = name))
p + geom_line(col = "darkgrey", linetype = 2) +
  geom_point() +
  scale_color_teams() +
  scale_y_continuous(limits = c(0, 1)) +
  scale_x_continuous(limits = c(0, 3600),
                     breaks = seq(0, 3600, by = 900),
                     labels = c("Q1", "Q2", "Q3", "Q4", "FT")) +
  labs(
    x = "time in game (s)",
    y = "LAC win probability",
    title = "Win Probability: KC @ LAC, week 11 2022"
  ) +
  guides(col = "none") +
  theme_bw()
```

We could also create this as a line plot showing the Kansas City win probability as one line and the Los Angeles win probability as another:

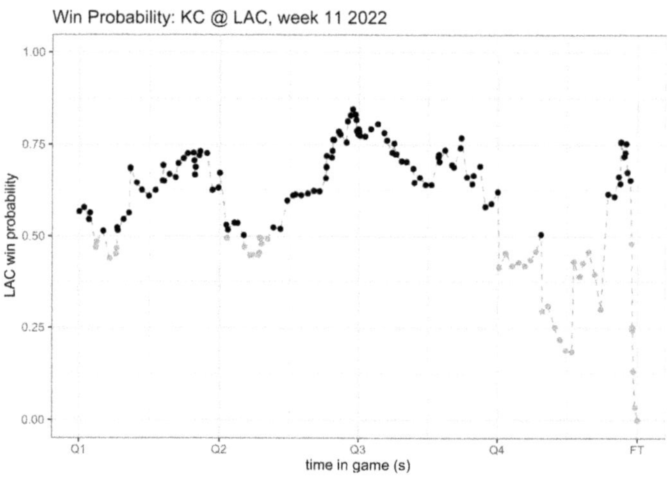

Figure 6.11: Los Angeles Chargers win probability versus the Kansas City Chiefs from the 2022–23 season playoffs.

```
kc_at_lac_pbp_tc <- kc_at_lac_pbp |>
  mutate(home_team_color = teamcolors |>
           filter(name == "Los Angeles Chargers") |>
           pull(primary),
         away_team_color = teamcolors |>
           filter(name == "Kansas City Chiefs") |>
           pull(primary)) |>
  filter(!is.na(home_wp))

p <- ggplot(data = kc_at_lac_pbp_tc,
            aes(x = 3600 - game_seconds_remaining,
                y = home_wp))
p + geom_line(color = kc_at_lac_pbp_tc$home_team_color[1]) +
  geom_line(aes(x = 3600 - game_seconds_remaining,
                y = away_wp),
            color = kc_at_lac_pbp_tc$away_team_color[1]) +
  scale_y_continuous(limits = c(0, 1)) +
  scale_x_continuous(limits = c(0, 3600),
                     breaks = seq(0, 3600, by = 900),
                     labels = c("Q1", "Q2", "Q3", "Q4", "FT")) +
```

```
  na.omit()

p <- ggplot(data = g1,
            aes(x = 3600 - game_seconds_remaining,
                y = home_wp,
                col = name))
p + geom_line(col = "darkgrey", linetype = 2) +
  geom_point() +
  scale_color_teams(name = "name") +
  scale_y_continuous(limits = c(0, 1)) +
  scale_x_continuous(limits = c(0, 3600),
                     breaks = seq(0, 3600, by = 900),
                     labels = c("Q1", "Q2", "Q3", "Q4", "FT")) +
  labs(
    title="KC win probability, Chiefs vs. Texans, Jan 12 2020",
    x = "time in game",
    y = "Kansas City win probability"
  ) +
  guides(col = "none") +
  theme_bw()
```

If you want to pull this information in for another game, it requires a bit more code. While each team will only play another team one time in the playoffs, they may play multiple times in the regular season. One way to focus on a particular game would be to know what week it occurred in the schedule, use the `fast_scraper_schedules()` function in `nflfastR` to get the games for that particular week, and then search for the two teams from that week and proceed as before. Alternatively, you can just pull in a single game as follows in this example, a 2022 contest between the Kansas City Chiefs and the Los Angeles Chargers:

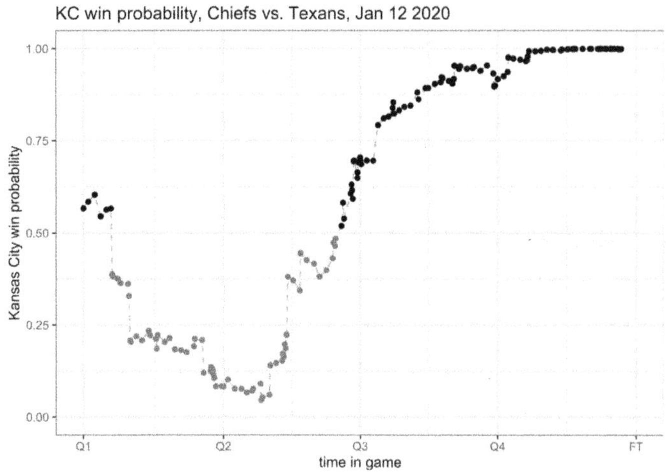

Figure 6.10: Kansas City Chiefs win probability versus the Houston Texans from the 2019–20 season playoffs. The points above and below 0.5 are shaded according to Kansas City's (light) and Houston's (dark) primary team colors.

```
week_11_ids <- fast_scraper_schedules(2022) |>
  filter(week == 11)
tc <- teamcolors |>
  filter(name %in% c("Kansas City Chiefs", "Los Angeles Chargers")) |>
  mutate(team = ifelse(name == "Kansas City Chiefs", "KC", "LAC"))

kc_at_lac_pbp <- week_11_ids |>
  filter(home_team == "LAC") |>
  pull(game_id) |>
  fast_scraper()
kc_at_lac_pbp_tc <- kc_at_lac_pbp |>
  mutate(team = ifelse(home_wp < .5, "KC", "LAC")) |>
  left_join(tc, by = "team") |>
  filter(!is.na(team))

p <- ggplot(data = kc_at_lac_pbp_tc,
```

```
             aes(x = 3600 - game_seconds_remaining,
                 y = home_wp,
                 col = name))
p + geom_line(col = "darkgrey", linetype = 2) +
  geom_point() +
  scale_color_teams() +
  scale_y_continuous(limits = c(0, 1)) +
  scale_x_continuous(limits = c(0, 3600),
                     breaks = seq(0, 3600, by = 900),
                     labels = c("Q1", "Q2", "Q3", "Q4", "FT")) +
  labs(
    x = "time in game (s)",
    y = "LAC win probability",
    title = "Win Probability: KC @ LAC, week 11 2022"
  ) +
  guides(col = "none") +
  theme_bw()
```

We could also create this as a line plot showing the Kansas City win probability as one line and the Los Angeles win probability as another:

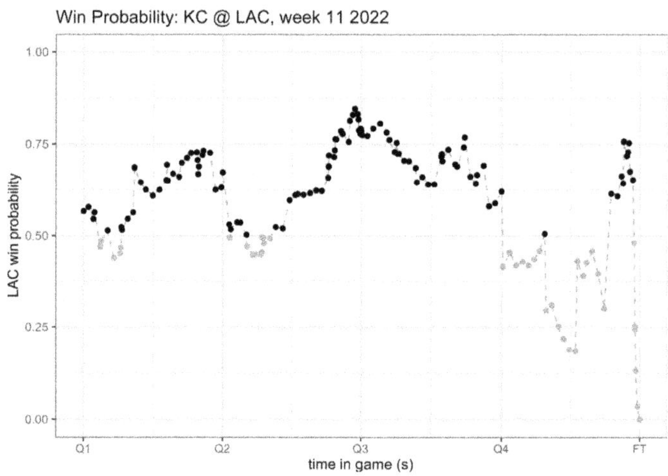

Figure 6.11: Los Angeles Chargers win probability versus the Kansas City Chiefs from the 2022–23 season playoffs.

```
kc_at_lac_pbp_tc <- kc_at_lac_pbp |>
  mutate(home_team_color = teamcolors |>
           filter(name == "Los Angeles Chargers") |>
           pull(primary),
         away_team_color = teamcolors |>
           filter(name == "Kansas City Chiefs") |>
           pull(primary)) |>
  filter(!is.na(home_wp))

p <- ggplot(data = kc_at_lac_pbp_tc,
            aes(x = 3600 - game_seconds_remaining,
                y = home_wp))
p + geom_line(color = kc_at_lac_pbp_tc$home_team_color[1]) +
  geom_line(aes(x = 3600 - game_seconds_remaining,
                y = away_wp),
            color = kc_at_lac_pbp_tc$away_team_color[1]) +
  scale_y_continuous(limits = c(0, 1)) +
  scale_x_continuous(limits = c(0, 3600),
                     breaks = seq(0, 3600, by = 900),
                     labels = c("Q1", "Q2", "Q3", "Q4", "FT")) +
```

```
  labs(
    x = "time in game",
    y = "win probability",
    title = "Win Probability: KC @ LAC, week 11 2022"
  ) +
  guides(col = "none") +
  theme_bw()
```

We would never suggest this type of visualization, however, as the additional line creates more nondata ink without supplying more data (see Edward Tufte's "The Visual Display of Quantitative Information," `https://www.edwardtufte.com/tufte/books_vdqi`), but we do it to show the power of the packages to create lines with the colors using the `teamcolors` package.

Who would use these data and visualizations? Programming directors, when trying to decide whether to switch their national feed from one game to another, might decide to never do this unless the win probability is over 99.4% and the game is in the fourth quarter. Gamblers who are trying to use more information to find an edge might compare the win probabilities to current live betting odds and see if there is a mismatch and, in theory, a market opportunity. We will discuss this more in chapter 10.

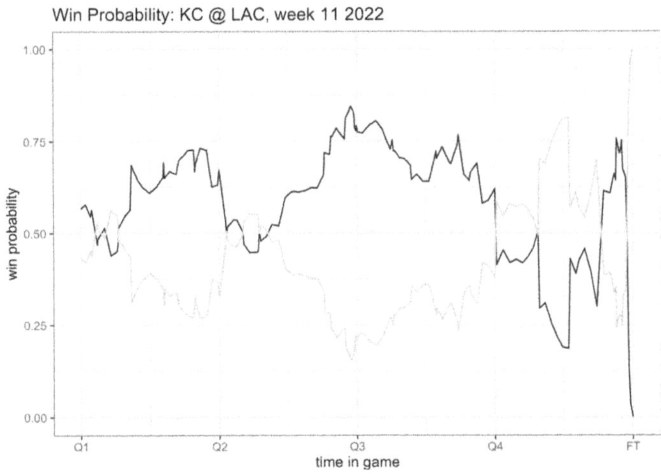

Figure 6.12: Los Angeles Chargers and Kansas City Chiefs win probabilities from the 2022–23 season playoffs.

6.12 Lab: Simulation with `NFLSimulatoR`

Now we turn our attention to a framework for doing a similar task to what is given above using the `NFLSimulatoR` R package. This package is written more specifically for NFL simulations, but it requires the data to be uploaded from outside sources to use as the basis for simulations.

Prep the Data

To use the package, you need to use the data from `NFLfastR` as we described earlier in this chapter. We also need to run that data through the package's preparation function (`prep_pbp_data`) to make it ready for simulation:

```
nfl_pbp_sim <- prep_pbp_data(nfl_pbp)
```

Sample Play

Let's sample a first-down-and-10-yards-to-go play starting from a team's 45-yard line. The yard line of 45 was arbitrarily chosen to illustrate a functionality rather than a meaningful football play. Note that we are calling the following functions while referencing the functions' namespace `NFLSimulatoR` so that we don't confuse these function calls with the functions defined earlier in this chapter:

```
set.seed(3)
play <- NFLSimulatoR::sample_play(
  what_down = 1,
  yards_to_go = 10,
  yards_from_own_goal = 45,
  play_by_play_data = nfl_pbp_sim,
  strategy = "normal"
)
play$desc
```

```
[1] "(3:23) 8-K.Cousins pass incomplete deep right to 17-K.Osborn."
```

You can see that it returns a play that happened in the 2022 game involving the Minnesota Vikings. In this case, Kirk Cousins attempted a pass to Kendrick Osborn, but it was incomplete. You will also see a strategy argument, which is mainly concerned with sampling drives if we want to employ a particular strategy. That is, we might have to have an equal mix of passes and rushes, or we might want to always go for it on fourth down. Or maybe we only want to go for it on fourth down if we have less than a certain number of yards to go to pick up the first down. There are many different possibilities.

Sample Drives

Here is how we might sample a series of drives. Note that we use the `set.seed()` function, with an integer as its argument, for the explicit purpose of reproducing our results. That is, if we set the random number generator's initialization seed to 98, for example, prior to running `sample_drives` with the same arguments, we will get the exact same set of drives in our `drives` object every time we use that seed. This can be important for testing and reproducibility, because when you do not set the seed, you will get a different (random!) set of plays every time you run it.

```
set.seed(98)
drives <- NFLSimulatoR::sample_drives(
  n_sims = 100,
  from_yard_line = 25,
  play_by_play_data = nfl_pbp_sim,
  strategy = "fourth_downs",
  fourth_down_strategy = "always_go_for_it",
  single_drive = T,
  progress = T #shows progress bar for simulations
)
```

As can be seen above, there are a multitude of arguments associated with this function, and we encourage the reader to read the NFLSimulatoR website for more details `https://datacolorado.com/r/nflsimulator/`. In this example, we are sampling 100 drives (`n_sims`) starting at the 25-yard line (`from_yard_line`), and we will never punt or kick a field goal on fourth down (`strategy = "fourth downs"` and `fourth_down_strategy = "always go for it"`). The data frame of drives is stored in the `drives` object.

Now let's consider a strategy that specifies a certain proportion of passes and runs:

```
set.seed(101)
drives_pr <- NFLSimulatoR::sample_drives(
  n_sims = 100,
  from_yard_line = 25,
  play_by_play_data = nfl_pbp_sim,
  strategy = "passes_rushes",
  prop_passes = 0.25,
  single_drive = T,
  progress = T #shows progress bar for simulations
)
```

Below we display each type of play that was run. While our distribution of passes to runs in the resulting set is 25.5% rather than exactly 25%, it is well within the variation we would expect from a simulation. In fact, we would almost never expect exactly 25%.

```
group_by(drives_pr, play_type) |>
  summarize(n = n())
```

```
# A tibble: 4 × 2
  play_type       n
  <chr>       <int>
1 field_goal     32
2 pass          128
3 punt           54
4 run           374
```

Now that we know how to use `NFLSimulatoR`, we can practice with it.

1. Sample 500 fourth-and-goal plays from the opponent's one-yard line. Find how often a team did the following:
   a. Kick a field goal
   b. Run the ball and score a TD
   c. Run the ball and not score a TD
   d. Pass the ball and score a TD
   e. Pass the ball and not score a TD
2. Based on just this information in question 1, what is your recommendation for a play in this situation?
3. Build a sample of 500 fourth-quarter drives and 500 first-quarter drives. Is there a difference in how often a team scores in the first quarter as opposed to the fourth quarter?

6.13 Conclusion

In this chapter, we looked mostly at situational analysis. Due to the large amounts of data and the discrete-play nature of football, there are almost endless situations that we can analyze. Of course, what we have done is just scratching the surface of the possibilities. Many NFL teams will have the lead analyst on the headset with the head coach, offering suggestions either proactively or when asked.

There is even more that could be done when considering player evaluation. Many decisions need to be made at the beginning of each year, long before the season starts, concerning the roster. Who does our team want to draft, resign, cut, trade and trade for, claim on waivers, or bring in as a free agent? How do we evaluate performance in a prior year and/or league and equate that to future performance for our team? No one wants to be the team that cut a player too early (e.g., the New England Patriots in 2020, when Tom Brady won the Super Bowl for the Buccaneers that year) or picked up a player a year too late (as appears to be the case with the Denver Broncos' 2022 signing of Russell Wilson). Teams must continue to make these decisions during the year when a major injury makes a player unavailable (e.g., the 2023 New York Jets and Aaron Rodgers) and they have to backfill that position for the season.

Anyone who has ever played Madden NFL (a video game series produced by EA Sports) is familiar with the player ratings in categories such as speed, agility, and strength contributing to an overall rating. NFL players have been known to lobby the programmers at EA Sports to make their ratings higher than they have been listed in the video game—everyone wants to be an Overall 99! These analytics are used in the video games, but others are based on the outcomes of real plays. Pro Football Focus creates their PFF ratings for players at a given position, and these are used to compare players. This is presumably more accurate than simply counting statistics, as humans review every play.

Moreover, there is more that can be done with opponent scouting and evaluation. Analytics can be used to identify a coach's or team's tendencies in certain situations, or perhaps which players from the roster to make available on a given day. An entire book could be written simply on American football analytics, but we do not have that luxury here! However, if you are interested, we recommend the book *Introduction to NFL Analytics with R*, which can be found at `https://bradcongelio.com/nfl-analytics-with-r-book/`.

6.14 Case Study: Overtime Strategy in the NFL

On November 14, 2021, the Detroit Lions and Pittsburgh Steelers played to a 16–16 tie. A tie game is an unusual result in the NFL, occurring about once per year out of a 256-game schedule that was expanded to 272 games in the 2021 season. The outcome of the game did little to affect the Detroit Lions, who at 0–8 had little still left to play for other than to avoid being the first 0–17 team in NFL history, a dubious distinction especially since in 2008, the Lions became the first team to record an 0–16 team season (the Cleveland Browns would be the only other team to duplicate that "feat" in 2016).

However, for the Pittsburgh Steelers, the tie left their record at 5-3-1, or half a win behind the AFC North division–leading Baltimore Ravens at 6–3. At the end of the season, it will not matter if they finish half a win or a full win behind as far as the standings are concerned and playoff positions (or qualifications) are determined.

Overtime in the NFL is a 10-minute sudden death–like period where a coin toss determines which team gets to choose to kick or receive the kickoff or choose which goal to defend. Afterward, the first team to score wins the game, with one caveat: If the team that possesses the ball first (Team A) in the overtime period scores a FG, they must kick off and give Team B a chance to possess the ball. If Team B scores a FG, they must kick off to Team A, and the period continues. If any team scores a TD at any time or any defense records a safety, the game is over, and the team scoring the TD or safety wins. If the game remains tied at the end of the overtime period, the game is a tie.

While a team always begins a game wanting to win, the strategy employed for overtime can adjust depending on the team's record and how close to the end of the season it is at the time. Moreover, a team's strategy could change depending on the situation of the game. There are many decision points that a team could face, and as analysts, we would use data to support or refute our decisions. Consider the following questions:

1. If a team wins the coin toss, is there ever a situation where one would choose to kick the ball instead of receiving it? What data would you need and how would you test it?
2. What happens to our consideration of the expected points variable in overtime?
3. Imagine the following scenarios. In each scenario, determine what decision you make and how you would use data to support that decision:
   a. You as Team A possess the ball first, and it is fourth down and 8 yards to go at the opponent's 15-yard line. Do you try to make the first down or do you attempt a 33-yard FG?
   b. Same as above, but it is fourth down and 2 yards to go.
   c. Same as (b), but instead, you are Team B, and Team A possessed the ball first and has already kicked a FG and has a three-point lead.
   d. There is one minute left in the overtime period, and you have the ball on fourth down and 4 yards to go from the opponent's 43-yard line. Do you try to get the first down, punt, or attempt a FG? What are the consequences of being unsuccessful at the attempt for a first down or for a FG?
   e. Suppose a team is faced with a fourth down at each yard line between 1 and 45, and each yards-to-go parameter is set at 1, 2, . . . , 10. Construct a heat map–like figure showing your decision in two colors for each combination of yard line and yards to go.

6.15 Exercises

1. Using the field goals dataset that we generated earlier in this chapter, fit a `glm` that uses `fg_distance`, `game_seconds_remaining`, and `year_of_season` (as a factor) as predictor variables for `success`. You will have to create the variable `year_of_season` by using the `mutate()` function from `dplyr` and the `substr()` function on the `game_id` variable.
2. In question 1, is `game_seconds_remaining` a significant predictor of field goal success? If not, refit the model from question 1 without that variable, using both a `glm` and `gam` approach.
3. Using the "best" model from problem 2, compare your estimates of the probability of successfully making a field goal by distance for the years 2011 and 2022. Show your answer graphically as a single plot with both lines.
4. After each kickoff that goes into the end zone, a player catching the ball in the air has the option to give himself up ("take a knee"), called a touchback, or attempt to return the kick. On a touchback, the receiving team gets the ball at the 25-yard line with 100% certainty, whereas returning the kick creates the possibility to score a touchdown by returning the kick the length of the field—but the player could also be tackled before the 25-yard line, or fumble the ball and lose possession, or suffer an injury. It is a risk-reward decision.

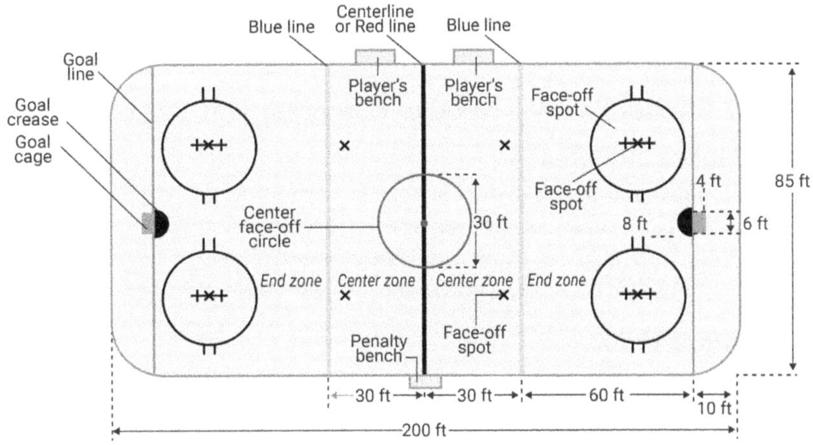

Figure 7.1: Hockey rink.

Hockey belongs to a family of sports where the objective is for a team of players to move an object from one end of a field or court to the other end and ultimately deposit it into a goal of some sort. While hockey is most similar to soccer in these regards, it also has elements of basketball.

In hockey, each team consists of five skaters and one goaltender. The game is played on an ice rink that is approximately 200 feet (60 meters) long and 85–100 feet (25–30 meters) wide. The skaters are divided into offensive players (left wing, center, and right wing) and two defenders, who are generally not classified as left or right. Each player carries a hockey stick, which is used to move the puck, a hard rubber disk about 3 inches (7.5 cm) in diameter, 1 inch (2.5 cm) thick, and weighing about 6 ounces (165 grams), along the ice. The sides of the rink are hemmed in by "boards" about 3 feet (1 meter) high and Plexiglas about another 6 feet (1.8 meters high), so in general, the puck does not go out of play with nearly the frequency of a soccer ball. A puck would have to be shot quite high to go out of play and/or into the seats with the spectators, who watch the game through the clear Plexiglas if they are close to the rink. The boards and glass allow spectators to be very close to the players, easily able to touch them if it weren't for the glass.

The object is to hit the puck with the stick into the net, a 6-by-4-foot (1.8-by-1.2-meter) target. The net is guarded by a goaltender, a player on the team whose job is primarily to keep the puck out of the net. The goalie, as he or she is colloquially known, wears many thick pads and a face mask to keep from getting hurt by a puck that can travel at over 100 mph (160 kph) off the sticks of players with the hardest shots. The net is anchored near each end of the ice, but unlike soccer or water polo, there is room to play behind the net. This requires goalies to have a neck like an owl, as they must look behind them even though the opening to the net is only in front of them.

Along with the skaters in play, there are approximately 15 players in reserve at any given time. Players may be substituted freely in and out of the game, and it is rare for a skater to play more than 90 seconds before going to the bench for a reserve skater. With skaters traveling sometimes more than 30 mph (50 kph), they tire quickly. It is quite rare for a skater to play more than 30 minutes of a normal 60-minute game (three 20-minute periods), with 19–25 minutes being the average time on ice. There is no stoppage in play for substitutes to come on and off the ice—players jump over the boards in front of their bench (where there is no Plexiglas) or exit through a door that opens in front of the bench. Hockey is full of action.

If a player commits a foul, such as hitting another player with the stick, tripping another player, or interfering with the fair course of action, it is called a penalty, and that player is sent to the penalty box for a period of time. While that player is in the penalty box, his or her team must play with one fewer player than the other team. The offending player's team is said to be short-handed, while the other team with one more skater on the ice is said to be on the power play. Most penalties are considered minor penalties, and the player is sent off for two minutes, but for dangerous plays like fighting or hitting someone even accidentally on or near the head with the stick, it is called a major penalty, and the player is sent off for five minutes. Five minutes is quite a long time to play with one fewer skater than your opponent, and it quite often results in giving up one or more goals to the opponents.

Figure 7.2: Substitution in hockey.
Source: Andrew Urbaczewski

Much like other chapters, this is just a basic introduction. For more details, you can read about ice hockey at `https://www.rookieroad.com/ice-hockey/what-is/`.

7.3 What You Will Need to Complete This Chapter

Hockey Reference

You may remember in our chapter on web scraping that we used data from Hockey Reference. We will use data again from this website. One word of warning: numbers will often come in as characters if you scrape Hockey Reference in R (or other reference.com sites). You will often have to change a particular field or variable to numeric (for example, use `as.numeric(variable)`) before creating a plot or making calculations with that data.

MoneyPuck

There is a great website that makes a ton of hockey data available for download called MoneyPuck. Almost all of their data are available as a `.csv` or a `.zip` file. You can download this data using the links given on their download page. For example, here is how you could get all of the skater (i.e., nongoalie) information for the 2022–23 season:

```
year <- "2023"
link <- paste("http://moneypuck.com/moneypuck/playerData/seasonSummary/",
              year,
              "/regular/skaters.csv",
              sep = "")
df <- read.csv(link)
```

Here are a few more links:

1. All game data going back to the 2008–9 season: `http://moneypuck.com/moneypuck/playerData/careers/gameByGame/all_teams.csv`
2. Shots (you can iterate over years): `http://peter-tanner.com/moneypuck/downloads/shots_2019.zip`

7.4 Exploring Ice Hockey through Basic and Advanced Statistics

The dataset that we used in the initial part of this chapter was obtained using the following code block. The dataset has 10,648 observations related to players from the 2011–12 season through the 2022–23 season. How do we know what season each variable/record is referring to? You have to look at the basic and advanced tables on `hockey-reference.com`. Please refer to chapter 3 on web scraping to refresh your memory.

```
years <- 2012:2023
for(i in seq_along(years)){
  cat(sprintf('Year: %s at %s\n', years[i], Sys.time()))
  reg_url <- paste("https://www.hockey-reference.com/leagues/NHL_", years[i],
                   "_skaters.html", sep = "")
  pg <- read_html(reg_url)
  nhl_reg_stats <- rvest::html_table(pg, fill = TRUE)[[1]]
  names(nhl_reg_stats) <- nhl_reg_stats[1, ]
  nhl_reg_stats_2 <- janitor::clean_names(nhl_reg_stats) |>
    filter(rk != "Rk")

  adv_url <- paste("https://www.hockey-reference.com/leagues/NHL_", years[i],
                   "_skaters-advanced.html", sep = "")
  pg_2 <- read_html(adv_url)
  nhl_adv_stats <- rvest::html_table(pg_2, fill = TRUE)[[1]]
  names(nhl_adv_stats) <- nhl_adv_stats[1, ]
  nhl_adv_stats_2 <- janitor::clean_names(nhl_adv_stats) |>
    filter(rk != "Rk")

  tmp_results <- dplyr::inner_join(nhl_reg_stats_2, nhl_adv_stats_2) |>
```

```
    mutate(season = years[i]) |>
    select(-rk)

  if(exists("nhl_data")){
    nhl_data <- dplyr::bind_rows(nhl_data, tmp_results)
  }
  else(nhl_data <- tmp_results)

}
```

```
Year: 2012 at 2023-12-24 13:29:12.333478
Year: 2013 at 2023-12-24 13:29:13.086999
Year: 2014 at 2023-12-24 13:29:13.820226
Year: 2015 at 2023-12-24 13:29:14.531736
Year: 2016 at 2023-12-24 13:29:15.368013
Year: 2017 at 2023-12-24 13:29:16.254139
Year: 2018 at 2023-12-24 13:29:17.343007
Year: 2019 at 2023-12-24 13:29:18.104753
Year: 2020 at 2023-12-24 13:29:18.860379
Year: 2021 at 2023-12-24 13:29:20.062596
Year: 2022 at 2023-12-24 13:29:20.793405
Year: 2023 at 2023-12-24 13:29:21.768902
```

```
nhl_data[, -c(1, 3, 4, 22, 41, 42)] <- sapply(nhl_data[, -c(1, 3, 4, 22, 41, 42)],
                                              as.numeric )
```

To help refresh your memory, you could explore the data. Some of these columns may seem quite obvious, but others might seem difficult to understand for the nonavid hockey fan.

7.5 Corsi and Fenwick Metrics

Among the first advanced analytics to be used in hockey to measure player effectiveness are Corsi and Fenwick. For over 100 years, basic metrics such as goals scored (or allowed, for goaltenders), assists, and penalty minutes were the primary metrics used to measure player effectiveness. Plus-minus also evolved as a metric, where a player's plus-minus rating was equal to the number of goals scored by their team while they were on the ice less the number of goals allowed by their team when that player was on the ice. This helped, but its flaw is that the metric often depends on how good a player's teammates are. A very low-level player might have an excellent plus-minus rating because he happens to be on the ice at the same time as a scoring superstar like Auston Matthews or Sidney Crosby.

Figure 7.3: Nathan MacKinnon. *Source:* Quintin Soloviev / CC BY-SA 4.0

Although not terribly advanced, Corsi and Fenwick are the next level, doing more than simply counting. Corsi is the difference in shot attempts (shots on goal + missed shots + blocked shots) when the player is on the ice and shot attempts by his opponent when he's on the ice. Note that only five-on-five scenarios are counted. Another measure, Fenwick, is similar but does not include blocked shots.

Though we describe Corsi and Fenwick as noting a difference, it may help to view them as percentages. For example, as a measure of effectiveness, we can see whether a player being on the ice is not just effective as a raw Corsi number but as a percentage of time on the ice. To do this, we can look at Corsi as a percentage of the Corsi "for" (SOG + missed shots + blocked shots for that player's team) while a player is on the ice, divided by the Corsi "for" plus the Corsi "against" (SOG + missed shots + blocked shots by the opponent while that player is on the ice). We can then plot the Corsi percent by year for one player, Nathan MacKinnon of the Colorado Avalanche:

```
mac <- filter(nhl_data, player == "Nathan MacKinnon")
p <- ggplot(data = mac,
            aes(x = age, y = cf_percent/100))
p + geom_line() +
  geom_point() +
  labs(x = "Age", y = "Corsi Percentage") +
  scale_y_continuous(labels = scales::percent) +
  scale_x_continuous(breaks = 18:28) +
  theme_bw()
```

As we see in the graph, as MacKinnon has gained experience in the NHL, his effectiveness on the ice has also increased. This graph indicates that not only are the scoring chances when he is on the ice more in favor of his team; they are increasingly in favor of his team as he has aged and become more proficient in the NHL game.

Corsi and Fenwick calculations are possible today with effective shot tracking, which began in 2007–8. As with all advanced metrics, it does make it difficult to compare modern players with those who played before these data were collected. This is true not just for players of lore like Maurice Richard, Johnny Bucyk, or Phil Esposito but even for Wayne Gretzky and Mario Lemieux.

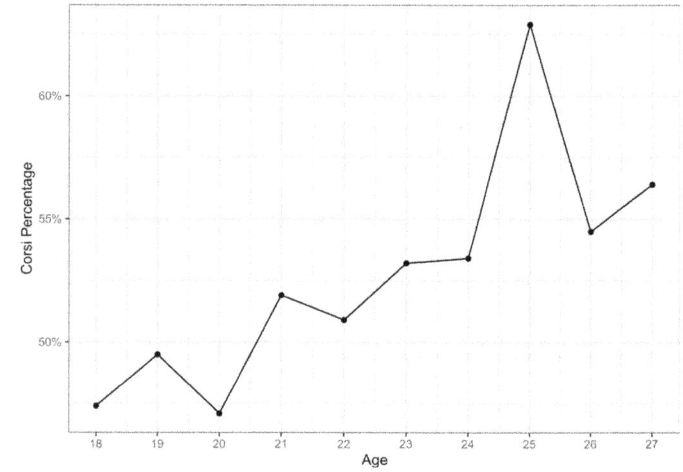

Figure 7.4: Corsi percentage values (y) by age (x) for Nathan MacKinnon of the Colorado Avalanche.

7.6 Time on Ice by Position

Earlier we mentioned that it is highly unusual for a skater to play even half the game. Goalkeepers generally play the entire game, but we will exclude them from this analysis. If we are managing a team, either at the highest professional level or in single-digit-aged youth, we want to ensure that players do not become overly fatigued in the waning minutes of a game or after several games in close succession, with few or no days off. To understand this, we should examine a metric called time on ice (TOI). First, we should note the differences by position played. As NHL teams generally carry four offensive lines (LW, C, RW) on the active roster for a game but only three pairs of defenders, we might expect that defenders are playing more minutes throughout a game and throughout the season. Thus, we can create a graphical distribution of TOI by position, first together and then in individual facets. To do this, we will take our NHL data and filter it by position, eliminating goalkeepers. We will also filter out anyone with a TOI of less than 200 minutes for the season, as that would be indicative of a bit player who played in perhaps a few games out of an 82-game season, and then create two different density plots:

```
p <- ggplot(data = nhl_data |>
              mutate(toi = toi) |>
              filter(toi >= 200,
                     !(pos %in% c("F", "W"))),
            aes(x = toi))
p + geom_density(alpha = .25, fill = "grey20") +
  facet_wrap(~ pos, nc = 2) +
  labs(x = "Time on Ice (min)") +
  theme_bw()
```

As we view the graphs, we see that the center, left wing, and right wing graphs look relatively similar. This is to be expected (as mentioned earlier), as normally, each team will group a center, left wing, and right wing as a "line" that will play together, as they know one another's strengths and weaknesses and tendencies. Having three defensive pairs to go with the four offensive lines means that defensemen tend to play more minutes on the ice each game.

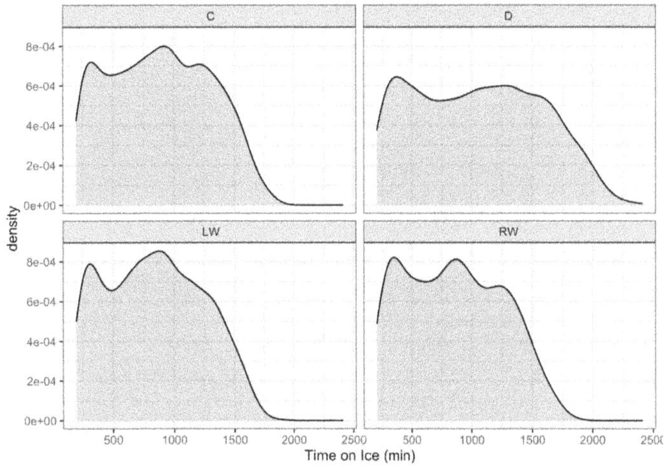

Figure 7.5: Density plots for time on ice by position.

7.7 Evaluating Players

As we mentioned earlier, Corsi percent is a newer metric for evaluating players. What if we wanted to see who had the maximum Corsi per year by position? We can take the NHL data that we've been working with in this chapter, and then

- filter out any player who didn't play at least 200 minutes,
- group the players by season and position, and
- list the maximum:

```
top_cor <- nhl_data |>
  filter(toi >= 200) |>
  group_by(season, pos) |>
  summarize(max_corsi = max(cf_percent)) |>
  arrange(desc(max_corsi))
head(top_cor)
```

```
# A tibble: 6 × 3
# Groups:   season [4]
  season pos   max_corsi
   <dbl> <chr>     <dbl>
1   2021 LW         67.2
2   2023 D          65.7
3   2023 C          64.9
4   2022 C          64.1
5   2013 D          64
6   2013 RW         63.4
```

The above data frame does not give us the entire dataset associated with this entry; it's only the season, position, and max Corsi, but not the player's name. How can we find that? Consider the following code:

```
top_cor <- nhl_data |>
  filter(toi >= 200) |>
  group_by(season, pos) |>
  filter(cf_percent == max(cf_percent)) |>
  select(season, player, pos, tm, cf_percent) |>
  arrange(desc(cf_percent))
head(top_cor)
```

```
# A tibble: 6 × 5
# Groups:   season, pos [6]
  season player           pos   tm    cf_percent
   <dbl> <chr>            <chr> <chr>      <dbl>
1   2021 Taylor Hall      LW    BOS         67.2
2   2023 Dylan Coghlan    D     CAR         65.7
3   2023 Jack Drury       C     CAR         64.9
4   2022 Patrice Bergeron C     BOS         64.1
5   2013 Jake Muzzin      D     LAK         64
6   2013 Justin Williams  RW    LAK         63.4
```

```
nhl_tmp <- nhl_data |>
  filter(toi >= 200) |>
  group_by(season, pos) |>
  summarize(avg_corsi = mean(cf_percent))
p <- ggplot(nhl_tmp,
            aes(x = season, y = avg_corsi, col = pos))
p + geom_line() +
  geom_point() +
  labs(y = "Average Corsi",
       x = "Season",
       linetype = "Position") +
  scale_x_continuous(breaks = 2008:2023) +
  scale_color_brewer("Position", palette = "Dark2") +
  theme_bw()
```

You can see here that the data are a bit confusing. It appears that starting in 2018, the position “W” was added, and in 2020, the position “F” also appeared. These are abbreviations for wing and forward, respectively, and they add some spice to the visualization. More on this later.

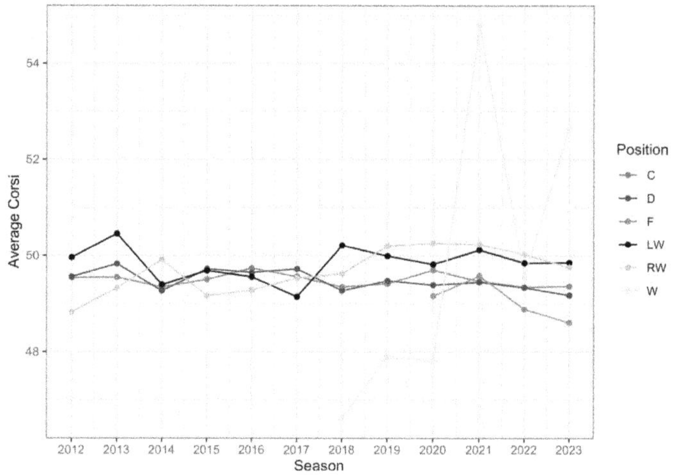

Figure 7.6: Average Corsi values over time by several positions.

7.8 Research Block: Fighting in the NHL

In the past, ice hockey was known for tolerating (to some degree) fighting between the players. When a particular player might have felt that some injustice occurred on the ice, such as a player being hit from behind or otherwise hit dangerously or needlessly, a fight might occur. Increasingly, teams would have players who might have had lesser technical skills than other skaters but were the ones who would be most likely to get into a fight. These skaters sometimes had nicknames like the enforcers, goons, or designated fighters. The result of the fight was usually that there would be some mild entertainment for the fans for a minute or two, the fighters would be sent to the penalty box for five minutes, and the game would resume.

Rules have changed throughout the years to limit the impact and frequency of fights, particularly as more serious acute injuries and chronic conditions like chronic traumatic encephalopathy (CTE) have led to much more than a few bruises or scars as the result of fights. Nevertheless, fighting itself has never been eliminated, particularly at the highest professional levels. Defenders of the practice have said this is how the players police the game themselves. They claim that without fighting, players would be enabled to take cheap shots at opposing players and fear nothing more than a two-minute minor penalty. They also claim that it can be used to change the momentum of a game—for example, to inspire a team that is losing. Opponents of the practice state that fighting takes a beautiful game like hockey and turns it into a medieval practice where skill is diminished by brawn. What would be called felonious assault if it happened on the concourses of the arena is somehow turned into "just a part of the game," and as such, they feel like they can't have their children watch the game. The NHL remains the only major hockey league in which fighting is considered a part of the game as opposed to an automatic ejection and suspension from further competition.

Figure 7.7: Hockey fight.
Source: Dan4th Nicholas / CC BY 2.0

While the authors here take no position on the role of fighting in the game, other researchers have examined different aspects of fighting and hockey. In the article "Do Not Drop Your Gloves: 'Winning' a Fight in the National Hockey League Does Not Improve Chances to Win the Game," available at `https://www.sciencedirect.com/science/article/abs/pii/S146902922100159X` and published in the journal *Psychology of Sport and Exercise*, Nadav Goldschmied and Michael Apostol study NHL games in which fights have occurred and if there was a change in momentum. As many fights in an NHL game occur when the game is out of hand, such as a 5–1 score late in the final period, the researchers only viewed games where the score was tied or there was a one-goal difference. They also had to determine which player "won" the fight. Of course, the NHL does not officially judge a winner or a loser of a fight or award different penalty minutes to the winner or the loser, so instead, the authors had to rely on online voting by fans as to who won the fight and used objective data from the fight to validate the fans' opinions.

The researchers found that the winning player's team was no more likely to win the game in a tied game than the losing player's team. Furthermore, when a team was down one goal, they also found no real momentum effect that would cause the team trailing at the time to change the game's outcome. What was not studied, however, was its effect later in the year, particularly when those two teams or players met again.

7.9 Accessing the NHL API

As mentioned at the beginning of this chapter, the textbook's `ISAR` package contains three datasets related to hockey: `avs_roster_2022`, `avs_stats_2022`, and `nhl_team_stats_2022`. These datasets were obtained using the `nhlapi` R package that was built on the NHL's pre-2023–24 season's API. Unfortunately, the API changed, and the `nhlapi` package no longer works. Fortunately, there is a tool that can acquire data directly from the NHL's new API itself. That tool, in R, is the `hockeyR` package.

Play-by-Play Data

The `hockeyR` package provides a handy function, `load_pbp()`, for accessing the play-by-play data in the NHL. The function downloads data from the `hockeyR-data` repository that is updated on a nightly basis. The repository includes all play-by-play data starting with the 2010–11 season. Let's access all play-by-play data for the 2022–23 season:

```
pbp_23 <- load_pbp('2022-23')
```

The pbp_23 object is loaded into memory with 429,879 observations across 111 variables. That is a lot of data! One column to note (among many) in this data frame is the xg (expected goals) field. The authors of the package include xg based on their gradient-boosted model contained in the hockeyR-models repository on GitHub.

Shot Charts

One point that helps us discern how teams are scoring goals is the location from where they are shooting. The NHL records this data using player tracking systems available in all arenas, and we can access this information using the pbp_23 data frame defined above. Furthermore, we can visualize this same data by plotting them on an NHL rink background using the sportyR package. This will give us similar results as the shot charts in the basketball chapter.

We will start by looking at all goals scored by the Colorado Avalanche during the 2022–23 season:

```
avs_pbp <- pbp_23 |>
  filter(event_team_abbr == "COL")
```

From this data frame, we need to focus on all shots. How can we isolate all shots? First, consider the event field and, in particular, the unique entries in the field:

```
unique(avs_pbp$event)
```

```
 [1] "Shot"                  "Faceoff"                "Hit"
 [4] "Missed Shot"           "Blocked Shot"           "Giveaway"
 [7] "Goal"                  "Penalty"                "Takeaway"
[10] "Official Challenge"   "Failed Shot Attempt"
```

Having reviewed the events, we can filter our data frame to only include shots where event == "Goal":

```
avs_goals <- avs_pbp |>
  filter(event == "Goal")
```

And now we plot the individual shots resulting in a goal:

```
nhl_rink <- geom_hockey('nhl')
nhl_rink +
  geom_point(data = avs_goals,
             aes(x = x_fixed, y = y_fixed),
             alpha = .5) +
  labs(caption = "")
```

Suppose we are interested in just the goals that were scored in the postseason. The play-by-play data includes a game_id having the format YYYYSSGGGG, where YYYY denotes the year (e.g., 2023), SS is the type of game (01 is preseason, 02 is regular season, 03 is playoffs, and 04 is the All-Star Game), and GGGG is the game number. We can use the substr() function to limit the data to just the playoff games:

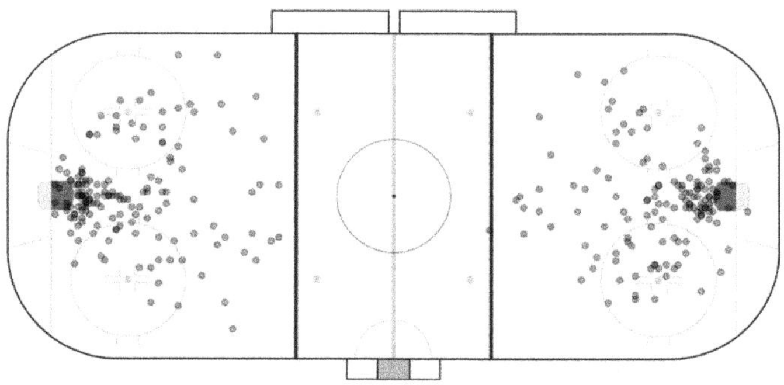

Figure 7.8: All shot locations with goals in Colorado Avalanche games from the 2022–23 season.

```
avs_goals_playoffs <- avs_goals |>
  filter(substr(game_id, 5, 6) == "03")
nhl_rink <- geom_hockey('nhl')
nhl_rink +
  geom_point(data = avs_goals_playoffs,
             aes(x = x_fixed, y = y_fixed),
             alpha = 1) +
  labs(caption = "")
```

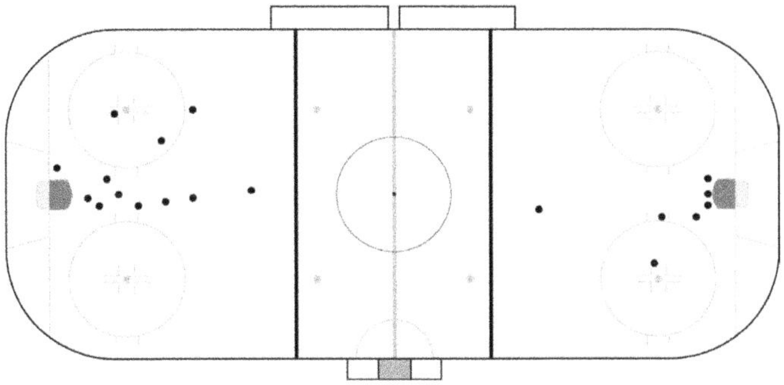

Figure 7.9: All shot locations with goals in Colorado Avalanche playoff games from the 2022–23 season.

7.10 Lab: Shiny Application

You are now two-thirds of the way through this book, and your instructor has certainly given you assignments to turn in by now. You may be wondering how to show your work effectively to people who do not have RStudio or know how to code in R or even care about coding. We can print pictures of our visualizations, but you may remember that in chapter 5, we started animating our graphical analysis, which is quite difficult to do on a piece of paper! It is high time to tackle this issue.

A useful tool for displaying complex, potentially high-dimensional datasets and the information they contain is to create an interactive dashboard for data exploration. In R, the best tool for creating dashboards is to use the functions provided in the Shiny package, described at `https://www.rstudio.com/products/shiny/`. The Posit website describes Shiny as "an open source R package that provides an elegant and powerful web framework for building web applications using R. Shiny helps you turn your analyses into interactive web applications without requiring HTML, CSS, or JavaScript knowledge."

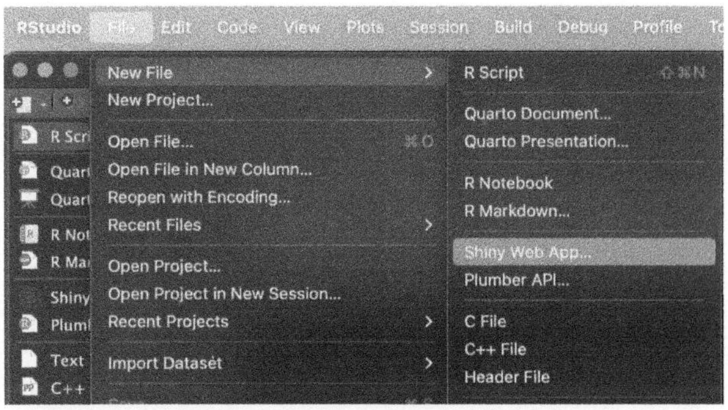

Figure 7.10: Creating a new `shiny` application.

Create a `shiny` Application

The first step in developing a `shiny` application is to create the necessary files. Given that Shiny is a Posit (RStudio) product, this step is simple when using their IDE (see figure 7.10 for a screenshot).

You can click on File → New File → Shiny Web App... and the following window will appear (figure 7.11). You specify the name of your app and have the choice between a single-file (`app.R`) and a multifile (`ui.R` and `server.R`) app. A new folder (whatever you name the app) is created in the directory of your choice.

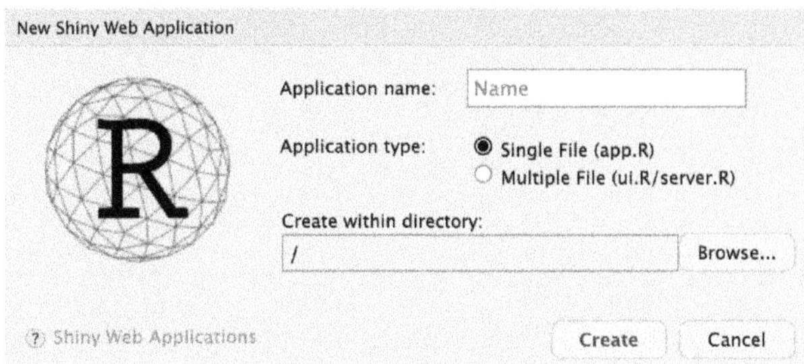

Figure 7.11: The dialogue box that appears after you initiate the creation of a new `shiny` application.

We will not get into all of the details surrounding complex Shiny web development. Rather, we will focus on the basics: the `ui()` and `server()` functions. As these dashboards are constructed as a web application, each app needs a UI (user interface) and a server to set up the app's display and serve its contents (data, figures, etc.), respectively. These functions are the basis for the files mentioned in the previous paragraph.

ISAR `shiny` Application

In order to highlight the utility of `shiny` applications, we created an NHL Shiny dashboard for the textbook (see figure 7.14). The dashboard can be found at the ISAR Dashboard website located at `https://ryan-elmore.shinyapps.io/ISAR-Dashboard/`, and the code used to generate the application is given below (saved in an `app.R` file). This file contains three components: the `ui`, a `server()` function, and Shiny's `shinyApp()` function, which ties everything together.

In this case, let's create a `shiny` application that mimics the output for what you see on the ISAR Dashboard. This allows us to create a scatterplot showing a list of possible variables on the x-axis and the same list on the y-axis. We will use a drop-down box to allow the user on a web page to pick his or her choice of team variables for each axis, and the scatterplot automatically updates.

For this `shiny` application to work, it exists as its own separate file. This means that we must start it like any other R script by loading any packages that we need. In this script, we will use `ISAR` and `ggplot2`, two packages that we have worked with in the past. We will also need to install two additional packages:

1. `plotly`, an interactive graphics package with a rich API
2. `shiny`, the package that lets us make the app:

```
library(shiny)
library(ISAR)
library(ggplot2)
library(plotly)
```

To make the data that we want to use available to the app, we should create a new data frame, `df`. We will populate it with our `nhl_team_stats_2022` data frame that we used earlier in the chapter, and then we will select everything that starts with `"stat"` and rename it to `"stat_"` to allow our data to be analyzed more cleanly:

```
df <- nhl_team_stats_2022 |>
  select(starts_with("stat"), team_name) |>
  rename_with(~ sub("stat_", "", .x), everything())
```

Next we will create the user interface, or the UI code that we mentioned earlier. You may remember some of these sections from when we examined the page source of web pages back in chapter 3. With the included comments, you can see that we have created a title for our app, and we then configured a sidebar layout. We will first put the input selectors in a sidebar panel. We give the selectors names, and we populate each of them with the variable names in our data frame in columns 2–31. We make "wins" the default for the x-axis and "losses" the default for the y-axis. We then create the main panel, and we put a scatterplot in that main panel:

```
ui <- fluidPage(

    # Application title
    titlePanel(div(HTML("Shiny Example for <em>Introduction to
                        Sports Analytics using R</em>"))),
    # Sidebar with a slider input for number of bins
    sidebarLayout(
        sidebarPanel(
          selectInput("selector_x", h4("X Variable"),
                      choices = names(df)[2:31],
                      selected = "wins",
                      width = '190px'),
          selectInput("selector_y", h4("Y Variable"),
                      choices = names(df)[2:31],
                      selected = "losses",
                      width = '190px'),
          width = 3
```

```
    ),

    # Show a plot of the generated distribution
    mainPanel(
      plotlyOutput("graph")
    )
  )
)
```

When we first mentioned the `ui` part of the application, we also mentioned there would be a `server` part of the application, so we will create that next. The `server` function that we create takes three arguments: the input, the output, and the session. Some of this may seem a bit confusing below, but for the output's actual graph (`output$graph`), we render the image by calling `renderPlotly` to render a `plotly` object. We use the `ggplotly()` function from the `plotly` package to transform a `ggplot` object into a `plotly` object. The key idea here is that the data are plotted dynamically depending on what the user has chosen in the selectors.

We use `aes_string` and `text` to get our column names from the selectors, and then we create our scatterplot points based on the aesthetics. The legend refers to the teams as the team name. We label our axes from what the users have chosen in the selectors, and finally, we run `shinyApp()` with our `ui` and `server` as inputs:

```
server <- function(input, output, session) {

  output$graph <- renderPlotly({
    ggplotly(ggplot(data = df,
                    aes_string(x = input$selector_x,
                               y = input$selector_y),
                    text = paste('X: ', input$selector_x, '\n',
                                 'Y: ', input$selector_y, sep = "")) +
               geom_point(aes(col = team_name)) +
               theme_bw() +
               labs(x = input$selector_x,
                    y = input$selector_y,
                    colour = "Teams"),
             tooltip = "text")
  })
}

# Run the application
shinyApp(ui = ui, server = server)
```

Run Shiny

If you are developing your analysis in RStudio and are not yet ready to deploy it, there is an integrated `Run` button in the IDE. The button is shown in figure 7.12. Running the app will spawn a local web server, and the app is displayed.

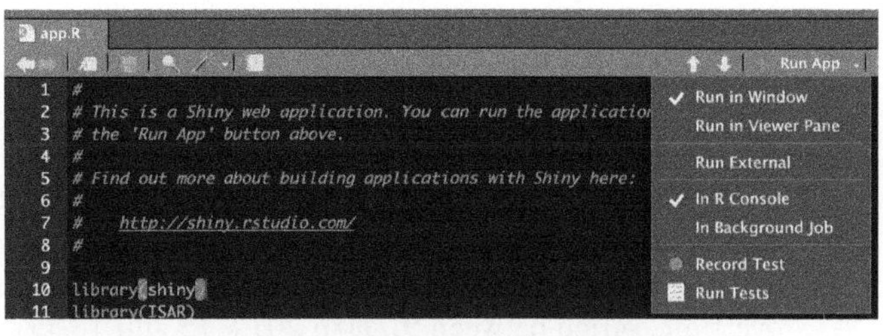

Figure 7.12: RStudio's button to run a `shiny` application.

Deploy Shiny

Finally, you might want to share your application with fellow students, your professor, or just the public at large. Once more, Posit comes to the rescue. `Shinyapps.io` by Posit is a web application hosting service that allows up to five free applications (and 25 user hours). Once you sign up for an account, you can publish to the website directly from RStudio using the blue publish button next to `Run` (see figure 7.13).

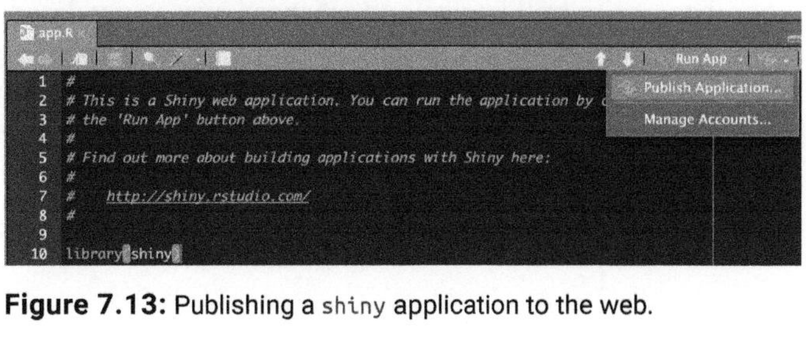

Figure 7.13: Publishing a `shiny` application to the web.

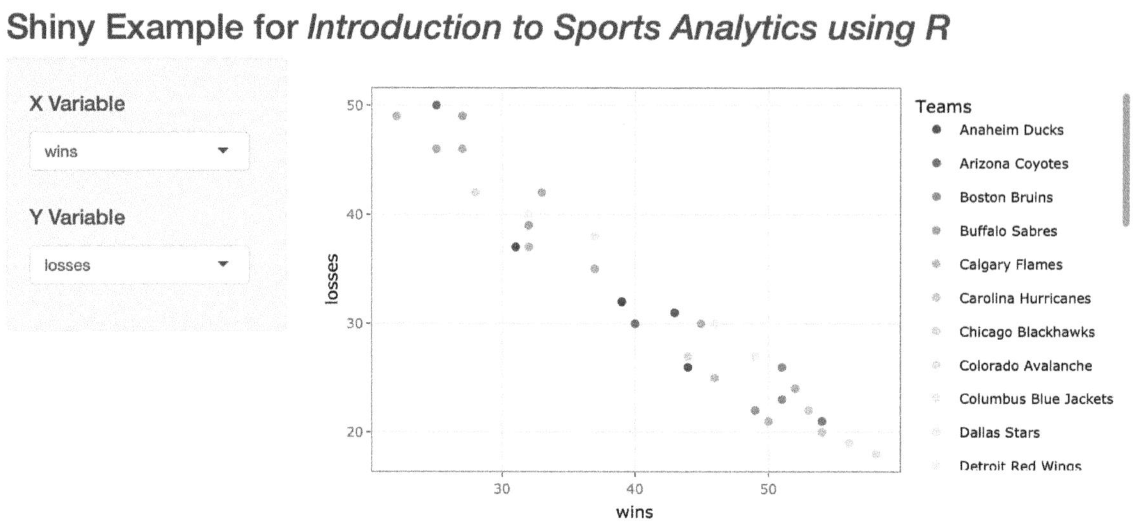

Figure 7.14: The resulting `shiny` application from the preceding code chunk.

You will see that there are many tools included by default with your app. Zoom and Select tools are the most obvious, plus the ability to download your graphic as a `.png` file.

We have only scratched the surface of what you can do with Shiny. It is a very powerful tool for distributing your work to others who know nothing about code. For more about what Shiny can do, we recommend once again a text by Hadley Wickham, *Mastering Shiny*, available at `https://mastering-shiny.org`.

7.11 Case Study: Pulling the Goaltender

There is nothing in the rules of ice hockey that requires a team to have a certain number of wingers or defensemen on the ice, nor is a team even required to have a goaltender playing. Due to this, one strategy that a team can employ is to remove the goaltender in favor of an extra attacking skater. This is a high-variance strategy, as having six skaters versus five creates an obvious offensive advantage, but of course, not having a goaltender creates an obvious defensive disadvantage for the same team. Because of this variance, this strategy is usually only employed late in a game when a team is behind and trying to tie the score.

Traditionally in ice hockey, a team who is trailing by one goal might take the goaltender off the ice in favor of an extra attacking skater in the last two minutes or so of the game. The idea is that if they can manage to tie the game, a tie is better than a loss (and in some leagues like the NHL, the game will go to overtime and give them a chance to win), but if they give up an empty-net goal, it doesn't really matter, as losing by two goals is virtually the same as losing by one goal.

The success rates of this strategy are not high, but then again, the likelihood of scoring an even-strength goal in any two-minute period is also not high. In the NHL, from 2013–14 to 2021, the success rate of pulling the goaltender when a team was losing by one goal, where success is defined as winning the game or reaching overtime, varied between 9.7% in 2014–15 and 18.1% in the shortened 2021 season.

While the strategy of pulling the goaltender when down one goal in the waning minutes of a game has been quite well known and practiced over many decades, there is much debate about expanding the strategy. For example, we could use the same logic and pull the goaltender at some point when a team was down two goals. Across the same seven seasons in the previous paragraph, it was tried about 2,500 times, and the success rate as defined above was approximately 1%. In that same time frame, no NHL team achieved a successful outcome by pulling the goaltender when down by three or more goals. Specifically, the success rate of tying or winning a game when down by one, two, or three or more goals was 13.6%, 1%, and 0%, respectively, from 2013–14 to 2021–22.

We also find that there are differences in the success rate depending on the average amount of time that the goaltender has been pulled. For example, across those same eight seasons, teams that achieved success had approximately 11 more seconds of extra attacker time than those that were unsuccessful (1:43 to 1:34). These differences cannot be attributed to simply a difference in coaching strategy, as hockey is a fluid game, and a team cannot wisely pull their goaltender when the puck is on their half of the ice, lest the opposing team have quite a large advantage. Furthermore, a team that has pulled their goaltender may also be strategically forced to put him back into the game if there is a face-off in the defensive half of the ice or in the neutral zone in the middle of the ice. Many of these visualizations are available on a beautifully created Tableau Public site by Meghan Hall, available at `https://public.tableau.com/app/profile/meghanhall/viz/GoaliePullTimes2018-19/GoaliePullTimes18-19`.

The point in a game when a trailing team should pull their goaltender is the subject of much debate. Much like fourth-down decisions in football (refer back to that chapter if you need more information), those not directly employed by the teams tend to suggest that the in-game strategy is far too conservative. While NHL teams traditionally for decades have waited for the last two minutes of a game to pull a goaltender, analysts not directly involved with teams suggest it should be done much earlier. In the 2018 paper "Pulling the Goalie: Hockey and Investment Implications," available at `https://papers.ssrn.com/sol3/papers.cfm?abstract_id=3132563`, authors Clifford Asness and Aaron Brown suggest that teams should pull the goaltender with 6:10 left in the game if they are down one goal and with 13:00 left if down two goals. In 2018, Rob Vollman developed `@ThePullBot`, a Twitter account created through statistical modeling, and suggests that a team down one goal should pull the goaltender at about the 4:10 mark. This account is no longer active, and Vollman is now the director of pro analytics for the NHL's Los Angeles Kings. Perhaps not coincidentally, the Kings have become much more aggressive about when they pull the goaltender since he arrived.

It is easy to see how the strategy affects the current game: If a team turns a loss into a tie or win, that's great. However, we know that about six times out of seven, this is not the case, at least in the NHL. For example, how might the psyche of a team be affected if they lose a game by two goals instead of just one, and is that effect stronger if the team plays the next day as opposed to two or more days later? Or is there an equally strong uplifting effect if a team manages a tie after pulling a goaltender? Or if the team loses in overtime after putting all the effort into getting tied by pulling the goaltender? Is the effect different in the playoffs, where an overtime loss counts for nothing in the stands, as opposed to in the regular season, where a loss in overtime counts as half of a win?

What kind of data would you need to study this effect, and how would you go about it?

7.12 Exercises

For problems 1 and 2, use the `nhl_data` that we used at the beginning of this chapter. This dataset is also given as `nhl_data_hockey_reference` in the R package.

1. What team won the Stanley Cup in 2022 (use Google)? Find the player who had the highest percent Fenwick value on that team. Interpret the value.
2. Find the correlation between the Corsi percent and Fenwick percent by year. Filter out all `NA` values on those variables (use `na_omit`).
3. Recall in figure 7.6 that we have to deal with data that have created two new positions for us, and it makes our graphic look a bit strange.
   - Explore the data for all players in that dataset who have the position W. How many unique players are there?
   - Explore the data for all players in that dataset who have the position F. How many unique players are there?
   - Is there a way to aggregate this data to allow for consistency with the existing data? What is your strategy to do it?
   - Re-create figure 7.6 following your strategy to make it look nicer and more informative.

4. Create a shot chart for the Vegas Golden Knights for their 2023 postseason games. Recall the play-by-play data includes a `game_id` having the format `YYYYSSGGGG`, where `YYYY` denotes the year (e.g., 2023), `SS` is the type of game (`01` is preseason, `02` is regular season, `03` is playoffs, and `04` is the All-Star Game), and `GGGG` is the game number. We can use the `substr()` function to limit the data to just the playoff games.
5. Color the Vegas playoff goals by expected goals.
6. Create a `shiny` application using the `avs_stats_2022` dataset in the `ISAR` package. For example, select a player and plot any two statistics.

Chapter 8

Soccer

> We lost because we didn't win.
>
> —Cristiano Ronaldo

8.1 R Packages

We will use the following R packages in this chapter that we have used in the past:

```
library(dplyr)
library(ggplot2)
library(lubridate)
library(rvest)
library(janitor)
library(scales)
library(ISAR)
```

We will also introduce the following new packages:

```
library(readr) # used to read rectangular data
library(ggrepel) # adds non-overlapping text labels to graphs
library(ggdendro) # create dendrograms and tree diagrams with ggplot2
library(mixtools) # tools for analyzing finite mixture models
library(factoextra) # visualize the results of multivariate data analyses
library(worldfootballR) # extract and clean world soccer data
```

8.2 If You Don't Know Anything about Soccer

Soccer* is the most popular team sport in the world. It flourishes in both the wealthiest of nations, such as Qatar, host of the 2022 World Cup, and the poorest of nations, where children often play without shoes or grass and perhaps with a ball made of recycled or discarded materials. At its most basic level, soccer is played between two teams each consisting of 11 people on a field approximately 100 meters long by 50 meters wide, with a goal at each end that is 2.44 meters high and 7.32 meters wide (or 8 feet by 24 feet). The object is to advance a ball down the field and into the goal using any part of the body except the hands and arms. One of the 11 players on the team is designated as the goalkeeper, or goalie. Goalkeepers wear a different-colored shirt to designate their position, as they are the only players on the team who are allowed to use their hands and arms to handle the ball.

For a more in-depth explanation of the laws of soccer, we refer you to `https://www.soccercoachingpro.com/soccer-rules/`, and if you would like to read the laws themselves as kept by the governing body FIFA, you can find them at `https://www.theifab.com/laws-of-the-game-documents/?language=all&year=2022%2F23`.

---

* While soccer is called "football" in much of the world, we will refer to it as soccer so as not to confuse it with American football in a previous chapter.

Perhaps the simplicity of the game is why it is so popular. There are but 17 basic rules (laws) to the game, and those laws govern the play of soccer worldwide. While you might think that with a game this simple, there is little place for analytics, its popularity and the money involved means that any possible advantage will be sought, and this includes through analytics.

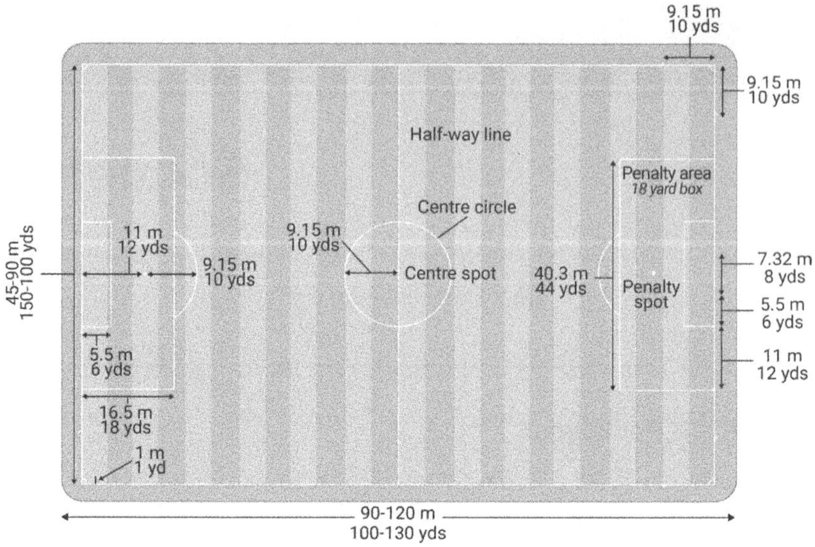

Figure 8.1: Diagram of a soccer field (pitch).

8.3 Soccer Data

In this chapter, we will explore soccer data using methods we have used before, but we will also learn several unsupervised learning methods—for example, hierarchical clustering—to apply to soccer analytics.

FB Reference

In October 2022, the Sports Reference website announced a partnership with Stats Perform Opta to dramatically increase the quantity and quality of soccer data that are available on its site. Soccer data are now hosted at `https://fbref.com/en/`, which includes data on most major professional leagues throughout the world at the team and player levels. More details related to this new partnership can be found at `https://www.sports-reference.com/blog/2022/10/fbref-leagues-🇵🇹-leagues-🇧🇷-leagues-🇲🇽-expanded-womens-and-mens-data-new-data-partner/`.

In this chapter, we will focus on using soccer data to cluster both teams and individual players using data from `fbref.com`.

Expected Goals and Assists

Soccer is notoriously low scoring. In the 2022 World Cup in Qatar, there were 172 goals scored over the 64 matches, for a mean of 2.68 goals per match. This was the highest-scoring World Cup ever, and even so, there were 7 matches that were scoreless. Moreover, there is certainly an element of luck in scoring a goal, and sometimes there are own goals, where a player inadvertently puts the ball into his or her own net. Therefore, one of the main developments in the soccer analytics space is the introduction of expected goals, or xG for short, as a means of measuring the likelihood of success on a given shot.

There are various models to compute xG, but at a high level, xG is simply the probability of scoring a goal from a given spot on the field when a shot is taken. Other factors that can be taken into account are whether the shot came from the head or the foot, how the shooter received the ball (cross, set piece, etc.), the position of the goalkeeper, the positions of other players (teammates and opponents) between the shooter and the goal, how tightly the defenders are playing (marking) the shooter, and a host of other situational variables that can be measured and calculated.

Given that most shots do not result in a goal, most passes to a shot taker will likely lead to a missed goal as well. Therefore, there is an analogous result for assists that is referred to as expected assists, or xA for short. You will often see these metrics normalized to 90 minutes so that a player who is a substitute and only plays 30 minutes can be directly compared to a starter who might play 60–90 minutes. The normalized expected goals and assists are often written as xG (or xA) per 90 (minutes).

A player who is consistently achieving a high number of xG will be one who is getting into a good position consistently on the field. Coaches and scouts can use this to evaluate whether a player is exceedingly (un)lucky over a given number of games, and this will help in evaluating that player's offensive skills beyond simple counts.

Player Statistics

We will initially focus our attention on individual players from the US National Women's Soccer League (NWSL). The NWSL is the largest women's soccer league in North America. In the 2023 season, there were 12 teams, and Gotham FC was crowned champion.

You might wonder why we examine a relatively minor league like the NWSL as compared to the English Premier League (EPL), German Bundesliga, Spanish LaLiga, Italian Serie A, or even Major League Soccer in the US. There is certainly more global interest in those leagues and, thus, likely a higher volume and quality of data. However, in data science, the greatest insights can often be gained by looking where others are not. Moreover, the talent in the NWSL is more evenly spread than in leagues like the EPL, where there are the "Big Five" clubs and everyone else, or the Bundesliga, where in the 25 seasons from 1999 to 2023, Bayern Munich won the title 19 times, including the last 11 consecutive seasons, and finished second on 3 of the other 6 occasions. The evenness of talent in the NWSL lends itself, then, to investigation by cluster analysis such that we can identify which players on which teams are most similar. This information could be used for talent acquisition by future team administrators.

For this textbook, we obtained a `.csv` file of NWSL player statistics from the aforementioned `fbref.com`, and those data are supplied in the book's `ISAR` R package as `nwsl_player_stats`. For reference, the code for transforming from the original `.csv` (saved locally as `nwsl-players.csv`) to the format in the R package is given below. Note that the column names are defined on the Football Reference website at `https://fbref.com/en/comps/182/stats/NWSL-Stats`.

```
nwsl_player_stats <- read.csv("nwsl-players.csv", header = T) |>
  clean_names() |>
  select(c(2:6, 8:10, 28:32)) |>
  rename(xGp90 = x_g_1,
         xAp90 = x_ag_1,
         xGxAp90 = x_g_x_ag,
         npxGp90 = npx_g_1,
         npxGxAp90 = npx_g_x_ag_1)
```

Exploratory Data Analysis

We will begin by exploring expected goals. In particular, let's create a plot of xG versus age in the NWSL. We will use the `xGp90` column as our xG value to normalize the number of minutes played across all players. In addition, we filter out goalkeepers, as they are not likely to score or assist on a goal:

```
p <- ggplot(data = nwsl_player_stats |>
              filter(pos != "GK"),
            aes(x = age, y = xGp90))
p + geom_point(alpha = .5) +
  labs(title = "xG per 90 by Player Age",
       x = "Age of Player",
       y = "Expected Goals per 90 (xGp90)") +
  theme_bw()
```

We can see that many of the players are clustered between 21 and 31 years old and between 0 and 0.3 xG per 90. However, there are certainly outlier players who are young or have a relatively high xG per 90. We can identify the players by name on the plot by using the `ggrepel` package to quickly add labels to certain points using the label aesthetic and the `geom_text_repel()` function. Suppose we want to identify players who are less than 20 years of age with a positive xG value as well as all players with an xG value greater than 0.6:

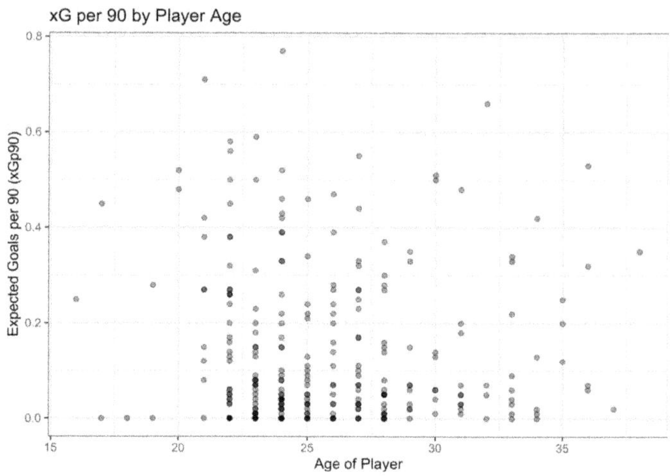

Figure 8.2: Player age (x) versus expected goals per 90 minutes played (y) during the 2022 NWSL season.

```
p <- ggplot(data = nwsl_player_stats |>
              filter(pos != "GK") |>
              mutate(new_player = ifelse((age < 20 & xGp90 > 0) | xGp90 > 0.6,
                                         player, "")),
            aes(x = age, y = xGp90, label = new_player))
p + geom_point(alpha = .5) +
  labs(title = "xG per 90 by Player Age",
       x = "Age of Player",
       y = "Expected goals per 90 (xGp90)") +
  geom_text_repel() +
  theme_bw()
```

These six players identified in the plot are either currently offensive stars or perhaps will be soon!

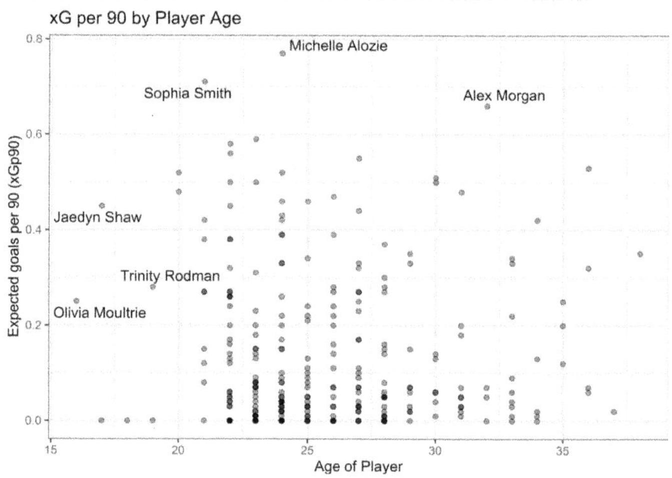

Figure 8.3: Player age (x) versus expected goals per 90 minutes played (y) during the 2022 NWSL season, with labels for players less than 20 years of age or expected goals per 90 above 0.6.

8.4 Clustering

After we plotted the xG per 90 for individual players in the previous section, we may now want to classify different groups of players. In the topic of soccer analytics, we will focus on several analytical tools that fall under the statistical, or machine, learning umbrella of unsupervised learning. Unsupervised learning is generally thought to be exploratory data analytic techniques that are designed to learn as much as possible about the data without the aid of labels, which are used in regression or classification models (supervised learning). Clustering, in particular, refers to the class of techniques concerned with finding groups within your dataset that are similar (in some sense) with respect to the measured variables (or covariates).

(a) Smith (b) Shaw (c) Morgan

Figure 8.4: Three stars for the US Women's National soccer team: Sophia Smith, Jaedyn Shaw, and Alex Morgan.
Sources: (a) Erik Drost / CC BY 2.0; (b) Hameltion / CC BY-SA 4.0; (c) Jamie Smed / CC BY 2.0

K-Means Clustering

In short, *k*-means clustering of data refers to assigning each observation in the dataset to one of the *k* clusters. The number of clusters, *k*, is specified a priori by the analyst. The algorithm for computing a *k*-means cluster of *n* observations is relatively simple and intuitive and easy to visualize when using two or three dimensions. Each observation is randomly assigned to one of the clusters, and the "center" of each cluster is computed—for example, the mean vector in *k*-means. Next, you assign each observation to the closest "center," recompute the "center," and reassign each observation until observations stop being reassigned. For more in-depth explanations of *k*-means clustering, you can visit the section on k-means clustering in the companion for the book *Introduction to Statistical Learning Using R* by Gareth James, Daniela Witten, Trevor Hastie, and Rob Tibshirani, available at `https://r4ds.github.io/bookclub-islr/k-means.html`.

Clustering Expected Goals and Assists with Age

First, let's look at a clustering based on the age of the player (`age`), total minutes played in the season (`min`), and expected goals and assists per 90 minutes played (`xGp90` and `xAp90`, respectively). We are going to consider three clusters initially, filter out goalkeepers, and also only include players with xG/xA per 90 of less than 1.5 to remove some outliers with little playing time who may have had good scoring chances in those few minutes and distort the overall results:

```
nwsl_cluster_df <- nwsl_player_stats |>
  select(player, squad, pos, age, min, starts, xGp90, xAp90,
         xGxAp90, npxGp90, npxGxAp90) |>
  filter(xGxAp90 < 1.5, pos != "GK") |>
  na.omit()

set.seed(9019)

km <- kmeans(select(nwsl_cluster_df, age, min, xGp90, xAp90) |>
               na.omit(),
             centers = 3)
```

How can we visualize these clusters? We are not able to visualize all the dimensions at once given the two-dimensional nature of this book. Understanding those limitations of visualization, let's look at some plots. First, we plot age versus minutes played with differing plot symbols based on their cluster membership in figure 8.5.

```
# add the cluster number to the data frame

nwsl_cluster_df <- mutate(nwsl_cluster_df, k_means = km$cluster)

p <- ggplot(data = nwsl_cluster_df,
            aes(x = age,
                y = min,
                shape = as.factor(k_means),
                col = as.factor(k_means)))
```

```
p + geom_point() +
  scale_color_brewer("cluster", palette = "Set1") +
  labs(title = "NWSL players clustered by PT and Age",
       x = "Age of Player",
       y = "Minutes Played") +
  guides(shape = guide_legend(title = "cluster"),
         col = guide_legend(title = "cluster")) +
  theme_bw()
```

What stands out among this clustering of points? Clearly, the clusters are dominated by different strata defined by minutes played. It looks like the first cluster is composed of players who played more than approximately 1,200 minutes, the second contains players playing (roughly) 500 to 1,200 minutes, and the last cluster contains players playing fewer than 500 minutes.

Is anything else evident if we omit minutes played and plot the age of the player versus expected goals (or assists)? Figure 8.6 shows the cluster memberships for `age` versus `xGp90`.

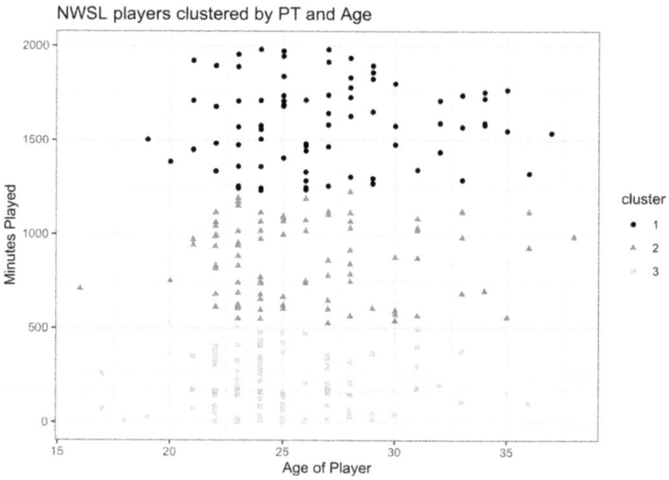

Figure 8.5: Player age (x) versus minutes played (y) during the 2022 NWSL season. Point symbols represent cluster membership using a *k*-means clustering with three clusters.

```
p <- ggplot(data = nwsl_cluster_df,
            aes(x = age, y = xGp90,
                shape = as.factor(k_means),
                col = as.factor(k_means)))
p + geom_point() +
  scale_color_brewer("cluster", palette = "Set1") +
  labs(title = "NWSL players clustered by xGp90 and Age",
       x = "Age of Player",
       y = "Expected Goals per 90") +
  guides(shape = guide_legend(title = "cluster"),
         col = guide_legend(title = "cluster")) +
  theme_bw()
```

Nothing is clearly evident from this figure, so we should do further analysis. Given that minutes played dominates the previous clustering, consider a *k*-means clustering on age, expected goals, and expected assists, both normalized by per 90 minutes played, and construct a similar plot as earlier:

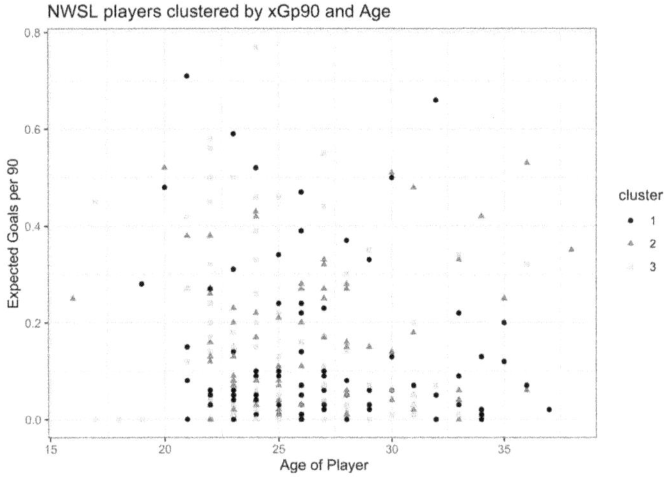

Figure 8.6: Player age (x) versus expected goals per 90 minutes played (y) during the 2022 NWSL season. Point symbols represent cluster membership using a *k*-means clustering with three clusters.

```
set.seed(9019)
km <- kmeans(select(nwsl_cluster_df, age, xGp90, xAp90) |>
                 na.omit(),
               centers = 3)

nwsl_cluster_df <- mutate(nwsl_cluster_df, clusters_two = km$cluster)
p <- ggplot(data = nwsl_cluster_df,
            aes(x = age, y = xGp90,
                col = as.factor(clusters_two),
                shape = as.factor(clusters_two)))
p + geom_point() +
  scale_color_brewer("cluster", palette = "Set1") +
    labs(title = "NWSL players clustered by xGp90 and Age",
      x = "Age of Player",
      y = "Expected Goals per 90") +
  guides(shape = guide_legend(title = "cluster"),
         col = guide_legend(title = "cluster")) +
  theme_bw()
```

As you might imagine, the clustering is now dominated by the age variable:

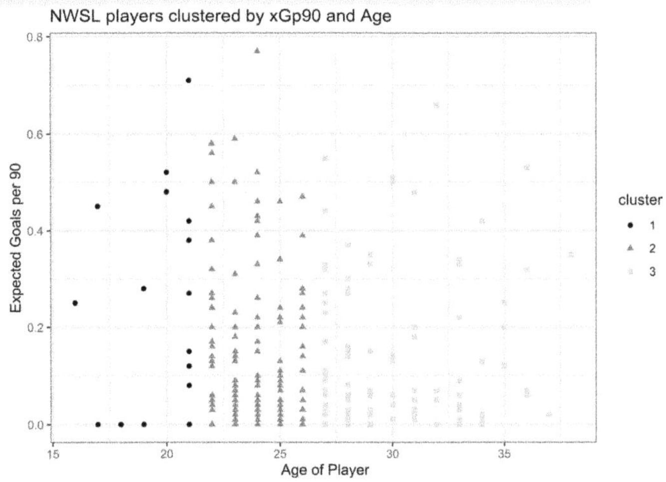

Figure 8.7: Player age (x) versus expected goals per 90 minutes played (y) during the 2022 NWSL season. Point symbols represent cluster membership using a *k*-means clustering with three clusters (no minutes played).

```
p <- ggplot(data = nwsl_cluster_df,
            aes(x = age, y = xAp90,
                col = as.factor(clusters_two),
                shape = as.factor(clusters_two)))
p + geom_point() +
  scale_color_brewer("cluster", palette = "Set1") +
  labs(title = "NWSL players clustered by xAp90 and Age",
       x = "Age of Player",
       y = "Expected Assists per 90") +
  guides(shape = guide_legend(title = "cluster"),
         col = guide_legend(title = "cluster")) +
  theme_bw()
```

It's obvious that including age and minutes seems to dominate the makeup of the clusters. So if we want to identify similar players based on their scoring ability, let's only consider the appropriate metrics. Here we perform an additional clustering using expected goals and assists (appropriately normalized) and plot the results:

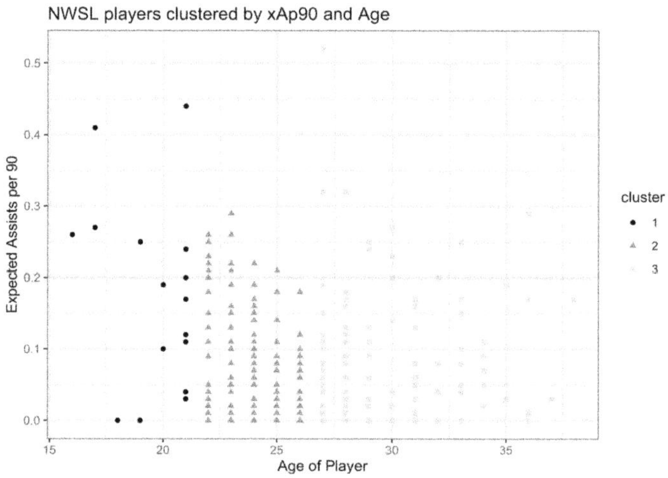

Figure 8.8: Player age (x) versus expected assists per 90 minutes played (y) during the 2022 NWSL season. Point symbols represent cluster membership using a *k*-means clustering with three clusters.

```
set.seed(9019)
km <- kmeans(nwsl_cluster_df |>
               select(xGp90, xAp90) |>
               na.omit(),
             centers = 3)
nwsl_cluster_df <- mutate(nwsl_cluster_df, clusters_three = km$cluster)
p <- ggplot(data = nwsl_cluster_df,
            aes(x = xAp90, y = xGp90,
                col = as.factor(clusters_three),
                shape = as.factor(clusters_three)))
p + geom_point() +
  scale_color_brewer("cluster", palette = "Set1") +
    labs(title = "NWSL players clustered by xGp90 and xAp90",
       x = "Expected Assists per 90",
       y = "Expected Goals per 90") +
  guides(shape = guide_legend(title = "cluster"),
         col = guide_legend(title = "cluster")) +
  theme_bw()
```

What if we wanted to further examine by position? We can change the color and/or shape of the points based on the position of the players. In this case, for simplicity, we change the original `position` variable in the dataset to just three positions: defender (`D`), midfielder (`M`), and forward (`F`):

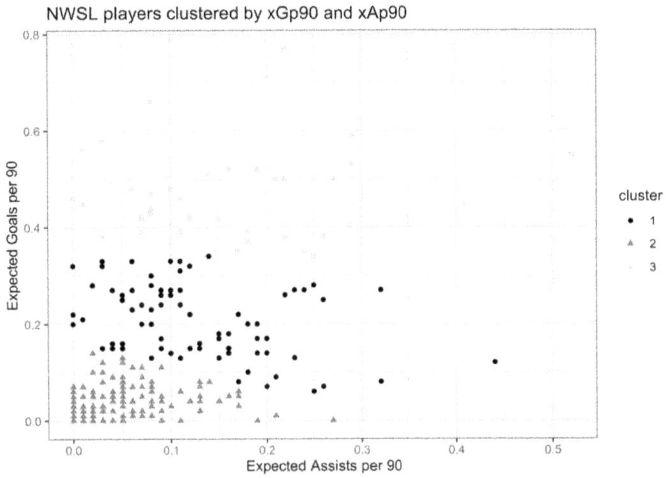

Figure 8.9: Expected assists per 90 (x) versus expected goals per 90 minutes played (y) during the 2022 NWSL season. Point symbols represent cluster membership using a *k*-means clustering with three clusters (no minutes played).

```
p <- ggplot(data = nwsl_cluster_df |>
              mutate(short_pos = substr(pos, 1, 1)),
            aes(x = xAp90, y = xGp90,
                pch = short_pos,
                col = as.factor(clusters_three)))
p + geom_point(alpha = .75) +
  scale_color_brewer("cluster", palette = "Set1") +
  labs(pch = "position",
       title = "NWSL players clustered by xGp90 and xAp90",
       x = "Expected Assists per 90",
       y = "Expected Goals per 90") +
  theme_bw()
```

Do certain positions dominate certain clusters? Yes, and this should be expected. The highest-scoring positions are the forwards, followed by the midfielders, and finally, by the defenders. Similarly, they seem to each be largely in their own clusters.

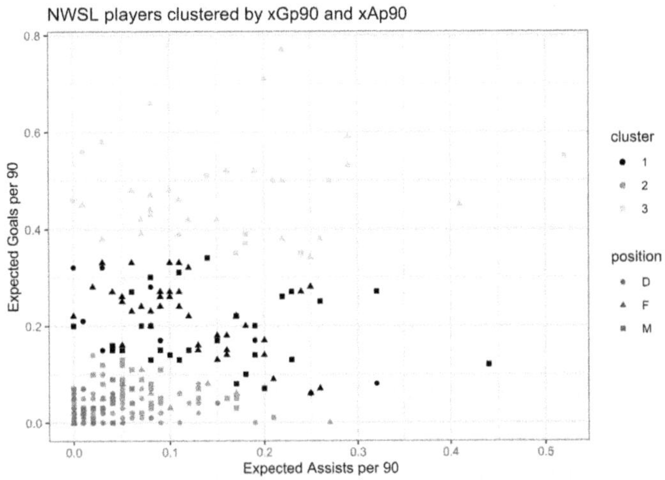

Figure 8.10: Expected assists per 90 (x) versus expected goals per 90 minutes played (y) during the 2022 NWSL season. Shades represent cluster membership using a *k*-means clustering with three clusters (no minutes played), and plot symbols represent positions.

8.5 Research Block: When and How to Pass the Ball?

As mentioned at the beginning of the chapter, soccer is a notoriously low-scoring game. With so many games being decided by scores like 1–0 or 2–1 or ending in a 0–0 or 1–1 draw, every goal matters. It is so low scoring because it is extremely difficult to move the ball up the field without using your hands or arms through a defense of 10 highly skilled players, all trying to stop the ball from getting farther up the field, and a goalkeeper beyond the defense who is allowed to use his or her hands and arms to stop the ball as well. For a team to score, they need to possess the ball, which means keeping it away from the defending team. When a player becomes guarded (marked) too closely, usually he or she will have to kick the ball, either toward the goal as a shot or toward a teammate as a pass, to avoid being dispossessed of the ball by the defender. More often than not, he or she will attempt to pass.

Not all passes are created equally. Sometimes passes are quite aggressive and move the ball toward the goal, while other times they may be passive, even passing to a teammate much farther away from the goal. The purpose of the pass may be to try to set up a scoring chance, or it may be just to keep the ball away from the defense. Some passes also have a higher chance of being completed than others. Often the passing strategy used by teams is consistent with their overall strategy, such as one where a team tries to maximize the number of completed passes, constantly looking for a striking opportunity, as opposed to the counterattacking strategy used by 2016 EPL champions Leicester City, where their success relied more on the long pass up the field from their defensive end.

Passing is a difficult metric to measure. One can easily measure the number of passes attempted and completed by a team, but how is that measure meaningful when trying to understand how a team can ultimately score more goals than their opponents? It would be relatively easy for two teammates to stand two meters apart and pass the ball back and forth to each other, and they would likely remain unmolested by the defense if they were nowhere near the attacking positions. Indeed, even in the title of the paper "Decomposing the Immeasurable Sport: A Deep Learning Expected Possession Value Framework for Soccer," available at `http://www.lukebornn.com/papers/fernandez_sloan_2019.pdf`, authors Javier Fernandez, Luke Bornn, and Dan Cervone refer to this possibility while they discuss their strategy for measuring pass efficiency.

With player tracking data becoming more available and relevant, there are data now ready for analysis and the processing of on-field movements and ball movements. The authors of the paper analyze the data to determine all the possible passing vectors available to a player possessing the ball at any given time and then attempt to calculate the "best" pass that the player could make, depending on the strategy of the team at that given time. They do this by defining a new metric, expected possession value (EPV), which ranges from 1 if the possessing team scores a goal and −1 if the ball is taken from them and the opposing team immediately scores a goal. Their deep learning model shows how EPV would increase or decrease based on a player attempting the pass. This allows for a measurement of passes that have a high probability of being completed but hardly increase the chance of scoring a goal versus ones that may have a lower probability of being completed but yet more greatly increase the chances of scoring a goal. Indeed, the authors compare the 2010 and 2018 Spanish national teams, which employed the same "tiki-taka" strategy of moving the ball around but by 2018 were merely completing a lot of low-value passes.

The EPV framework provides a look into a possible expansion over xG and xA that we have discussed earlier in this chapter and breaks it down into opportunities for moving the ball into those higher-value positions.

8.6 Hierarchical Clustering

Hierarchical clustering methods are a commonly used class of alternatives to k-means clustering. As the name suggests, the methodology will produce a hierarchy among the observations relative to some distance measure, and the results can be easy to visualize. There are several competing hierarchical methods from which to choose; however, we will only focus on those that are agglomerative in nature. That is, each observation is considered its own cluster initially, and they are paired up in subsequent steps based on dissimilarity measures between observations and clusters:

```
nwsl_hclust_df <- nwsl_cluster_df |>
  select(player, squad, age, starts, xGp90, xAp90, xGxAp90,
             npxGp90, npxGxAp90)
hc <- hclust(dist(nwsl_hclust_df), "average")
```

Figure 8.11 shows that with hierarchical clustering, we can ultimately assign each observation to its own cluster. Obviously, this is not useful and defeats the purpose of clustering. We have to cut the clustering at a certain level in order to make this a meaningful methodology:

```
p <- ggdendrogram(hc, labels = F, size = 2)
p
```

As you can see, it is extremely difficult to visualize the dendrogram in its entirety. We can, however, visualize specific pieces and try to identify individuals within clusters. We can easily see how many elements fall into a particular clustering—for example, five clusters or groups—using the `cutree` function:

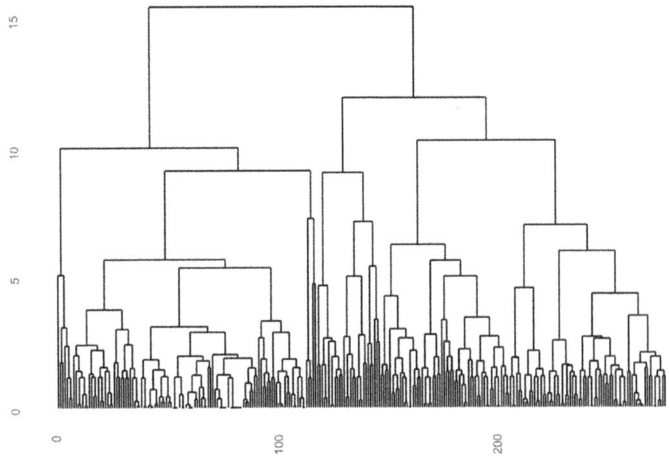

Figure 8.11: Dendrogram based on the hierarchical clustering using average linkage.

```
clusters <- cutree(hc, k = 5)
table(clusters)
```

```
clusters
  1   2   3   4   5
110  71  59  29   7
```

Do we see any patterns in the data with respect to clusters? We can append the cluster memberships to the data frame used in the clustering. This allows us to visualize cluster membership in two dimensions, as the following plot illustrates:

```
nwsl_hclust_df <- nwsl_hclust_df |>
  mutate(clusters = clusters)
p <- ggplot(data = nwsl_hclust_df,
            aes(x = age, y = starts,
                col = as.factor(clusters)))
p + geom_point(alpha = .75) +
  scale_color_brewer("cluster", palette = "Set1") +
  labs(title = "NWSL players clustered by starting frequency",
       x = "Age of Players",
       y = "Number of Starts") +
  theme_bw()
```

After making this two-dimensional plot, it seems that there is a strong separation between the clusters when we consider player age and the number of starts. Therefore, we can deduce that the hierarchical cluster is dominated by the `age` and `starts` variables.

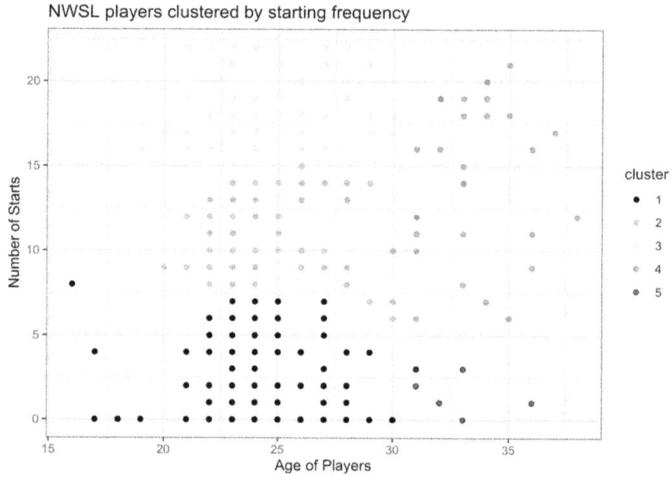

Figure 8.12: Player age (x) versus number of starts (y), with point shapes representing cluster membership based on the hierarchical clustering using average linkage.

8.7 Gaussian Mixtures

This section is one of the more advanced topics in the textbook; however, we feel that its utility in a host of differing domains is worth noting. The class of algorithm that we will explore here is often referred to as Gaussian, or normal, mixture models.

The two preceding clustering algorithms result in a "hard" clustering of observations into groups, as there is no room for ambiguity in the cluster assignments. We now turn our attention to a probability-based clustering algorithm using mixtures of K Gaussian distributions. The result is a "soft" clustering in which each observation is assigned to a cluster using a probability. We write the probability of observation x_i belonging to cluster $k = 1, 2, \ldots, K$ as $P(i^{th} \text{ observation} \in k|x_i)$, with

$$\sum_{k=1}^{K} P\left(i^{th} \text{ observation} \in k \mid x_i\right) = 1.$$

The Gaussian (normal) mixture model can be written as

$$f(x) = \sum_{k=1}^{K} \pi_k f\left(x; \mu_k, \Sigma_k\right),$$

where each $f(x;\mu_k, \Sigma_k)$ is itself a multivariate Gaussian distribution characterized by its mean, μ, and covariance matrix, Σ_k. An often-used simplifying assumption is that each component shares a common covariance matrix—say, $\Sigma_k = \Sigma$. The individual mixing proportions, π_k, represent the probability of an individual observational unit belonging to the kth cluster with $\sum_{k=1}^{K} \pi_k = 1$—that is, every unit belongs to one of the clusters.

Although the theoretical details of Gaussian mixture models are well beyond the scope of this text, the implementation details are relatively straightforward. We will use the `mixtools` R package to fit a Gaussian mixture model using an expectation-maximization (EM) algorithm and making cluster assignments. We will start with a two-component, or two-cluster, mixture using the expected goals and expected assists variables. In order to initialize the algorithm, you must specify a priori the mean vector and covariance matrix of the individual components as well as the initial mixing probabilities. We assume a common covariance matrix in our initial example given next. Further, we take $\mu_1 = (21, 0.1)'$, $\mu_2 = (30, 0.5)'$, $\pi_1 = 0.15$, and $\pi_2 = 0.85$. This initializes the algorithm with clusters having average age equal to 21 and average xG/xA per 90 equal to 0.1 and the other with average age equal to 30 and xG/xA per 90 equal to 0.15. The two clusters are initialized to consist of 15% and 85% of the population, respectively:

```
set.seed(109823)
nwsl_mix_df <- nwsl_cluster_df
mix_model <- mvnormalmixEM(nwsl_mix_df[, c("age", "xGxAp90")],
                           arbvar = FALSE,
                           mu = list(c(21, .1), c(30, .5)),
                           lambda = c(.15, .85),
                           k = 2,
                           epsilon = 1e-02,
                           verb = T)
```

```
iteration= 1 diff= 847.8347 log-likelihood -734.566
iteration= 2 diff= 0.1086601 log-likelihood -734.4573
iteration= 3 diff= 0.06638859 log-likelihood -734.3909
iteration= 4 diff= 0.0438556 log-likelihood -734.3471
iteration= 5 diff= 0.03125344 log-likelihood -734.3158
iteration= 6 diff= 0.02416589 log-likelihood -734.2916
iteration= 7 diff= 0.0204981 log-likelihood -734.2711
iteration= 8 diff= 0.01928716 log-likelihood -734.2519
iteration= 9 diff= 0.02022809 log-likelihood -734.2316
iteration= 10 diff= 0.02352684 log-likelihood -734.2081
iteration= 11 diff= 0.02996533 log-likelihood -734.1781
iteration= 12 diff= 0.04120394 log-likelihood -734.1369
iteration= 13 diff= 0.06049156 log-likelihood -734.0764
iteration= 14 diff= 0.09422249 log-likelihood -733.9822
iteration= 15 diff= 0.155386 log-likelihood -733.8268
iteration= 16 diff= 0.27134 log-likelihood -733.5555
iteration= 17 diff= 0.5011215 log-likelihood -733.0544
iteration= 18 diff= 0.970478 log-likelihood -732.0839
iteration= 19 diff= 1.921815 log-likelihood -730.1621
iteration= 20 diff= 3.69554 log-likelihood -726.4665
iteration= 21 diff= 6.296351 log-likelihood -720.1702
iteration= 22 diff= 7.995901 log-likelihood -712.1743
iteration= 23 diff= 5.789614 log-likelihood -706.3847
iteration= 24 diff= 2.010316 log-likelihood -704.3744
iteration= 25 diff= 0.4107738 log-likelihood -703.9636
iteration= 26 diff= 0.09269801 log-likelihood -703.8709
iteration= 27 diff= 0.03713044 log-likelihood -703.8338
iteration= 28 diff= 0.02066821 log-likelihood -703.8131
iteration= 29 diff= 0.01245683 log-likelihood -703.8006
iteration= 30 diff= 0.007616735 log-likelihood -703.793
number of iterations= 30
```

The individual observations are clustered according to their estimated posterior probabilities of cluster assignment. The `mix_model` object stores these estimates in the `posterior` object. Look at the first six values in this list:

```
head(mix_model$posterior)
```

```
           comp.1       comp.2
[1,] 4.566354e-05 9.999543e-01
[2,] 1.702920e-01 8.297080e-01
[3,] 6.215476e-03 9.937845e-01
[4,] 9.927770e-01 7.222963e-03
[5,] 3.458898e-02 9.654110e-01
[6,] 9.999985e-01 1.495544e-06
```

The first line in the posterior output shows 0.00005 and 0.99995 for `comp.1` (cluster 1) and `comp.2` (cluster 2), respectively. These numbers represent the posterior probability of belonging to the first and second components, or clusters. In particular, the model classifies someone having `age = 23` and `xGxAp90 = 0` as belonging to the second cluster, given that the first cluster's posterior probability is lower than the second. On the other hand, someone with `age = 22` and `xGxAp90 = 0.62` is assigned to the first cluster. As mentioned before, this is referred to as a "soft" clustering, given that we are assigning group membership based on the posterior probabilities:

```
head(nwsl_mix_df[, c("age", "xGxAp90")])
```

```
  age xGxAp90
1  23    0.00
2  24    0.36
3  22    0.20
5  22    0.62
6  23    0.28
7  24    0.99
```

```
mix_model$mu
```

```
[[1]]
[1] 24.6725491  0.5894699

[[2]]
[1] 25.998017  0.146694
```

Let's add the centers to our scatterplot and color the points according to their classification. The first variable (`pp`) would be our soft classification probability, whereas the `class` variable is a hard classification. We can visualize both using some of the tools that we have used previously. The centers, or means, of the individual cluster distributions, f_k, are given as solid black triangles. Figure 8.13 shows the points with shapes representing their cluster membership, whereas figure 8.14 shows the points colored by their probability of cluster membership as a continuum.

```
nwsl_mix_df <- nwsl_mix_df |>
  mutate(pp = mix_model$posterior[, 1],
         class = ifelse(pp <= .5, "one", "two"))
p <- ggplot(data = nwsl_mix_df,
            aes(x = age, y = xGxAp90,
                col = class,
                pch = class))
p + geom_point() +
  geom_point(data = data.frame(age = c(mix_model$mu[[1]][1],
                                        mix_model$mu[[2]][1]),
                               xGxAp90 = c(mix_model$mu[[1]][2],
                                           mix_model$mu[[2]][2])),
             aes(x = age, y = xGxAp90),
             col = "black",
             shape = 17,
             size = 3) +
  scale_color_brewer("cluster", palette = "Set1") +
  guides(pch = "none",
         col = guide_legend(title = "cluster")) +
  labs(title = "Gaussian Mixture Clustering of NWSL players",
       x = "Age of Players",
       y = "Expected Goals plus Assists per 90") +
  theme_bw()
```

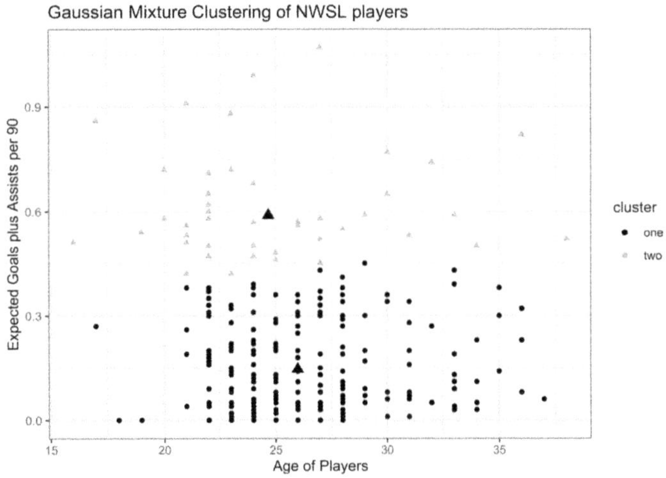

Figure 8.13: Player age (x) versus expected goals plus assists per 90 (y), with point shapes representing cluster membership based on the two-component Gaussian mixture model.

```
p <- ggplot(data = nwsl_mix_df,
            aes(x = age, y = xGxAp90, col = pp))
p + geom_point() +
  geom_point(data = data.frame(age = c(mix_model$mu[[1]][1],
                                       mix_model$mu[[2]][1]),
                               xGxAp90 = c(mix_model$mu[[1]][2],
                                           mix_model$mu[[2]][2])),
             aes(x = age, y = xGxAp90),
             col = "black",
             shape = 17,
             size = 3) +
  scale_color_distiller("Probability", palette = "Spectral", limits = c(0, 1)) +
  labs(color = "cluster",
       x = "Age",
       y = "Expected Goals and Assists per 90") +
  theme_bw()
```

The `lambda` parameter in the `mvnormalmixEM` object yields the estimated mixing proportions for each component. In this example, we have $_1 = 0.1707153 $ and $_2 = $ `0.8292847`:

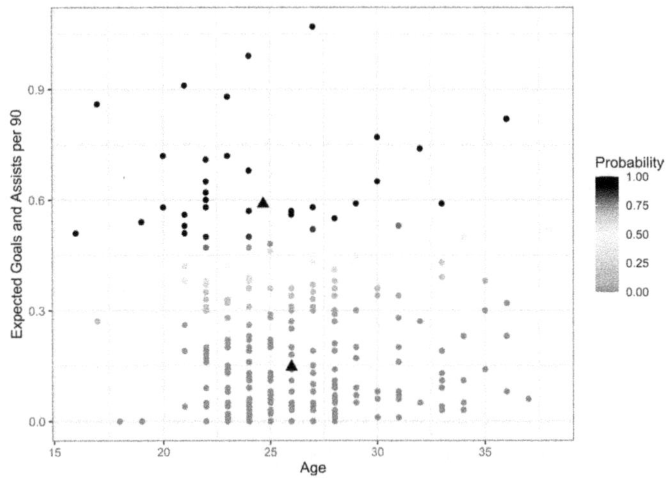

Figure 8.14: Player age (x) versus expected goals plus assists per 90 (y), with point shades of gray representing the probability of cluster membership based on the two-component Gaussian mixture model.

```
mix_model$lambda
```

```
[1] 0.1707153 0.8292847
```

One thing to note about using the `mixtools` package specifically or EM algorithms in general is that you should always initialize the algorithm using multiple initial values in order to ensure convergence to a global maximum. You can check the log-likelihood in the output to see if you (hopefully) arrive at a global maximum. Consider a different initialization of the same function call and examine the log-likelihood:

```
set.seed(109823)
mix_model_2 <- mvnormalmixEM(nwsl_mix_df[, c("age", "xGxAp90")],
                              arbvar = FALSE,
                              mu = list(c(25, .1), c(20, .5)),
                              lambda = c(.5, .5),
                              k = 2,
                              epsilon = 1e-02,
                              verb = T)
```

```
iteration= 1 diff= 843.6957 log-likelihood -734.2906
iteration= 2 diff= 0.00217201 log-likelihood -734.2885
number of iterations= 2
```

8.8 Case Study: Soccer Roster Economics

Soccer teams throughout the world are no different from other teams we have examined in that they are businesses that need to operate within a budget and make a financial return for their owners and shareholders. Some teams have very wealthy owners, especially in England, where in the 21st century, club ownership has become a status symbol for royalty, oligarchs, and sovereign wealth funds. Anyone can commission a superyacht, but there are only 20 teams in the English Premier League.

While teams in the biggest European leagues do not have the same salary cap restrictions as NBA, NFL, or NHL teams, they are subject to UEFA Financial Fair Play (FFP) restrictions. These rules were created in 2010 to ensure that clubs did not spend so much money on player salaries that it threatened their existence. FFP was implemented after a 2009 study showed that approximately half of European clubs were losing money, and as many as 20% were in financial danger. FFP rules have continued to evolve over the years but currently state that clubs can only lose a total of €60 million over three years. They also have something of a spending cap (as opposed to a salary cap), where salaries, transfer fees (fees paid to another club when acquiring playing rights to that player), and money paid to player agents cannot exceed 70% of the club's total revenue. Of course, these rules are frequently broken, perhaps most often by the richest clubs, but FFP rule enforcement is not the purpose of this section.

The purpose of this section is to talk about the need for the administration of soccer teams to think carefully about the players that they acquire and the salaries that they pay in order to make their team competitive both on the pitch and in the boardroom. While the rules these teams play under may seem unfair, this also should be familiar by now. The subtitle of Michael Lewis's groundbreaking sports analytics book *Moneyball* is, after all, *The Art of Winning an Unfair Game*. Billy Beane's thinking in *Moneyball* was that general managers should be buying runs, not players. Perhaps the same thinking should be applied to buying goals, or buying xG.

So if you readers of the text are administration and general managers of soccer clubs, how do you go about accurately valuing the fair worth of and appropriate salary for a player? We can use the `worldfootballR` package to match player valuations based on `Transfermarkt.com`. In particular, use the `tm_player_market_values()` function to pull all EPL valuations for nongoalkeeper players in the 2021–22 season and join these valuations with the `ISAR` package's `epl_player_stats_2022` data. Perform a full accounting of valuations in order to identify under- and overpaid players:

```
epl_valuations <- tm_player_market_values(country_name = "England",
                                          start_year = 2021)
epl_stats_val <- dplyr::left_join(epl_player_stats_2022, epl_valuations,
                                  by = c("player" = "player_name"))
```

Choose the covariates that you think would be appropriate. Some might include `age`, `position`, `xG`, and `xA`, among other characteristics. Do some calculations to determine which players you believe are overvalued and undervalued. What else do you notice? What strategies could you derive from this analysis?

8.9 Lab: Goalkeeper Styles in the English Premier League

In this lab, we will investigate the playing styles of goalkeepers in the English Premier League. The data for the lab can be found in the `ISAR` package under `epl_gk_stats_2022`. The dataset consists of 42 observations (goalkeepers) across 32 variables. We will perform a *k*-means clustering of the players to gain insights into their shot-stopping and passing styles.

1. Create a *k*-means clustering (two clusters) of goalkeepers based on the following variables: post-shot expected goals per shot on target (`post_shot_xG_per_shot_on_target`), postshot expected goals minus goals scored per 90 minutes (`post_shot_xG_minus_goals_p90`), launch completion percent (`launch_completion_percent`), pass launch percentage (`pass_launch_percent`), average pass length (`avg_pass_len`), goal kick launch percent (`gk_launch_percent`), and defensive actions outside the penalty area per 90 minutes (`def_actions_out_pen_area_p90`). Set your seed at 8675:

```
set.seed(8675)
epl_gk_kmean <- kmeans(select(epl_gk_stats_2022,
                              post_shot_xG_per_shot_on_target,
                              launch_completion_percent,
                              pass_launch_percent,
                              avg_pass_len,
                              gk_launch_percent,
                              def_actions_out_pen_area_p90) |>
                         na.omit(),
                       centers = 2)
epl_gk_kmean
```

```
K-means clustering with 2 clusters of sizes 23, 19

Cluster means:
  post_shot_xG_per_shot_on_target launch_completion_percent pass_launch_percent
1                       0.2834783                  32.43478            27.55652
2                       0.2994737                  35.62105            53.35789
  avg_pass_len gk_launch_percent def_actions_out_pen_area_p90
1     29.84783          32.65652                    1.4708696
2     40.48421          75.59474                    0.9294737

Clustering vector:
 2  3  4  5  6  7  8  9 10 11 12 13 14 15 16 17 18 19 20 21 22 23 24 25 26 27
 1  2  1  2  2  1  2  2  2  1  2  1  2  2  1  1  1  2  1  1  1  2  1  1  1  2
28 29 30 31 32 33 34 35 36 37 38 39 40 41 42 43
 1  1  2  2  2  2  2  1  1  2  1  1  1  1  1  2

Within cluster sum of squares by cluster:
[1] 8441.624 6535.225
 (between_SS / total_SS =  64.7 %)

Available components:

[1] "cluster"      "centers"      "totss"        "withinss"     "tot.withinss"
[6] "betweenss"    "size"         "iter"         "ifault"
```

2. Create a data frame showing the players, their nationalities, and their cluster assignments. Sort the data by cluster:

```
epl_gk_stats_2022 |>dplyr::mutate(k_means = epl_gk_kmean$cluster) |>
  dplyr::select(player, nation, k_means) |>
  dplyr::arrange(k_means)
```

```
                player  nation k_means
1              Alisson  br BRA       1
2     Kepa Arrizabalaga  es ESP       1
3          Jack Butland eng ENG       1
4              Ederson  br BRA       1
5      Álvaro Fernández  es ESP       1
6          David de Gea  es ESP       1
7       Vicente Guaita  es ESP       1
8            Angus Gunn eng ENG       1
9     Caoimhín Kelleher  ie IRL       1
10 Kristoffer Klaesson  no NOR       1
11             Tim Krul  nl NED       1
12          Hugo Lloris  fr FRA       1
13          Jonas Lössl  dk DEN       1
14    Emiliano Martínez  ar ARG       1
15        Edouard Mendy  sn SEN       1
16        Illan Meslier  fr FRA       1
17           John Ruddy eng ENG       1
18              José Sá  pt POR       1
19    Kasper Schmeichel  dk DEN       1
20         Jason Steele eng ENG       1
21            Jed Steer eng ENG       1
22         Zack Steffen  us USA       1
23           Danny Ward wls WAL       1
24      Alphonse Areola  fr FRA       2
25      Daniel Bachmann  at AUT       2
26        Asmir Begović  ba BIH       2
27      Willy Caballero  ar ARG       2
28          Karl Darlow eng ENG       2
29      Martin Dúbravka  sk SVK       2
30     Łukasz Fabiański  pl POL       2
31       Fraser Forster eng ENG       2
32           Ben Foster eng ENG       2
33      Wayne Hennessey wls WAL       2
34           Bernd Leno  de GER       2
35        Alex McCarthy eng ENG       2
36          Robin Olsen  se SWE       2
37      Jordan Pickford eng ENG       2
38            Nick Pope eng ENG       2
39       Aaron Ramsdale eng ENG       2
40           David Raya  es ESP       2
41       Robert Sánchez  es ESP       2
42      Freddie Woodman eng ENG       2
```

3. Plot the average pass length by the number of defensive actions outside the penalty area per 90 minutes. Color the points by the cluster membership:

```
epl_cluster_df <- dplyr::mutate(epl_gk_stats_2022,
                                k_means = epl_gk_kmean$cluster)

p <- ggplot(data = epl_cluster_df,
            aes(x = avg_pass_len,
                y = def_actions_out_pen_area_p90,
                col = as.factor(k_means)))
p + geom_point() +
```

```
  scale_color_brewer("cluster", palette = "Set1") +
  labs(title = "Clustering Goalkeepers in the EPL",
       x = "Average Pass Length",
       y = "Defensive Actions Outside the Penalty Area per 90") +
  theme_bw()
```

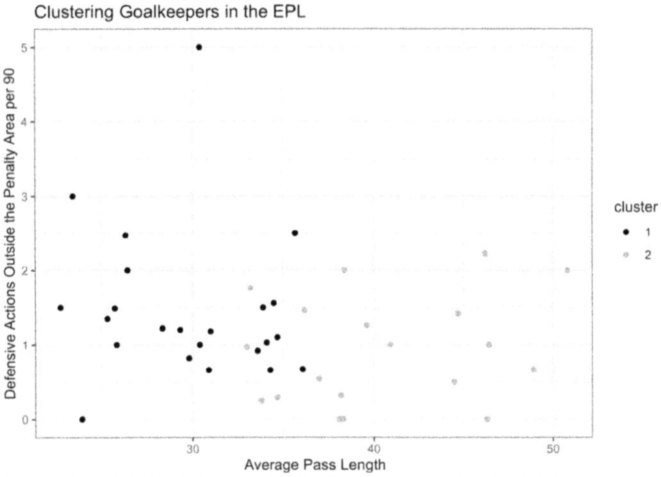

4. Add simple linear regression trend lines for each cluster. What can you infer based on these trend lines?

```
p <- ggplot(data = epl_cluster_df,
            aes(x = avg_pass_len,
                y = def_actions_out_pen_area_p90,
                col = as.factor(k_means)))
p + geom_point() +
  scale_color_brewer("cluster", palette = "Set1") +
  labs(title = "Clustering Goalkeepers in the EPL",
       x = "Average Pass Length",
       y = "Defensive Actions Outside the Penalty Area per 90") +
  geom_smooth(method = "lm") +
  theme_bw()
```

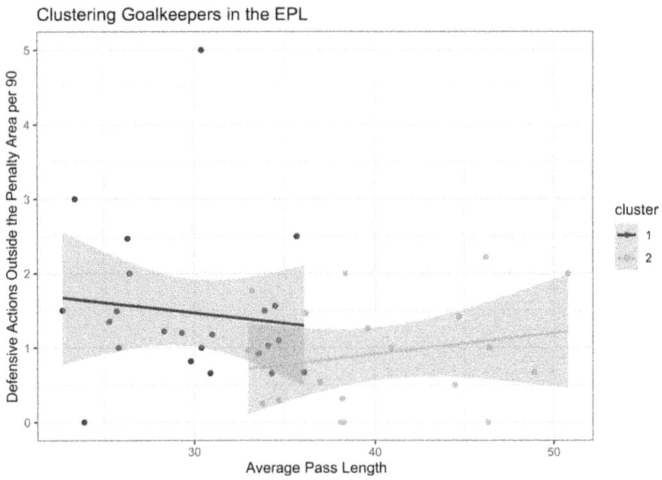

8.10 Exercises

Problems 1–5 of the exercises will use the `epl_team_stats` dataset in the authors' `ISAR` package. Problem 6 will use `epl_player_stats_2022`.

1. Plot the average age of a team age (`age`) versus expected goals and assists per 90 minutes (`xG_xA_p90`).
2. Add a smooth trend line to the plot given and comment on your observations.
3. Label all points that are above 3 in `xG_xA_p90` by team and season.
4. Remove Manchester City and redo the trend plot. Add a linear trend line to the plot as well.
5. Repeat steps 1–2 using only data from 2018–19 to 2021–22. Show each season separately as its own plot in a faceted graph.
6. Using the `epl_player_stats_2022` data frame from the `ISAR` package, plot expected goals plus assists per 90 (`xG_xA_p90`) on the y-axis and minutes played (`min`) on the y-axis. Label the players having an `xG_xA_p90` value greater than 1.
7. Filter the dataset to players who played more than 90 minutes. Regress expected goals plus assists per 90 (`xG_xA_p90`) on minutes played (`min`). Does the result surprise you?
8. Redo steps 6 and 7 using expected goals plus expected assists as the dependent variable.
9. Given the previous exercises, what are your overall interpretations?

Chapter 9

Golf

> Competitive golf is played mainly on a 5.5-inch course . . . the space between your ears.
>
> —Bobby Jones

9.1 R Packages

We will use the following R packages in this chapter:

```
library(ggplot2)
library(dplyr)
library(tidyr)
library(factoextra)
library(ISAR)
```

We only introduce one new package in this chapter:

```
library(fmsb) # used to help us make radar charts
```

9.2 If You Don't Know Anything about Golf

Some of you may not be as familiar with golf as the other sports mentioned in this text. Golf differs from these other sports in many ways. First, golf is an individual sport, not a team sport like the other sports considered in individual chapters in this text. Second, the participants compete against each other only indirectly: each participant plays the golf course, and the actions of any one player do not change the ability of any other player to play the shot he or she wants to play. Third, at the highest levels of the game and at courses in cities every weekend, the players generally compete in a tournament format. That is, they do not compete one-on-one with a winner and a loser; rather, scores are aggregated across the entire tournament to determine the winner and subsequent positions. In any given week on the PGA Tour, you could say that there is one tournament winner and 155 losers, but players determine their relative performance by position finished, such as a runner-up, a top-10 finish, or perhaps a top-25 finish.

Yet in other ways, golf is similar to the sports we have studied elsewhere in this book. For example, each stroke in golf is a discrete event, much like a pitch in baseball or a play in football. It is played exclusively outdoors, meaning it is subject to the weather conditions that you see in sports like baseball and soccer. The strategy that a player selects for his or her own shot, combined with its execution, will determine the score a player achieves on any given hole. When we examine the strokes gained metrics later in this chapter, we will see how these decisions, and their results, compound to create a score on each hole, much like the strategy used in American football when choosing conservative or aggressive strategies on offense and defense.

In case you are not familiar with some of the terminology used here, we refer you to the Wikipedia page for the "Glossary of Golf," available at `https://en.wikipedia.org/wiki/Glossary_of_golf`.

9.3 The Evolution of Golf Analytics

Golf does not have the long history of analytics the way that a sport like baseball does. Sportswriters do not create box scores for golf the way they do for baseball or football. This may be due to the relatively simple nature of the game (the low score wins) and the small numbers being easy to count. Moreover, through the first half of the 20th century, the most popular form of the game at the professional level (and still the most popular form today at weekend games between friends at golf clubs) was match play, where one player competes against one other player and the winner of the match is the player who has the lowest score on the largest number of holes rather than the lowest total score over all 18 holes.

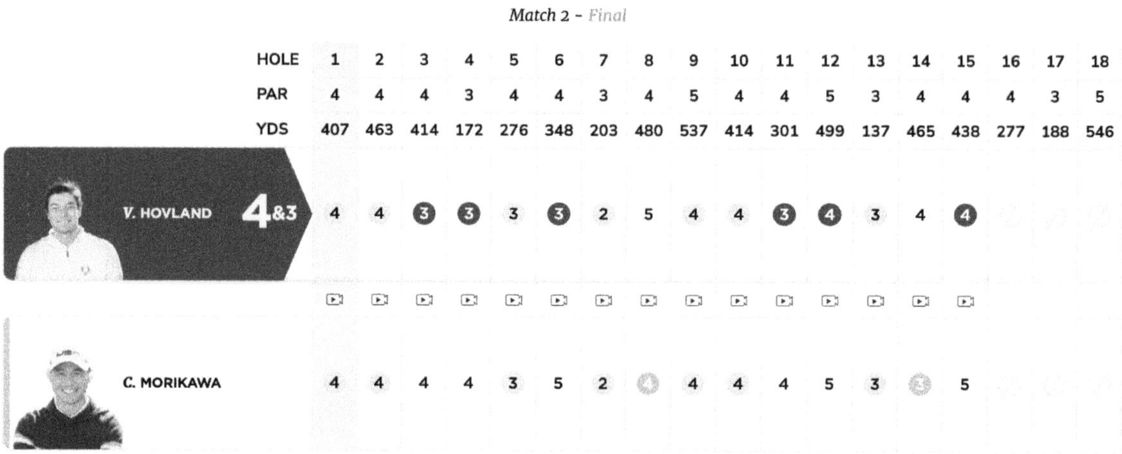

Figure 9.1: Scorecard from the 2023 Ryder Cup.
Source: `rydercup.com/scoring`

Due to the above, early golf metrics were very simple. Usually, the best professional player of the year was judged by the amount of prize money won that year, or perhaps the number and importance of tournaments won, and sometimes even by just a vote of his or her peers. But any statistics beyond those were generally not kept.

In 1980, the PGA Tour began to publish statistics about the players in their events. While these are basic by today's standards, at the time it was considered a revolutionary way for players to be compared and evaluated in several different ways instead of just their score on a hole. These statistics included driving distance, driving accuracy, greens in regulation percentage, scrambling percentage, sand save percentage, putts per round, and par breakers. So many of these statistics have their inherent flaws when viewed in isolation. For example, one player might have very few putts per round, so it looks as though this person is a superior putter. One explanation could be, however, that this player was not very good at hitting the green from the fairway and, as such, chipped a lot. It is much easier to get the ball close to the hole when chipping from 20 yards than when hitting from 200 yards. Thus, the starting distance on the green is strongly correlated with the number of putts it takes to get the ball into the hole.*

* Famously, in the final tournament round of 1984, PGA Tour player and later television announcer Gary McCord, who had over 400 PGA Tour starts but 0 wins, intentionally attempted to miss all 18 greens in regulation with his approach shots in order to increase his chances of leading the average putts per round statistic for the year. He was successful both in missing every green that day and in subsequently winning the average putts per round (28.57) statistical category for the year over Hubert Green (28.69).

9.4 Advanced Golf Metrics

In 2001, the PGA Tour began the ShotLink program to more accurately track each stroke that players make in PGA Tour tournaments. Operated largely by volunteers, three people would shoot a laser at the ball after it had come to rest. This data would then be fed into computers that would triangulate the ball's position relative to the hole and the location of the previous shot to determine how far that shot traveled, its condition (fairway, rough, sand, green, etc.), and how far the ball remained from the hole. This enabled far more accurate tracking of distances than previously used for simply measuring driving distance (which was only done on two holes per tournament) and enabled the announcers to have more accurate data as well. The next-generation ShotLink+ is adding camera data in and around greens to gather even more granular data.

Figure 9.2: ShotLink camera.
Source: Michael Cohen / Stringer / PGA TOUR via Getty Images

With the advent of ShotLink came a whole new era in golf statistics under the umbrella of strokes gained. Strokes gained calculations allow a comparison of how many strokes someone is expected to take to get the ball in the hole from a certain location and lie, such as from 400 yards away off the tee, 170 yards away in the fairway, or 110 yards out in the rough, based on a baseline established from data collected on all PGA Tour players. For an in-depth explanation of the formulas used, see `https://www.pgatour.com/news/2016/05/31/strokes-gained-defined.html`.

Figure 9.3: Mark Broadie.
Source: Permission granted by Mark Broadie, February 8, 2024

Mark Broadie at Columbia University is credited with first creating the strokes gained concept. He used this as a way to get rid of the complicating factors mentioned in the previous section on one category of data unduly influencing another category. Professor Broadie has since become well known in the golf analytics community, authoring the book *Every Shot Counts*, writing a monthly column for *Golf* magazine, and working with the United States Golf Association (USGA) on their handicap research team.

9.5 Exploring Golf through Basic and Advanced Statistics

Until 2019, the PGA Tour had a partnership with academics that allowed researchers to get access to ShotLink data to use for academic research. Many researchers were able to get this data and publish papers about it. However, at the beginning of 2019, the PGA Tour suspended this partnership and not only stopped allowing access to ShotLink data but ordered academics to destroy all ShotLink data that they had been provided. At about the same time, the PGA Tour announced several partnerships with sports gambling companies. Perhaps these are related efforts? So now we have to get creative about how we gather data for analysis.

For the purposes of this text, we have been supplied with data for our analyses and problems by Matthew Courchene, one of the cofounders of `Datagolf.com`. Data Golf, as the title proclaims, is an analysis of all things data that relate to golf, particularly helping predict golf performance. It pays particular attention to daily fantasy sports contests and other betting opportunities. While in this space we could not hope to accomplish even a tiny fraction of what Data Golf does for its customers and golf fans in general, we do thank them for their data and point those who may have more interest in golf toward their website and their free and paid subscription options.

Calculating Strokes Gained

To explain strokes gained in statisticians' terms, we will define a function $J(d,c)$. This function represents the average number of strokes it takes a PGA Tour golfer to finish a hole, considering the distance from the hole, d, and the condition of the stroke about to be played, c. To calculate the strokes gained on a given shot, i, we want to take the difference between the average number of shots it takes a player to complete the hole before shot i and after shot i. We then subtract 1 from that difference because the player just completed a shot. Represented mathematically, the equation is

$$g_i = J(d_i,c_i) - J(d_{i+1}, c_{i+1}) - 1.$$

As an example, let us borrow from the explanations on `PGATour.com` and consider tour player Rickie Fowler on the 18th (final) hole in the fourth (final) round of the Players Championship in 2015. The hole is a 446-yard par four, and the PGA Tour average for a 446-yard hole is 4.1 strokes.

Shot 1: Fowler hit his tee shot 330 yards in the fairway, leaving himself 116 yards to the cup. From 116 yards in the fairway, the average tour player needs 2.825 strokes to complete the hole. So the calculation of his strokes gained on the tee shot is

$$g = 4.1 - 2.825 - 1 = +0.275.$$

Shot 2: Fowler then hit his shot from 116 yards in the fairway onto the green, to a distance of 16 feet, 11 inches from the cup. The average tour player needs 1.826 shots from this distance on the green. Therefore, his strokes gained on the second shot is

$$g = 2.825 - 1.826 - 1 = -0.001.$$

Shot 3: Fowler then proceeded to make the putt (and win the tournament later in a playoff). He has no more strokes to take once the ball is in the cup. Thus we calculate his strokes gained putting as

$$g = 1.826 - 0 - 1 = +0.826.$$

We can calculate the strokes gained or lost on every hole, or for the round, or for the year. Often, strokes gained when evaluating a player are grouped into four categories:

1. Strokes gained off the tee (SG: OTT): tee shots on par-four and par-five holes
2. Strokes gained approach (SG: APP): all shots not from the tee on par-four and par-five holes that are not included in strokes gained around the green (also includes tee shots on par-three holes)
3. Strokes gained around the green (SG: ARG): any shot that happens within 30 yards of the edge of the green but is not on the green
4. Strokes gained putting (SG: PUTT): shots from the putting surface

You will often see 1–3 grouped as strokes gained tee-to-green.

Obviously, the permutations of these statistics are endless. For example, a player wanting to study how he is performing on shots with full-swing wedges relative to the field might look at strokes gained 100–150 yards.

Visualizing the Strokes Gained Data

One method we could use to visualize the strokes gained data for all the players is to plot the data on a radar chart. A radar chart allows for the display of multidimensional data on a two-dimensional chart. What we might think of as a normal graph normally has just an x- and y-axis, and as such, it makes it impossible to display data with three or more dimensions, but the radar chart allows us to overcome this limitation.

Figure 9.4 is an example of a radar chart that shows six-dimensional data for an organization, comparing budgeted funds to actual spending. This is sometimes referred to as a spider chart, as it somewhat resembles the web of a spider. We will use R to analyze data and display it in a radar chart to show the relative importance of the four types of shots gained data relative to player success in PGA Tour events for the 2022 season right up to the split with LIV Golf as a competing tour.

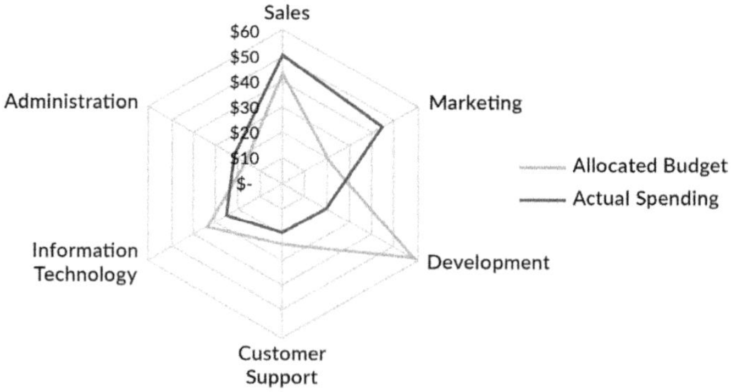

Figure 9.4: A sample radar chart.
Source: Public domain

To do this, our script will use the `dplyr` and `tidyr` packages for data retrieval and manipulation and the `ggplot2` and `fmsb` packages for graphing the data in a radar plot. We will use two datasets in the `ISAR` package: `ow_golf_rankings` (Official World Golf Rankings) and `pga_tournaments` (from Data Golf). First, we will merge the two datasets using the `left_join()` operator:

```
df <- left_join(pga_tournaments,
                ow_golf_rankings,
                by = "Player_initial_last")
```

Exploring the data, we see that for each tournament, we have player data such as name, whether he made the 36-hole cut, total number of strokes taken in the tournament, fantasy points earned in various competitions by DraftKings and FanDuel, and finishing position in the tournament, all merged with the OWGR points from above. We clean these data a bit by assigning anyone who was not in the top 300 in the OWGR a ranking of 301. Moreover, we see that if a player misses the cut, his finishing position is listed as N/A, and we instead assign each N/A a value of 999. We also remove rows where a player's SG data are, for whatever reason, missing.

We are mainly interested in the SG data and OWGR data, so we are going to select only those columns into a new data frame and then create another data frame that has the averages of each of the four main SG categories for each player:

```
df_sub <- df |>
  select(Player_initial_last, sg_putt, sg_arg,
         sg_app, sg_ott, sg_t2g, sg_total, WGR_June_2022) |>
  na.omit()
df_summarized <- df_sub |>
  group_by(Player_initial_last) |>
  summarize(mean_sg_ott = mean(sg_ott, na.rm = TRUE),
            mean_sg_app = mean(sg_app, na.rm = TRUE),
            mean_sg_arg = mean(sg_arg, na.rm = TRUE),
            mean_sg_putt = mean(sg_putt, na.rm = TRUE),
            mean_WGR = mean(WGR_June_2022, na.rm = TRUE)) |>
  mutate(top_50 = ifelse(mean_WGR <= 50, T, F))
```

Our objective in this exercise was to see how the SG stats compared between players who were currently the best in the world and those who were not quite there yet. So we create a flag in the dataset to delineate players as being either in the top 50 or outside the top 50.

Now we summarize the data to get the mean SG scores for the top 50 players in the OWGR and those who played in the PGA Tour tournaments who were not in the top 50:

```
df_summarized_top_50 <- df_summarized |>
  group_by(top_50) |>
  summarize(SGOTT = mean(mean_sg_ott, na.rm = TRUE),
            SGAPP = mean(mean_sg_app, na.rm = TRUE),
            SGARG = mean(mean_sg_arg, na.rm = TRUE),
            SGPUTT = mean(mean_sg_putt, na.rm = TRUE))
```

Next, we need to prepare the data for use in the `fmsb` package for the radar chart. The data frames used in creating these charts must fit a peculiar format, where the first two rows have the minimum and maximum values for each of the axes. We create these and then bind them to our summarized data while changing the column names so the `rbind()` function knows how to bind the data frames. Then we can construct the radar chart, and we provide some labels to add some meaning to the visualization:

```
df_SG_radarchart <- data.frame(SGOTT= c(0.4, -0.5),
                               SGAPP = c(0.4, -0.5),
                               SGARG = c(0.4, -0.5),
                               SGPUTT = c(0.4, -0.5)) |>
  bind_rows(df_summarized_top_50 |> select(-top_50))
areas <- c(rgb(1,0,0,.25), rgb(0,1,0,.25))
radarchart(df_SG_radarchart,
```

```
           title = "Shots Gained Metrics for Professional Golfers",
           axistype = 1,
           caxislabels = c("-0.6","-0.3", "0", "0.3", "0.6"),
           plty=1,
           pcol=2:3,
           pfcol = areas)
legend("topright",
       legend = c("Not Top 50 Players", "Top 50 Players"),
       bty="n", pch=20, col=areas,
       text.col = "black", pt.cex = 2)
```

We can now see the gaps between the players in the two groups. From looking at the radar chart, it seems that the biggest difference between the groups is in SG: APP and the smallest is in SG: ARG. So a player who is ranked 200 and wants to move into the top 50 might decide to spend the majority of his practice time working on his shots from 100–200 yards and less time on chipping and putting.

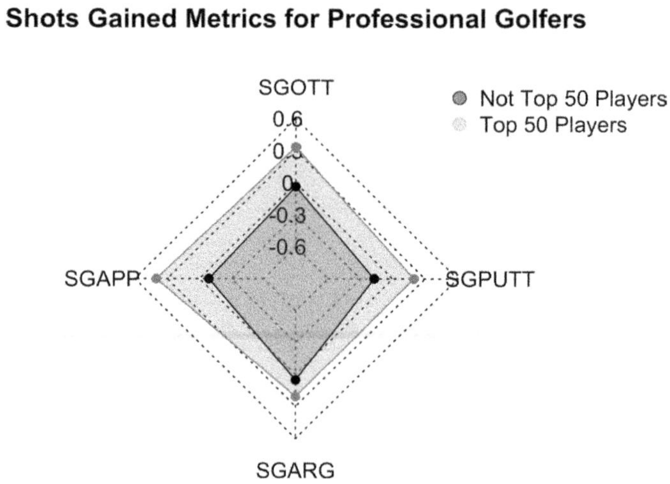

Figure 9.5: Radar plot showing four average strokes gained metrics for golfers in the top 50 versus those not in the top 50 of the OWGR.

9.6 Cluster Analysis

Much like we did in the soccer chapter, we can use *k*-means clustering for unsupervised learning. As a reminder, in *k*-means clustering, we specify a number of clusters (say, *k* clusters) that potentially underlie our data. We then calculate *k* centroids (usually group means or medians) and minimize the total distances between the data and the centroids. Given that we have four different types of shots gained data, we can use them as dimensions and see if we can identify which of the shots gained metrics are most important in identifying the OWGR points of our players.

In R, we will start with a script similar to the one we used above in creating the radar chart. We will also add the `factoextra()` package to assist us with some of the visualizations. At this point, though, we will do a few things differently. For example, we may want to group players into the top 50 in the OWGR (usually this will get a player invitations to the Masters and World Golf Championship events), top 100 in the OWGR (usually this will get a player an invitation to the PGA Championship), and everyone else:

```
df_clusters <- df_summarized |>
  select(Player_initial_last, mean_sg_ott, mean_sg_app, mean_sg_arg,
         mean_sg_putt) |>
  na.omit()
df_summarized <- df_summarized |>
  mutate(three_tiers = ifelse(mean_WGR <= 50, "top_50",
                        ifelse(mean_WGR <= 100, "top_100",
                               "outside_100")))
set.seed(90283)
cluster_strokes_gained <- kmeans(df_clusters |>
                                   select(-Player_initial_last),
                                 centers = 3, nstart = 20)
cluster_strokes_gained
```

```
K-means clustering with 3 clusters of sizes 66, 39, 68

Cluster means:
  mean_sg_ott mean_sg_app mean_sg_arg mean_sg_putt
1  -0.0101011  -0.1057341 -0.05390755  -0.48821092
2  -0.3401341  -0.4883770  0.11011648   0.29965069
3   0.2085267   0.3464833  0.04506881   0.04231509

Clustering vector:
  [1] 3 3 1 2 2 1 3 1 3 1 1 3 2 1 3 3 2 2 1 1 2 1 3 1 3 1 3 3 1 1 1 3 3 2 3 1 1
 [38] 3 3 3 3 1 1 1 3 1 3 2 3 1 1 1 1 1 2 1 3 1 2 2 2 3 1 3 2 2 1 3 2 1 3 1 1 3
 [75] 3 1 3 2 3 3 3 3 1 3 1 2 1 3 3 3 1 2 1 3 2 1 1 1 1 1 3 3 3 2 1 1 2 1 3 3 3
[112] 3 2 2 1 2 1 1 3 3 1 1 2 2 3 2 3 2 1 3 3 2 1 1 1 1 2 1 3 1 3 2 3 2 3 3 1 2
[149] 1 3 1 3 3 2 1 3 3 3 2 3 2 3 1 1 1 3 2 2 3 3 3 1 2

Within cluster sum of squares by cluster:
[1] 27.49616 26.09684 23.30980
 (between_SS / total_SS =  36.3 %)

Available components:

[1] "cluster"      "centers"      "totss"        "withinss"     "tot.withinss"
[6] "betweenss"    "size"         "iter"         "ifault"
```

```
df_cl_results <- df_clusters |>
  mutate(clusters = cluster_strokes_gained$cluster) |>
  left_join(df_summarized)
table(df_cl_results$clusters, df_cl_results$three_tiers)
```

```
    outside_100 top_100 top_50
  1          52      12      2
  2          21      10      8
  3          15      15     38
```

One of the first things we may notice is that we only have 48 of the top 50 players and only 37 of the second 50 players. We must have eliminated many of these players when we cleaned the data to remove some of the rows with `NA`. It is also probable that many of these players did not play in any of the PGA Tour tournaments during this time frame. This could be due to injury or because those players primarily played on other tours like the DP World (European) Tour or Japan Golf Tour.

This output gives us the three clusters we requested. Cluster 1 has negative means/averages in all four categories, but especially so in putting, where they lose (on average) about 0.49 strokes. In cluster 2, it seems that the players are not necessarily very good off the tee, as they lose 0.34 shots off the tee and 0.49 shots on approach but are better around the green (0.11 shots) and above average on the green while putting (0.30 shots). Cluster 3, which has the majority of our top players, has positive strokes gained in all categories. On average, these players are excelling on their approach shots (0.37 shots).

As is usually the case with clustering as an exploratory tool, it would be useful to explore clustering results using differing numbers of clusters. That is, we could change the `centers = 3` argument in the `kmeans()` function to either `centers = 2` or `centers = 4` to see whether our interpretations still hold or something more informative might emerge. We leave those tasks to the interested reader.

9.7 Research Block: Does Par on a Hole Matter?

On a standard golf course, every hole has a par rating. Par for a given hole is almost always rated as a three, four, or five, which is the number of shots a skilled golfer should expect to take to reach the green, plus two for the number of putts a skilled golfer would expect to take on that green. Even on minigolf courses at beach resorts, one can find each hole rated by the number of putts expected to complete the hole. But what does that number really mean in the grand scheme of things, and does it affect a golfer's psyche?

In a competition, par on a hole or for a course does not really matter. It merely creates a reference point that allows someone to refer to their status at a given point in the tournament not by the number of strokes taken but in relation to par. For example, at the 2023 AT&T Pebble Beach Pro-Am, Justin Rose was the winner, needing 269 strokes to complete 72 holes. The next closest competitor needed 272 strokes. Normally, reporters and players alike refer to their score not by the total number of strokes but by the score in relation to par. It would be reported that Rose was −18 (or 18 under par) and won by 3. For the purposes of the competition, it would not matter if we decided that 268 strokes was −18, −28, or +8, as he would still be the winner by completing the 72-hole tournament in the lowest number of strokes.

Curiously, research by the textbook authors published in the paper "Loss Aversion in Professional Golf," in the *Journal of Sports Economics* and available at `https://journals.sagepub.com/doi/abs/10.1177/1527002520967403`, shows that professional golfers do indeed suffer from the behavioral economic bias of loss aversion. Professional golfers anchor on whether a hole is rated as a par five or a par four and exhibit behavior that causes them to try harder to ensure that they score a par as opposed to trying for one stroke below par (known in golf parlance as a birdie). A natural experiment where the USGA played the US Open on the same golf courses (Pebble Beach in California as well as Oakmont in Pennsylvania) but in one year called the same hole a par five as opposed to in the following year calling it a par four resulted in players playing the hole approximately .25 strokes better as a par four, all other things accounted for. Quotes from several players even indicated that they knew in the grand scheme of things that par didn't matter, and yet it still affected their attitudes toward playing the hole, particularly after hitting a bad shot.

9.8 Lab: Simulating the Cut

Currently, the tournaments on the PGA Tour have a curious financial structure for the participants. Each player in the tournament covers his own travel, coaching, and caddie expenses and pays a nominal entry fee. Then normally after the second day of the four-day tournament, the field of 120–60 players is "cut" to the top 65 players plus any ties. This results in about half of the field coming to play each week earning nothing—in fact, losing money due to ancillary expenses.* The players who survive the cut then play for two more days, and the prize money is distributed according to their place in the tournament. It is a top-heavy structure, where normally 18% of the prize pool goes to the winner, 10.9% to 2nd place, 6.9% to 3rd place, and in continuing smaller increments down to 0.215% for the person finishing 65th and beyond. In a tournament with a $10 million prize pool, a player would have to finish 23rd or better to earn a 1% payout of $100,000.

In addition to the short-term financial incentives for finishing high in a tournament, there are also many incentives for winning. A tournament winner receives not only 18% of the prize pool but also other incentives such as a two-year automatic exemption from qualifying for the PGA Tour and automatic entry into other prestigious tournaments for the following year like the Masters.

So when a player is playing on the PGA Tour, he makes various decisions each time he has a shot. An aggressive strategy to aim directly at a hole that is located near a pond might bring the player a reward of a low score if he executes it perfectly but also brings in danger and penalty strokes if his ball were to land slightly offline in or near the water.

We can use analytics, of course, to help us make a better decision, but it depends on how one defines *better*. One player may choose a strategy with the best chance of making cuts and ensuring that he has a job for the following year, but another player may say he is ignoring the money and playing to win. This lab helps us start modeling some of these strategy decisions.

Suppose we have two players, Player X and Player Y. They are professional golfers, and both are competing in the National Open. We want to model their potential outcomes in the tournament.

Player X has probabilities of recording a one, two, three, four, five, and six on any par-three hole as 0.0001, 0.25, 0.6, 0.1, 0.04, and 0.0099, respectively. We write this as $\pi_3^X = (0.0001, 0.25, 0.6, 0.1, 0.04, 0.0099)$. His probability

* The authors would not enjoy teaching against 154 other professors for half the semester to then see who actually gets paid and who gets sent home broke.

of recording a two through seven on par fours and par fives can be written as $\pi_4^X = (.0005,.2,.6,.1,.09,0.0095)$ and $\pi_5^X = (0,0.05,0.35,0.5,0.0901,0.0099)$, respectively. Player Y is a little more volatile and has a slightly higher probability of making a birdie or better, or a bogey or worse, than Player X. His probability vectors can be written as $\pi_3^Y = (0.0001,0.30,0.5,0.14,0.05,0.0099)$, $\pi_4^Y = (0.0005,.25,.5,.15,.09,0.0095)$, and $\pi_5^Y = (0,0.05,0.375,0.45,0.1151,0.0099)$ on par threes, par fours, and par fives, respectively.

1. Given that the course used in the National Open tournament has 4 par-three holes, 10 par-four holes, and 4 par-five holes, which player do you think is more likely to make the cut if we predict that players need to shoot 146 or lower after two rounds to play the weekend?
2. Which player is more likely to have a better overall (four-round) score?

For both of the above questions, assume that holes are independent. That is, a player's performance on one hole is independent of his performance on any other hole, including the same hole the next day. Each hole's score can be sampled from a multinomial distribution given the probability vectors defined above.

To do this lab, we will use simulation. You may recall that we used simulation in the football chapter when we simulated drives based on actual plays from an NFL player database. We will do this again here, and this time we will draw 10,000 Monte Carlo samples.

First, we will define vectors `x_scores` and `x_probs`. The `x_scores` vector will hold the sampled scores, while the `x_probs` is actually a matrix with three vectors. Each vector in the `x_probs` matrix corresponds to the probabilities mentioned above for each player's different score on par-three, par-four, and par-five holes.

The `for` loop that follows runs 10,000, or `B`, times, one for each tournament outcome we are simulating. We create three different vectors (threes, fours, fives), which are the results of both Player X's and Player Y's simulated results on par threes, par fours, and par fives. We use `rmultinom()` to sample scores from a multinomial distribution. We sample from the multinomial distribution 8 times for the par-three and par-five holes and 20 times for the par fours. Recall that in the two rounds before the cut in the National Open, each player will play 8 par threes, 20 par fours, and 8 par fives for their 36 holes. We will then sum the scores on those holes and repeat for each of the 10,000 times. The two players' scores will be recorded in the `x_scores` and `y_scores` vectors.

We then calculate the mean probability of making the cut by counting the number of scores in each vector that are less than or equal to our projected cut number (146) and dividing by the number of times the simulation was run. Furthermore, we create a 95% confidence interval for the mean by calculating the standard deviation and adding and subtracting 1.96 standard deviations from our mean.

We can then plot the two distributions on top of each other and see that, as expected, Player Y has a wider distribution of scores, whereas the more consistent Player X has a narrower distribution:

```
set.seed(19831)
B <- 10000
x_scores <- numeric(length = B)
x_probs <- matrix(c(0.0001, 0.25, 0.6, 0.1, 0.04, 0.0099,
                    0.0005, .2, .6, .1, .09, 0.0095,
                    0, 0.05, 0.35, 0.5, 0.0901, 0.0099),
                  nr = 3, byrow = T)
y_scores <- numeric(length = B)
y_probs <- matrix(c(0.0001, 0.30, 0.5, 0.14, 0.05, 0.0099,
                    0.0005, .25, .5, .15, .09, 0.0095,
                    0, 0.05, 0.375, 0.45, 0.1151, 0.0099),
                  nr = 3, byrow = T)
for(b in 1:B){
  threes <- c(sum(rmultinom(8, size = 1, prob = x_probs[1, ])*1:6),
              sum(rmultinom(8, size = 1, prob = y_probs[1, ])*1:6))
  fours <- c(sum(rmultinom(20, size = 1, prob = x_probs[2, ])*2:7),
             sum(rmultinom(20, size = 1, prob = y_probs[2, ])*2:7))
  fives <- c(sum(rmultinom(8, size = 1, prob = x_probs[3, ])*2:7),
             sum(rmultinom(8, size = 1, prob = y_probs[3, ])*2:7))
```

```
  x_scores[b] <- sum(threes[1]) + sum(fours[1]) + sum(fives[1])
  y_scores[b] <- sum(threes[2]) + sum(fours[2]) + sum(fives[2])
}
```

The estimated probability of making the cut for each player can be found as follows:

```
px <- sum(x_scores <= 146)/B
px
```

```
[1] 0.7616
```

```
py <- sum(y_scores <= 146)/B
py
```

```
[1] 0.75
```

Are these differences meaningful in a statistical sense? You can easily calculate a 95% confidence interval using the rationale mentioned above:

```
c(px - 1.96*sqrt(px*(1-px)/B), px + 1.96*sqrt(px*(1-px)/B))
```

```
[1] 0.7532483 0.7699517
```

```
c(py - 1.96*sqrt(py*(1-py)/B), py + 1.96*sqrt(py*(1-py)/B))
```

```
[1] 0.741513 0.758487
```

Because these two confidence intervals overlap, they are not statistically different. Let's plot the distributions of the simulations:

```
df <- data.frame(name = rep(c("Player X", "Player Y"), each = B),
                 scores = c(x_scores, y_scores))
 p <- ggplot(data = df, aes(x = scores, fill = name))
 p + geom_density(alpha = .5) +
   scale_fill_brewer(palette = "Set1") +
   theme_bw()
```

Suppose a total score of seven under par (–7) will give you the lead after two rounds. Which player is more likely to be in the lead? To calculate this, let's count the number of scores in the simulation that were –7 or better and then divide that sum by the total number of trials in the simulation:

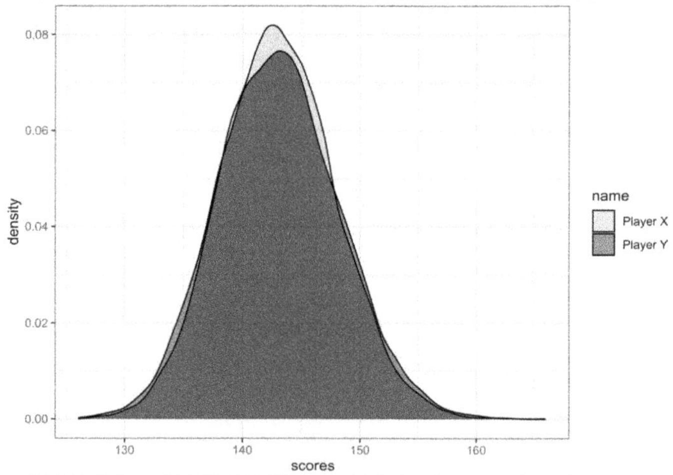


```
sum(x_scores <= 137)/B
```

```
[1] 0.1207
```

```
sum(y_scores <= 137)/B
```

```
[1] 0.137
```

From the results of our simulation, we believe it is more likely that Player Y is in the lead after two rounds than Player X.

9.9 Case Study: Ranking Golfers from Different Tours against One Another

Every day around the world, amateur golfers of different skills compete against one another based on the World Handicap System. This system requires players to enter their scores into a certain structure every time they play, along with the course they played and from what set of tees they played. The formula, simplified a bit for the purposes of this exercise, for calculating a player's handicap is as follows:

1. Identify the 20 most recent 18-hole scores that a player has posted.
2. Identify the relative difficulty level of the courses where the rounds were played. For example, it is probably easier to shoot an 80 at your local town municipal golf course than it is at Augusta National Golf Club. The USGA has determined two different ways of assessing a course's difficulty: course rating and slope. Course rating is the score that a scratch golfer (i.e., a golfer with a handicap of 0) should shoot, on average, at that course. For example, the course rating from the black (back) tees at the University of Denver Golf Club is 72.9, which means that a scratch golfer should shoot, on average, about 73. The course rating is heavily influenced by the length. Each course also has a slope rating, which is to help identify how much more difficult a course is for less skilled golfers than scratch golfers. Less skilled golfers will be more affected by deep sand bunkers, water hazards, thick grass, narrow fairways, undulating greens, and other similar difficulties than a more skilled player. The USGA decided that the slope rating for a golf course of average difficulty is 113 and that courses could be as easy as 55 or as difficult as 155, though one will rarely find the extremes. TPC Sawgrass is a 155 from their tournament tees. The same University of Denver Golf Club mentioned above has a slope rating of 129 from the black tees. As a result, you will generally find these metrics on the scorecard for the course (and in the USGA database), often with the nomenclature "rating/slope." For the University of Denver Golf Club, on the scorecard next to the information for the black tees, you will see "72.9/129."
3. Calculate the handicap differential for the round. The formula for the handicap differential is the difference between the player's score for the day and the course rating, multiplied by 113 and divided by the slope rating for the course. For example, a player who shot 95 on the aforementioned University of Denver Golf Course from the black tees, a course rated at 72.9 and with a slope rating of 129, would have a handicap differential for that round of (95 – 72.9) × (113 / 129) = 19.36, rounded to 19.4.
4. Identify the best 8 of those last 20 handicap differentials, calculate the mean, and take 96% of that mean.

So (once again, a bit simplified) Player A with a handicap of 5 would be expected to beat Player B with a 17 handicap by 12 strokes, and as such, in a match between those two players, an allowance should be made for that skill difference to give each player an equal chance of winning. As a matter of reference, the USGA reports that 1.6% of golfers with an official handicap have a rating of 0 or better (reported as a plus handicap, such as +1.2), and these players would be expected to score better than the course rating at least half of the time.

Professionals do not use the handicap system; it is simply that the best score wins. If they were to keep a handicap, it would be significantly on the plus side.* However, players need to be ranked against one another for various purposes. For example, in 2023, the top 70 players in the FedEx Cup points system on the PGA Tour qualify for the PGA Tour playoffs, a system of tournaments to identify a season-long champion. Also as of this writing, the top 30 in the FedEx Cup points system qualify for the PGA Tour's Sentry Tournament of Champions in January in Maui.

The FedEx Cup points system is how the PGA Tour ranks golfers each year within their organization, but it does not include players who are not members of the PGA Tour. The PGA Tour, the predominant golf tour in North America, is not the only golf tour in the world. The DP World Tour is primarily in Europe, the Sunshine

* In January 2023, Twitter user `@MichaelVerity` calculated the current handicap of Jon Rahm to be +13.2. This means that he is approximately one stroke per hole better than the aforementioned five-handicapper.

Tour is primarily in South Africa, the Japan Golf Tour is the highest level for players there, and there is also an Australasian tour. The Official World Golf Ranking (OWGR) at `owgr.com` is a means to try to rank golfers from many different tours in the world. It normalizes player performances in professional events based on many factors, such as the number of players competing in the tournament and the relative strength of the field based on the skill levels of the competitors in the event. When a player is referred to as "the number-one player in the world," it generally means that this player is ranked first in the OWGR. The formula that the OWGR uses has changed over the years since its founding in the 1980s, as have the formulas that the individual tours use (which, at first, were primarily based on prize money earned by each player), but the formula attempts to assign points for each professional competing in a sanctioned tour no matter where it is located.

While the OWGR started as a project by an agent to rank players for the purpose of sponsorship deals, these rankings are now used in determining the fields for the most prestigious tournaments in the world. Interestingly, the four most important golf tournaments in the world (the United States Open, the Masters, the PGA Championship, and the Open Championship [also known as the British Open]) are not controlled by any of the professional tours. Collectively known as the majors, the tournaments are controlled by the USGA, the Augusta National Golf Club, the PGA of America,* and the R&A,† respectively. In determining the fields for these championships, these organizations rely on the OWGR. For example, at the Masters, the top 50 players in the OWGR at the end of a calendar year are typically issued invitations to the following year's tournament, and the USGA exempts the top 60 in the OWGR from having to qualify for the US Open. There are many ways to qualify for these tournaments, but these are the primary ways used for professional golfers, particularly at invitationals like the Masters. Professional golfers on the cusp of the top 50 will try to play well at the end of the year to secure a coveted invite to the Masters.

In 2022, the Saudi Public Investment Fund founded and funded LIV Golf, a worldwide tour with comparatively large prize pools and smaller fields to have golf in both individual and team formats. Viewing this tour as a competitor, the PGA Tour and DP World Tours gave indefinite suspensions to any player competing in a LIV event. While most of the 48 players competing in LIV were earning far more money than they would on the PGA or DP World Tours, the one thing they could not earn on the LIV tour was OWGR points.

OWGR points are awarded for playing in tournaments on a rolling, two-year basis. A player who won a tournament in October 2020 would continue to keep those points until October 2022.‡ The OWGR calculates the average number of points won by adding the number of points earned in the previous two years and dividing it by the number of tournaments played, with a minimum divisor of 40. While this system works well for players who are continuing to play in events on OWGR-recognized tours, the LIV tour was not immediately recognized by the OWGR, and it has not committed to a time when it will recognize the LIV tour, if ever. Many LIV players have qualified for the majors through other means, such as being a past champion with a long-term exemption into that major. For others, though, and for other majors, the road is far less clear. Given that the players have been suspended by the tours where they previously played and provided the opportunities to earn the most points, the OWGR points of the LIV players are bound to drop as the tournaments they played two years prior are now no longer counting toward their points, while their opportunities to earn new points are extremely limited. Moreover, as their collective rankings drop, the strength of field metric (as measured by the field's OWGR average points) also drops, creating a vicious cycle for the competitors.

There are many reasons that have been confirmed or suspected as to why the OWGR has not as of yet awarded points to competitors in LIV tournaments. Many of these are procedural, such as needing to be in existence for at least a year and completing an application. Others are perceived as political, such as the OWGR board of directors being composed of people (like the PGA Tour commissioner) who have expressed open disapproval of LIV and their means of signing players to contracts with guaranteed money signing bonuses as well as their

---

* The PGA Tour is a separate entity from the PGA of America, with the tour having broken off in 1968.

† The Open Championship was run by the Royal and Ancient Golf Club of Saint Andrews until 2004, when the R&A was formed to support golf around the world and run several championships, including the Open Championship.

‡ Note that this relationship is constantly changing through this book's writing in 2023 and may not be current when you read it. However, the question of this case study remains.

disapproval of LIV's funding source. Yet another, however, has to do with the nature of the competition itself. LIV tournaments are conducted over 54 holes of stroke play with no cut, and 20% of the prize pool goes to four-person teams, while most professional tournaments consist of 72 holes of completely individual stroke play where the field is cut approximately in half after 36 holes. Moreover, the tour has no clear way of having new players qualify and underperforming players relegated.

While as sports analysts we are not generally asked to deal with political or procedural concerns, we can develop analytical methods for ranking players or comparing competitions. How would you develop a new OWGR method for incorporating LIV tournament results into the rankings? Would it look like the USGA handicap method? Would it have a correction factor for the length of the tournaments? Would it be just the same as the current method? Discuss and defend your answers.

9.10 Exercises

1. Earlier in the chapter, we showed how to calculate strokes gained on a hole. How might you calculate strokes gained by Rory McIlroy on the rest of the field for a hole that day? Or for the round? (Hint: The answer is simpler than you might think.)
2. Using multiple linear regression and the data from earlier in this chapter, which strokes gained statistic is most important to predicting a golfer's OWGR?

For problems 3–7, we will use the 2019 Masters dataset `masters` given in the `ISAR` R package.

3. Compute histograms of the scores and facet by round.
4. Add the average score per round to the plots above as a reference. We will use this average per round in the next question.
5. Calculate strokes gained for each player round. Note that you will have to compute the average score per round and compare each player's score relative to that average.
6. Repeat question 4 using strokes gained.
7. Plot strokes gained (y) versus player score (x) by round. Do you find the resulting plot surprising? Why or why not?
8. How would you model pressure in professional golf? What would be the inputs and how would you identify the players who are affected the most, either positively or negatively, by pressure?
9. Visualize the clusters from the `cluster_strokes_gained` object defined earlier in the chapter.
10. Perform a four-cluster k-means clustering on the `df_clusters` data frame given earlier in this chapter. Visualize and interpret the clusters to the best of your ability.

Chapter 10

Sports Wagering and Daily Fantasy Sports

> To be successful in sports betting, you need three things: brains, guts, and money. If you are missing one of them, you're dead.
>
> —Charles K. McNeil

10.1 R Packages

We will use the following R packages in this chapter:

```
library(ISAR)
library(remotes)
library(dplyr)
library(janitor)
library(bettoR)
library(lpSolve)
library(scales)
library(ggplot2)
```

We also introduce the following new packages for this chapter:

```
library(bettoR) #functions for wagering operations and calculations
library(lpSolve) # solves linear, integer, and mixed integer programs
```

Note that `bettoR` can be installed from GitHub using the `remotes` package:

```
remotes::install_github("a-i-sports/bettoR")
```

10.2 If You Don't Know Anything about Sports Wagering

Sports wagering has likely existed since the beginning of athletic competitions. Some of the earliest mentions of sports wagering refer to the ancient Olympic Games in Greece. It is also widely suspected that some of those earliest Olympians may have been paid to not perform their best, thus altering the outcome of the events to the advantage of certain wagerers who were in the know. It is also well known that the Romans wagered feverishly on the outcome of chariot races and gladiator contests, and many other societies have since adopted sports wagering.

Today, people can wager on just about any type of sport. Football is the most wagered-upon sport in the US, while in the rest of the world, most bet on soccer and tennis. But not only major sports see wagering. Cricket, darts, and lacrosse are wagered upon. During the early days of the COVID-19 pandemic, table tennis matches in Russia were close to the only athletic competitions being held worldwide, and they were wagered upon aggressively in a world with very little to do but sit at home in quarantine. The US was no exception to this, with a 2018 US Supreme Court decision paving the way for legal gambling to expand across the US instead of simply Nevada. According to a Statista report at `https://www.statista.com/statistics/1126480/sports-betting-revenue-us/`, the size of the legal sports betting market in the US went from $430 million in 2018 to $7.56 billion in 2022 and is forecast to only keep growing* as sports betting becomes legal in more and

* In September 2023, $12 million was still being wagered in the state of Colorado alone on table tennis matches.

more jurisdictions. Moreover, the size of the underground/illegal betting market in the US is estimated to be 10 times the size of the legal market, though of course, no one knows for sure.

Sports wagering can be not only on individuals or teams but often on the outcomes of animals racing, such as horses and dogs.

In this chapter, we will cover the various types of sports wagers that can be made. We will discuss probabilities versus odds and converting between the two. We will also cover daily fantasy sports (DFS) and setting lineups in a separate subsection after the wagering section.

10.3 Sports Wagering and Morality

The authors of this text take no moral stance on sports wagering and attempt to present it as such. We do not try to promote or dissuade it any more or less than we might any other financial market. This market, in its simplest form, represents the "buying" or "selling" of a team or player rather than the buying or selling of stocks or bonds in the traditional financial market. The biggest difference between these markets and other financial markets is that there is no "buy and hold" strategy, as the "accounts" are settled each day at the conclusion of each sporting event. In that way, it is more like a financial options market, where the market settles each day. Like investing in any other financial product, we recommend these methods be applied wisely and only where legal.

10.4 Sports Wagering and Legality

The legality of sports wagering varies around the world. In the UK, for example, it is a largely open market where many companies can each serve as market makers, more commonly known as "bookies." In Finland, sports gambling is a regulated market with one market maker (Veikkaus) that is owned by the government. In other countries, wagering on sports is strictly illegal. Countries with Islamic backgrounds, such as Qatar, Brunei, and the UAE, are perhaps the most salient examples of nations banning gambling of all forms, and yet underground/illegal gambling exists even there despite the threat of strict penalties if caught.

In the United States, each of the 50 states and the District of Columbia has its own set of laws regarding sports betting. As of November 2023, 34 states and Washington, DC, have some form of legalized sports betting, and 2 more states have approved sports betting laws but do not expect to launch until 2024. At this time, the three most populous states (California, Texas, and Florida) do not yet have legalized sports betting, so it may not be quite as available (legally) to all as it appears. Utah and Hawaiʻi currently have no legal gambling (lotteries, casinos, horse racing, etc.) of any kind, and there is no reason to believe that they will allow it anytime soon.

Even in places where sports wagering is licensed and regulated, there continue to be illegal bookmakers. These bookmakers do virtually the same thing as the licensed bookmakers, except they do not advertise and likely do not pay taxes on their profits. Illegal bookmakers may also operate on credit, allowing people to make wagers over the phone and then settling the bets perhaps each week or each month or when one side has reached a limit of liability. These services are sometimes operated by organized crime figures or their affiliates and have a reputation for nefarious ways of collecting their debts.

10.5 Basics of Sports Wagering

In its most basic form, individuals can wager on the outcome of a match. For example, let's say that Roger Federer is playing a tennis match against Rafael Nadal. While both are highly skilled tennis players, a sports wagering market maker (often called a bookmaker, bookie, or sportsbook) calculates that Federer is likely to win this match 75% of the time. The sportsbook offers to accept bets on Federer as a 3-to-1 favorite (he will win three times for every loss). This means that if a bettor wanted to place a wager that Federer would win, they would have to risk \$3 in order to win \$1. These odds, or the market price, can be expressed in a variety of ways, which will be shown in detail later.

If a bettor wanted to wager that Nadal would win the match, it would make sense, then, that since Nadal is not as likely to win as Federer, the return should be greater. A completely fair market would then allow a bettor to win \$3 for every \$1 risked on Nadal to win. However, it is extremely rare to find a completely fair market, and it might be more likely that a bettor would win \$2.25 for every \$1 risked on Nadal to win.

10.6 The Role of the Bookmaker

Figure 10.1: A typical scene in a sportsbook.
Source: Baishampayan Ghose / CC BY-SA 2.0

Why the discrepancy between the sides of the market as mentioned in the previous section? This is essentially the fee that the bookmaker charges to provide the market service. This differential is called juice, vig, or vigorish. The wider the differential between the price on the two sides of the market, the more money the bookmaker stands to make.

Traditionally, the role of the bookmaker is to set the price of the market such that the outcome of the event does not matter and they will make the same amount of money regardless of the outcome. To use the previous example, the bookmaker would like to attract $123.08 of wagers on Nadal to win for every $300 that is attracted on Federer to win. If this happens, the bookmaker will win $23.08 no matter who wins:

```
#Federer Wins or Nadal Wins
federer_exposure = 300
nadal_exposure = 123.08
bookmaker_profit_federer_wins = nadal_exposure -
  (federer_exposure/3) #federer backers had to lay 3 to 1 odds
bookmaker_profit_nadal_wins = federer_exposure -
  (nadal_exposure * 2.25) # nadal backers receive 2.25 to 1 odds
cat("When Federer wins, the bookmaker profits",
    bookmaker_profit_federer_wins)
```

```
When Federer wins, the bookmaker profits 23.08
```

```
cat("When Nadal wins, the bookmaker profits",
    bookmaker_profit_nadal_wins)
```

```
When Nadal wins, the bookmaker profits 23.07
```

When a bookmaker starts to have more money attracted on one side of a market (e.g., Federer to win) than the odds might indicate, the bookmaker then has a liability and, as such, a vested interest in the outcome of the match. In the above example, let's say that the bookmaker takes $300 in wagers on Federer to win but only $50 on Nadal to win. If this happens, the bookmaker will keep $187.50 if Nadal wins but will lose $50 if Federer wins:

```
# Nadal Wins
300-(50*2.25)
```

```
[1] 187.5
```

```
# Federer Wins
50-(300/3)
```

```
[1] -50
```

The bookmaker, of course, cannot force people to bet on Nadal any more than a stock market maker can force people to buy a put option on Google stock instead of a call option. So how does the bookmaker avoid having financial exposure to the outcome, which is referred to as getting sided? Much like the stock market maker, the bookmaker changes the prices to make bets on Federer seem less attractive and bets on Nadal seem more attractive. The bookmaker might change the price to require people to risk $3.50 to win $1 if the bettors prefer Federer. At the same time, the bookmaker may now offer a return of $2.75 for every $1 risked on a wager for Nadal to win. This should cause the balance of money wagered to flow away from Federer and toward Nadal.

It is important to note that sports betting is unlike parimutuel betting on horses, where the odds for everyone change as the bets are placed up to the event. In sports betting, the odds that are presented at the time of the event are the odds for the person who made that bet. So in the above example, if a bettor placed a bet on

Federer at 3-to-1 odds, and Nadal twists his ankle in warm-ups and the odds change to Federer being a 10-to-1 favorite just before the match starts, that bettor would still receive payment at 3-to-1 odds.

In recent years, bookmakers have hired teams of analytics consultants, and now many are not just interested in balancing the market. They will have an opinion on the outcome of a match and may try to move the market prices in such a way that the market appears tilted more toward one outcome than it might appear to the general public. In essence, the bookmaker becomes like a bettor, gambling in his own casino. We mention this not so much to teach individuals how to be profitable bookmakers but rather to inform the reader about the contemporary state of events.

More recently, exchanges that more resemble equity markets have begun to appear in the sports betting world. In these exchanges, sometimes also called peer-to-peer betting, the exchanges attempt to match buyers and sellers of a particular market at the same price. To take the example above, an exchange might offer Federer at 3-to-1 odds and Nadal at the exact opposite, 1-to-3 odds. The winner of the bet would then pay a small amount as a commission so that the exchange operator could make a profit for operating the service. These exchanges also allow bettors to offer a wide variety of bets and prices and see if anyone is willing to take those bets.

10.7 Popular Types of Wagers

Moneyline

The simplest type of wager, which is just on one person or team to win an event against another person or team, is referred to as moneyline. The mythical tennis match mentioned above is a moneyline wager. Because two people or teams that are competing against each other are rarely equally matched and one person/team is generally perceived as being more likely to win, the prices on the matches are set to where the team who is more likely to win (the favorite) generally returns less than $1 for every $1 wagered, whereas the team less likely to win (the underdog) returns more than $1 for every $1 wagered. In the example above, Federer is the favorite and Nadal is the underdog.

Point Spread

Another way to equalize the differences between the favorites and the underdogs is to provide the underdog with a handicap. The favorite has to win by a certain number of points in order to win (cover) the point spread wager, whereas the underdog does not need to win the match—just lose by less than the handicap (also referred to as cover) for wagers on the underdog to be winners. Once the handicap is set, generally, the odds are the same whether a bettor chooses to wager on the favorite or the underdog.

For example, in the 2022 Super Bowl (championship game of American football), the Los Angeles Rams were the favorite, and most bookmakers required a bettor to risk $1.90 to win $1 if betting on the moneyline, whereas bettors who thought the Cincinnati Bengals would win the game would receive about $1.70 for every $1 risked on them to win. However, most bookmakers also established the Rams as a four-point favorite. This means that a bettor could bet on the Rams to win by more than four points and only have to risk $1.10 to win $1. Similarly, a bettor could choose the Bengals to win or lose by less than four points, but they would also have to risk $1.10 to win $1. This means that for every $11 the bookmaker attracted on the LA Rams -4, if he also attracted $11 on the Cincinnati Bengals +4, he would guarantee a profit of $1. If the Rams win, he would return the $11 to the Rams bettor plus their $10 profit while keeping the $11 from the Bengals bettor. The math is similar if the Bengals would win. The bookmaker would not want the Rams to win by exactly four points, as then all the point spread bets would be voided, the wagers returned to the bettors, and the bookmaker would earn zero profit.

The result of the game was that the Rams defeated the Bengals 23–20. This means that people who made moneyline wagers on the Rams were winners, but on the point spread, the Bengals were winners, as they only lost by three points.

Totals

The moneyline and point spread examples are what are called wagers on a side, as a bettor chooses one team or the other. Another popular type of bet is called betting on a total, or sometimes called an over/under bet. For a total bet, a bookmaker sets a total number of points that would be scored in the match, and then the bettor can wager on whether the actual total number of points scored is over or under than total. Usually, the amount risked versus the potential reward is similar to the point spread bet, where a bettor needs to risk $1.10 to win $1.00.

In the example of the 2022 Super Bowl, most bookmakers had set the total points scored at 48.5. In the actual game, only 43 points were scored (23 + 20). So people who wagered on under 48.5 won, while those who wagered on over 48.5 lost their wagers.

On both totals and point spread wagers, it is possible that the bookmaker could get sided, or attract more bets on one outcome of a match than desired and have an unbalanced market. To avoid this, a bookmaker will adjust the handicap (or the total) if necessary to inspire the market to move in one direction or another. For example, at first, the Los Angeles Rams were 4.5-point favorites, but initial wagers came in more heavily on the Cincinnati Bengals, so the market price moved to make the Rams only a 4-point favorite (and as such, encourage more wagers on the Rams).

Propositions

Propositions (prop bets) are bets that are offered on something smaller than the general outcome of the game. These might include scenarios such as will a hitter hit a home run, or will a pitcher achieve a certain number of strikeouts in baseball, or will a player have over or under a certain number of rushing yards in football, or will a goal be scored in the first 10 minutes of a hockey game? These bets tend to be offered at higher levels of juice to the player but allow for literally hundreds of different bets to be placed on a single contest. These first became popular in the Super Bowl to entice bettors to wager on many possible different outcomes (and thus increase the amount of money wagered on the game), but with the advent of mobile betting from your phone, these are offered by some online sportsbooks on virtually every game.

Live Wagering

All the previous examples are for wagers placed before the match starts, which is how wagering has taken place for thousands of years. In the 21st century, the advent of the Internet and computing technology has allowed for wagering to occur during a particular competition. Market prices can be updated every few seconds based on the outcome of a particular play or point and how it might affect the side or the total in that competition. An even quicker version of live wagering can allow a bettor to wager on the outcome of a particular play. This includes whether a player makes a free throw, a golfer makes a putt, or a kicker makes a field goal.

The market for live wagering is virtually infinite. It can be difficult for bookmakers to offer fair and accurate prices, and as such, these are often more heavily juiced than pregame bets, but it allows for revenue to be earned by the bookmaker throughout a contest. It also offers bettors opportunities to increase the amount they bet on an outcome or perhaps to hedge their bets based on in-game injuries.

10.8 Using Analytics to Set Market Prices

Many factors go into setting the market price in a contest. While, of course, these would include some rating of each team's perceived ability in a vacuum, there are additional factors that affect the predicted outcome of a particular contest. In a team sport like football, it could be which team is the home team, the surface of the field, the weather, the crew refereeing the game, any current injured players, the time of year, the amount of rest since the team previously played, staff changes, and results of previous contests between the teams. In an individual sport like tennis, it could be the weather, the surface, the conditions (indoor/outdoor), recent form, left-handers versus right-handers, number of matches played recently, perceived crowd support, or even travel and rest days.

As mentioned earlier, bookmakers can seek to guarantee profits by setting the market prices such that equal financial obligations fall on both sides. However, a bookmaker may also try to take advantage of market tendencies to maximize profits. For example, studies have shown that in sports like football and basketball, the betting public (otherwise known as squares) tends to prefer favorites to underdogs and over to under in totals bets. This provides opportunities for the bookmakers to adjust the prices in a way that might attract more wagers on the favorites than their predictive models might indicate, and similarly for the over in a totals wager than the under, allowing for the potential for profit maximization.

Bookmakers employing the above strategy will be held in check by savvy professional bettors (otherwise known as sharps) who are aware of these tendencies of the public, spend many hours building their own predictive models, and tend to place much larger wagers than your average square. Bookmakers are aware of the sharps and will place limits on the amounts wagered by an individual in order to limit exposure to sharp money. In more extreme cases, some bookmakers will even refuse to take wagers from the sharpest of sharps.

Much of the analytic modeling in predicting the outcomes of games and then using them to set the market prices derives from other financial markets. For example, Cantor Fitzgerald, a large financial services firm that was deeply affected by the 9/11 attacks on the World Trade Center in New York, started a division of the company called Cantor Gaming in the early 20th century to provide market prices to Las Vegas casinos for live wagering markets, among other products and services. While it was subsequently sold in 2020 to rival bookmaker William Hill, these models and others are continuously refined to take advantage of real and perceived market inefficiencies, much as a Wall Street portfolio manager adjusts her trading strategies.

10.9 Displaying and Calculating Market Prices

The prices on wagers are displayed in many different formats around the world, but they can be converted.

American Odds

American odds are displayed in a format of either a positive or negative number. A negative number would indicate how much money a bettor would have to wager to win \$100. A positive number indicates an underdog and shows how much money a bettor would win if he risked \$100. In the Super Bowl example, the Rams would have been listed as a –190 favorite, meaning that a bettor would have to risk \$190 to win \$100 on the moneyline. The Bengals would have been listed as +170, meaning that a \$100 bet would have won the bettor \$170.

Decimal Odds

Decimal odds are used in most of the world outside of the US. They are given in a format where a bettor can multiply the wager by the number listed to show how much would be returned to the bettor if he wins his bet. This would include the original wager plus the amount won. A bettor who wagers \$100 on a team at 1.91 decimal odds and wins would get back \$191 if he wins (100×1.91) and lose his wager of \$100 if he loses.

Fractional Odds

Fractional odds are seen primarily in the UK and other commonwealth countries and also in horse and dog racing. They are displayed as a ratio of the amount won to the amount risked, usually reduced as far as possible as a fraction. So in the previous examples in the point spread and the totals wagers, where a bettor must risk \$1.10 to win \$1.00, this would be expressed as 10/11 in fractional terms.

Probabilities

Probabilities are expressed as an implied probability of the outcome happening. This is usually calculated as the amount risked divided by the amount risked plus the amount won. So in the previous example in fractional odds, the probability would be $1.10/(1.10 + 1.00) = 52.38\%$. The implied probability, of course, is not the actual probability, as there is juice built in for the bookmaker. An additional calculation can be done to see the real probability when the juice is removed.

Table 10.1 shows the equivalent odds for the hypothetical tennis match mentioned throughout this chapter.

Of course, we can also use R and functions in the `bettoR` package to convert one odds format to another. The `implied_odds()` function starts with a probability and gives you the odds in all other formats:

Table 10.1: Hypothetical tennis match odds in the various formats discussed in this chapter

Winner	American	Decimal	Fractional	Probability
Federer	-300	1.33	0.3333333	0.75
Nadal	+225	3.25	2.2500000	0.30

```
implied_odds(0.75, type = "all")
```

```
  Decimal American Fraction Implied.Probability
1  1.3333     -300      1/3                0.75
```

You may notice that the probabilities add up to more than 1, which usually would violate every rule that we know about statistics. The reason for this is that the probabilities also include the bookmaker's implied commission for providing the market, which we can calculate. In this case, this commission is referred to as the hold:

```
hold_calc(-110, -110)
```

```
[1] 0.04545455
```

This implies that if a sportsbook were to take two $110 bets on this market, one bet on Team A and a similar bet on Team B, both at -110 odds, the bookmaker's commission would be 4.545%. This is the total amount of the wagers (220) less the amount paid back (100 winnings + 110 posted by the winning bettor) all divided by the amount of the wagers taken (220), or 10/220 = 0.045.

10.10 Straight Wagers versus Parlays

All the wagers we have mentioned previously are called straight wagers. This means that the wager is graded as a win or a loss based on the outcome of a single event, like a tennis match or a football game. However, another type of wager with a higher payoff, albeit with a larger chance of losing, is called a parlay. In a parlay, two or more outcomes are combined into a single wager. For the bettor to win the parlay, she must correctly predict the outcome of both events; otherwise, it will be judged as a loss.

An example of a parlay bet that we now know would have been successful with the benefit of hindsight would be for the Los Angeles Rams to win the 2022 Super Bowl *and* for the total points of the game to be under 48.5 points. We know that a bettor could have wagered $10 on the outcome of each event, and he would have won both bets to win a total of $14.40:

```
side_wager = 10
side_multiplier = 1.53 # -190 in decimal odds
total_wager = 10
total_multiplier = 1.91 #-110 in decimal odds
payout = side_wager * side_multiplier + total_wager * total_multiplier
profit = payout - side_wager - total_wager
profit
```

```
[1] 14.4
```

However, if he had instead taken that $20 and placed a parlay wager to win both of these events, he would have profited much more, a total of $38.45. The amount of a parlay payout is the combination of both events happening, so we need to multiply the probabilities together to find the outcome of two uncorrelated events. The most straightforward way to calculate the fair parlay odds is a four-step process:

1. Make sure odds are converted to decimal odds:

```
convert_odds(-190)
```

```
  Decimal American Fraction Implied_Probability
1  1.5263     -190    10/19           0.6551724
```

```
convert_odds(-110)
```

```
  Decimal American Fraction Implied_Probability
1  1.9091     -110    10/11           0.5238095
```

2. Multiply the decimal odds together to get the parlay multiplier:

```
convert_odds(-190)[1]*convert_odds(-110)[1]
```

```
   Decimal
1 2.913859
```

3. Multiply the parlay multiplier by the amount wagered:

```
convert_odds(-190)[1]*convert_odds(-110)[1]*20
```

```
   Decimal
1 58.27719
```

4. Subtract the original amount to get the payout:

```
convert_odds(-190)[1]*convert_odds(-110)[1]*20 - 20
```

```
   Decimal
1 38.27719
```

So this $20 parlay wager had American odds of +192 ((2.9223 – 1) × 100), which resulted in a profit of $38.45. However, if either of these events did not happen, the bettor would lose his entire $20 wager, whereas if he wagered on them as two separate $10 events, he would have received a partial payout and only lost his entire stake if he lost both wagers.

In general, parlays are much more profitable to the bookmaker due to these combined odds, and much of a Nevada sportsbook's profits can be attributed to parlays.

10.11 Research Block: Are Sports Wagering Markets Efficient?

Much of modern finance and its applications rely on the efficient market hypothesis (EMH). Closely tied with Eugene Fama based on his 1970 review of prediction literature (available at `https://onlinelibrary.wiley.com/doi/abs/10.1111/j.1540-6261.1970.tb00518.x`), EMH states that one cannot make abnormal profits, or "beat the market," consistently over time. A market is thus efficient when the price of a financial instrument reflects all available information and the information is available to all market participants who are all able to instantly absorb this information and use it in their investment strategies. EMH holds that an individual might be able to beat the market return for a day, week, month, or year, but eventually, all participants will regress to the market average returns.

As mentioned at the outset of this chapter, the authors view legalized and regulated sports wagering markets as another financial market. Given that the markets settle at the end of each event and the bookmakers charge the vig as a commission for offering wagers, if sports markets are truly efficient, then bettors should, on average, achieve a commission-free return on investment (ROI) of zero, and then the market participants should all lose the vig over time. For example, if the point spread NFL wagering market is efficient, if a bettor wagers on 100 NFL games and wagers $110 on each of them at the usual –110 point spread market price, he should win 50 of those games and, as such, win $5,000 on the games he wins and lose $5,500 on the games he loses, meaning that he should lose $500 for the $11,000 wagered. There are short-term variations, but an efficient market would then create a –4.54% return (–500/11000). But are the markets truly efficient?

In their 1997 *Journal of Finance* paper "Testing Market Efficiency: Evidence from the NFL Sports Betting Market," available at `https://www.jstor.org/stable/2329455`, authors Philip Gray and Stephen Gray examine whether the betting market is efficient. They gathered data on over 4,200 NFL games played from 1976 to 1994, along with the closing line (the number of points that the favorite would have to beat their opponent by in order to win the game when the game kicked off) for each game. The examined several strategies that would be relatively naïve by today's analytics and yet discovered that there were several market inefficiencies that also worked when tested against games not included in the sample. For example, they found that by simply wagering on every home team who was an underdog (i.e., had points added to their total for the purpose of the wager), a bettor could have earned a return of approximately +4.5%. However, they also found that the success of many of these strategies dissipated over time, presumably as more bettors learned about them and more bookmakers adjusted their prices to give the home team underdog less of a handicap than in past years.

So is the NFL point spread betting market efficient? Many professional gamblers will attest that it is the toughest market to consistently beat. As the bettors build their own models, which include extraneous factors like wind speed and direction, the bookmakers also incorporate more and more information when setting their market prices. An aspiring bettor would do well to focus on different markets than the NFL point spread.

10.12 Kelly Criterion

When investing in traditional financial markets, participants often seek to hold a diversified portfolio of assets. These might include stocks, bonds, real estate—and today, even cryptocurrency. Within each category, they might hold several different types of stocks (such as tech companies, energy, and banks) or real estate (commercial office space, warehouses, apartment complexes, and single-family houses, for example). The idea behind holding these different assets or different asset classes is to try to reduce the risk of the portfolio's value crashing because of an issue in one company (e.g., Enron) or one market sector (such as Russian stocks in March 2022) through diversification. While this limits the possibilities for extreme profits, it also limits the exposure to extreme losses.

In sports wagering, bettors also have to examine these criteria. A bettor's bankroll (the total amount of money available to wager) could be doubled or more by wagering it all on one game and winning. However, the bettor also could lose all of her money by wagering it on one game and losing. The rational bettor would never wager all of her bankroll on any one sporting event, but then is also faced with the problem of how much money to risk on each wager while trying to keep the likelihood of several bad wagers in a row bankrupting her to a minimum.

No stock picker is going to be correct 100% of the time, and no one is going to be able to predict sporting events correctly 100% of the time. If someone could predict them correctly 90% or 80% or even 70% of the time, no sportsbook would take the person's wagers. Billy Walters, widely regarded as the best and most successful sports wagerer in the world, was only correct about 57% of the time (or 4 out of 7 times). If you are betting football and basketball games on the point spread, where generally the odds on either team are –110, you need to be correct 52.38% of the time (11 times out of 21) to break even. Given these odds, professional sports wagerers seek to be correct in the 54%–56% range. The nature in which random events occur also ensures that in the long run, wagerers with a 55% success rate will also have periods of time where they perform well above 55% and well below 55%. While performing above 55% may be great, performing below it for longer periods of time creates a risk of ruin, something the mathematician J. L. Kelly models. He also provides advice about how to minimize the risk of ruin while maximizing returns.

The formula for the Kelly criterion is

$$F = p - \frac{q}{b} = p - \frac{1-p}{b},$$

where F is the fraction of your bankroll to wager, p is the probability of a win, q is the probability of a loss (1 - probability of a win), and b is the proportion of the bet gained by winning (also equal to the decimal odds on a bet – 1).

So if you have a $100 bankroll and someone is offering you even money bets (e.g., American odds +100 or decimal odds of 2.00) on flipping a coin, and you know the coin is weighted such that it lands on heads 60% of the time, how much should you wager?

```
0.6 - (0.4/1)
```

```
[1] 0.2
```

The chances that you would go bankrupt on your first five wagers in this case are 0.4^5, or approximately 1% of the time. Your average outcome would be that you would win three of these flips and lose two of them, so your bankroll would increase on average by 20%.

It is unlikely that anyone would find this example in the real world, so let's apply this math to the point spread sports wagering examples mentioned earlier. Let's say that we believe we will win a particular point spread wager 55% of the time, and the odds being offered are −110 American (1.91 decimal). What percentage of your bankroll should you wager on that contest?

```
0.55 - (0.45/0.91)
```

```
[1] 0.05549451
```

The `bettoR` package also includes a function, `kelly()`, which allows us to calculate these percentages:

```
kelly(win_prob = 0.55, odds = -110, type = "us")
```

```
[1] 0.055
```

```
kelly(win_prob = 0.55, odds = 1.91, type = "dec")
```

```
[1] 0.0555
```

The difficulty here is that we don't know with absolute certainty our probability of picking correctly in the short term or the long term. We may believe it is 55%, but if everyone could pick 55% of the time correctly, then the market makers would be out of business. What if it were a 54% chance of success?

```
kelly(win_prob = 0.54, odds = -110, type = "us")
```

```
[1] 0.034
```

What about 53% or 52%? The negative percentage associated with the 0.52 win probability tells us not to bet!

```
kelly(win_prob = 0.53, odds = -110, type = "us")
```

```
[1] 0.013
```

```
kelly(win_prob = 0.52, odds = -110, type = "us")
```

```
[1] -0.008
```

Because a bettor cannot wager a negative amount, he should not bet anything. This makes sense, since we know that a bettor must be successful 52.38% of the time to break even in a −110 market.

There is a much longer proof of the Kelly criterion, but it is beyond the scope of this text.

10.13 Case Study: Stevin Smith, Tim Donaghy, and the Issues of Sports Fixing

In financial markets, one concern is often if the market is fixed. By a market being fixed, we mean that some market participants have access to information that is not generally public, and as such, the market price does not accurately reflect all the information. In stocks and options markets, we generally refer to this as inside information. Trading on inside information is illegal in the US and most markets around the world, and people can go to prison and pay large fines for acting on that information.

As another financial market, the sports wagering industry is not immune to these effects either. While there is nothing generally illegal about placing wagers knowing that a player might be injured or something similar, it is typically forbidden for players, coaches, and other employees to place wagers within their own sport and also to communicate such information to others on the outside who may then participate in wagering markets. The most famous recent case of gambling by players in these markets in the US is with the baseball player Pete Rose, who was permanently banned from the sport in 1989 when it was found he had placed bets on baseball.

Another danger in these markets is when a player might intentionally not perform at his or her best in order to affect the outcome of a game. If a bettor knows in advance that a player is intentionally not going to be performing optimally, the bettor stands to make abnormal profits. In an individual sport like tennis, it could be much easier for a player to intentionally lose a match (throwing the match) or to win by less than the game spread or lose by more than the game spread (point shaving). In a team sport, it can be a bit more difficult to have one player directly affect the outcome of a game, as a coach could decide whether or not to have a player play in the game or a player may not be in enough of a position to affect the outcome of scoring. Other cases you may have heard of include the 1919 "Black Sox" scandal in Major League Baseball (a subplot of the 1989 movie *Field of Dreams* starring Kevin Costner) and the Boston College basketball team in 1978–79. Most recently, University of Alabama baseball coach Brad Bohannon was fired in May 2023 after it was found he had ties to suspicious gamblers and fed information about an injury to a starting pitcher for a game against LSU.

If a bettor could pay a player to throw a game, she can make abnormal profits. If a bettor pays a tennis player $5,000 to not win a match but can then profit $50,000 in the wagering markets by betting on that compromised player to lose and be virtually assured that the person will indeed lose, then there is great temptation to try to find a player who could be compromised. While this is illegal in most locales for both the player and the bettor, the payoff can be great if the player and bettor can get away with fixing that match.

Currently, in the most popular professional sports in America—such as football, baseball, basketball, and hockey—it is almost impossible to fix a game by compromising a player. The reason is not morality or law enforcement but likely simple economics. The salaries have gotten so high that the bettor could never pay the player enough money to throw a game and still be able to wager enough money to make an abnormal profit.

Table 10.2: A survey of salaries in the MLB, NFL, NBA, and NHL

Sport	Maximum salary	Average salary	Minimum salary
MLB (2023)	$43.33M	$4.9M	$720K
NFL (2023)	$55M	$3.3M	$750K
NBA (2023–24)	$51.9M	$10.28M	$1.12M
NHL (2023–24)	$16.5M	$3.49M	$775K

Given the salaries of players today, it is hard to believe that a player would jeopardize his criminal status and professional career for a $5,000 or $10,000 payout from a bettor. If a bettor were to pay a player $500,000 to throw a game, that might be tempting, but it is unlikely that the bettor would be able to bet enough money on the game to make a profit, and certainly that amount of money coming in would raise suspicions that something is likely wrong with this market, and market makers and law enforcement would then investigate. But there are other potential weak points in the market.

Referees are paid far less than players, and they too have the ability to affect the outcomes of games. While it may be obvious if a particular referee is biased toward one team in getting that team to win, less obvious could be totals bets. For example, in basketball, the more fouls that are called by a referee, the more points will be scored on free throws and the less tight defense will be played, which will then cause more points to be scored in the normal course of the game. If a referee is calling many fouls but calls them equally on both teams, it may not appear that the game is fixed for one team to win, but a bettor who bets on the over in the total bet with a referee who is going to call an abnormal number of fouls would be able to profit.

Tim Donaghy was an NBA referee from 1994 to 2007. During those 13 seasons, he refereed approximately 60 games per year and also officiated a total of 20 playoff games during that time. However, Donaghy himself had a gambling problem and was alleged to have bet tens of thousands of dollars on NBA games from 2005 to 2007 in an effort to get out of debt. Donaghy also admitted to having been paid $30,000 by organized crime affiliates to pass them information about players' physical conditions and game situations. He was found guilty of participating in the gambling scheme and sentenced to 15 months in prison and three years of probation following the prison term. While he was the one convicted, he also claimed (but never proved) that several other referees had conspired to fix games because it was in the interest of the NBA to fix them, such as to extend playoff series or ensure that teams in larger media markets would win games and thus make the NBA more money.

While the players in professional sports likely make too much money to be corrupted by gamblers, collegiate sports are a different story. In comparison to the millions of dollars paid to professional athletes, intercollegiate athletes receive only a free college education and meal and travel expense reimbursement* for their participation in representing their schools on the athletic field. The annual men's college basketball 68-team single-elimination tournament in the spring, colloquially known as March Madness, is the second-biggest gambling event in the US behind only the Super Bowl. Over $16 billion was bet legally on the tournament in 2021, and much more was wagered illegally. Many millions of dollars are bet on an average Saturday during the college basketball season. In collegiate sports, football and basketball get the most betting action, but football is much more difficult to fix, given the number of players involved. With less betting action, it also becomes more difficult to fix (a single large attempted bet was enough to identify the aforementioned Alabama baseball issue). Combine the relative lack of player remuneration with the amount of money wagered, and you have the opportunity for a player to be compromised.

Stevin Smith was such a player. From 1991 to 1994, he was a point guard for the Arizona State University (ASU) basketball team. He was a two-time All-Pac-10 selection and, as of 2023, still holds the school record for three-point shots attempted and three-point shots made and shares the school record for steals. However, during his senior year, he and fellow player Isaac Burton agreed to a point shaving scheme with a campus bookmaker, Benny Silman, to whom he initially owed gambling debts from betting on other sports. He pled guilty and admitted to accepting $20,000 in bribes while conspiring to shave points in a game versus Oregon State and then more bribes for shaving points in three more games in the 1993–94 season and served a year in prison. The scheme cost him any real chance to play in the NBA, and he went undrafted. He played largely overseas for 14 years, playing only eight games in his career at the NBA level.

Smith's scheme was largely uncovered by the Las Vegas bookmakers due to highly unusual activity around the ASU-Washington game on March 5, 1994. As often happens around college campuses, the rumor mill was running wild, and this time it was about ASU men's basketball games being fixed. So many people around the ASU campus and in criminal syndicates went to Las Vegas with the information about the probability of a compromised player being in the game that the market price changed 42 times, starting with ASU as a 10-point favorite over Washington when the market opened but only a 1.5-point favorite when the game tipped off. The game would have normally attracted about $50,000 in action but had over $1 million bet on Washington. The Las Vegas bookmakers alerted the FBI, and the ASU coach was notified at halftime that the FBI and the Pac-10 Conference were looking into the game. Smith had an explosive performance in the second half, and ASU's lead went from 2 at halftime to 18 at game's end. The people who were in on the scheme ultimately lost over $1 million.

Given these possibilities for sports being fixed, consider the following discussion questions:

1. What is the likelihood that professional sports are fixed today? Which professional sports are most susceptible to being fixed?
2. How would you use analytics to ensure that a game is not fixed?
3. How do you compare the sports markets to financial markets in terms of their fairness?
4. What have individual states done to try to prevent games from being fixed? Are these methods effective? What else can be done?

10.14 Daily Fantasy Sports

Another type of contest that became popular in the 1970s and 1980s was fantasy sports, which allowed fans to act like their own general managers of a team. A group of people would get together at the beginning of a season, choose players for their team, and compete against one another throughout the year by measuring the accumulation of various statistics by each player. The games evolved throughout the year to allow for head-to-head competitions instead of simple statistical accumulations. The most tedious part of these competitions was keeping score, as it involved copying statistics from newspapers and tabulating them without error. In the

* In 2021, rules were changed in US collegiate athletics to allow the athletes to profit from their name, image, and likeness (NIL). Though they are not paid directly by their schools, some players are reported to be signing endorsement deals for greater than $1 million.

1990s, Internet services evolved that hosted fantasy leagues and tabulated scores, either for a fee or free, but they made the process much easier.

Often these friendly competitions among friends would include an entry fee, which was redistributed to the winners. For example, 10 people in a league might each pay $25 as an entry fee, and the winner of the league might get $125, the second-place finisher $75, and the third-place finisher $50. In some circles, this was seen as tantamount to gambling, but in many others, it was just seen as fun. When the United States Congress in 2006 passed the Unlawful Internet Gambling Enforcement Act (UIGEA), a law designed to combat online poker and sports wagering sites, fantasy sports were specifically exempted from the UIGEA.

While the carve out from UIGEA was designed for season-long fantasy contests, many of which were sponsored by media outlets and even the leagues themselves, by the early 2010s, many people desired quicker action. The idea of a fantasy contest that was settled in one day rather than one season was born, and the sites that sponsored these daily fantasy sports (DFS) contests became extremely popular and competitive. To get an idea of the popularity and ferocity of competition, on ESPN, the largest sports television network in the US, before the 2015 NFL season, an ad for either DraftKings or FanDuel, the two biggest sites for DFS contests, ran approximately every 90 seconds.

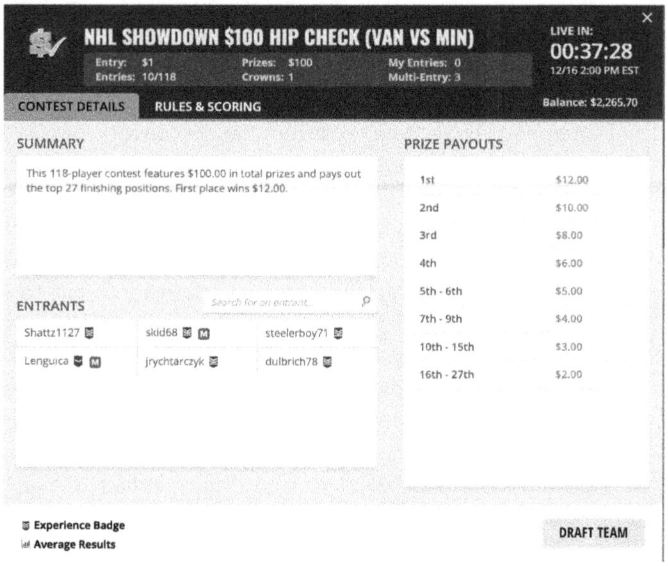

With direct sports wagering now more available and more popular, DFS is not quite as popular as before but still has quite the following in addition to season-long contests. As you might imagine since we are talking about it in this book, analytics plays a huge role in choosing an optimal lineup to give a player the best chance of winning the matchup. The sites know this and, to some extent, support it. It is a balancing act for them to welcome new players and make them feel comfortable while at the same time making it easier for big-volume players to participate as much as possible, as the fees they pay with each entry into a DFS contest generate revenue for the sites.

One way the sites support analytics is to make the data for each day, league, and contest downloadable. Each player on a team that is drafted has a particular fantasy salary for that day, and each lineup submitted has a maximum salary that is allowed, called the salary cap. This is to make the contests more challenging than just selecting the six best goal scorers in a DFS hockey contest and instead force the player to make choices when constructing his team between player skill and maximum salary.

Lineup Construction

Ultimately, DFS lineup construction is an optimization problem. At a high level, optimization is a mathematical technique of (usually)

1. maximizing or minimizing the value of a particular *objective* function, based on
2. *decision variables* that the person or computer solving the problem may affect, subject to
3. *constraints*, or limits, that a decision-maker must abide by.

To apply this to DFS, we might say that the objective function is to maximize the number of fantasy points scored by the team, and the decision variables are which players to select, subject to the constraints of not exceeding the team salary cap. Each sport requires additional roster considerations such as a maximum or minimum number of players at each position or who play for a particular team in real life.

Our first example involves a showdown contest on DraftKings. We use a showdown because it is one of the most basic contests, or optimization problems, on the DraftKings platform. The contest involves choosing six players from the two actual teams that are competing in a real-life game, subject to the following constraints: we can only spend, at most, $50,000 on the six players and we must select at least one player from each of the two teams. Skaters and goalies will accumulate points based on the distributions given in table 10.3 and table 10.4, respectively. In addition, we will designate one player as the captain, and they will accumulate points at a rate of 1.5 times the normal rate, and their salary is 50% higher than their noncaptain salary.

Table 10.4: DraftKings points (goalies) for an NHL showdown game

Statistics	Points
Win	4.0
Save	0.5
Goal allowed	-1.0
Shutout	4.0

Table 10.3: DraftKings points (skaters) for an NHL showdown game

Statistics	Points
Goal	8.0
Assist	5.0
Shot on goal	2.0
Blocked shot	1.1
Shorthanded goal	2.0
Face-off win	0.2
Shootout goal	1.5
Hat trick	3.0

To make this example more concrete, we examine a hockey showdown and, in particular, the data downloaded from DraftKings for Game 7 of the 2022 NHL playoffs between the New York Rangers and the Carolina Hurricanes. The dataset is given in the `ISAR` package and is named `dk_nyr_car`. We will ignore the `Captain` position in this initial solution. We will refer to this as the simplified showdown, and later we will see what happens when we introduce the captain position and the full showdown problem:

```
df <- dk_nyr_car |>
  filter(roster_position == "FLEX") #be sure we can include any player
```

Objective Function

We will define the objective to calculate the average points per game by reading those past data values from the data frame, and later we will set that to a maximum. The average points per game may not be a winning strategy in DFS, and we are only using it to illustrate the optimization problem. A professional DFS player will likely spend a lot of time building models to predict each player's expected points in order to use it as their objective function. We denote the objective function in R as `obj`:

```
obj <- df$avg_points_per_game
```

Constraints: Lineups, Salary, Teams

There are several constraints that we will implement. We will enter them in the form of left-hand side (`cons`), comparison operator (`dir`), and right-hand side (`rhs`). The left-hand side will be the variable being constrained, and the right-hand side will be the value for that constraint.

1. We need to select exactly six players.
2. Salary is contained in `df$Salary`.
3. We need players from both teams.

In R, we do this as follows.

Left-Hand Side

The following code will create a coefficient matrix. Note that each line represents the coefficients of our constraint inequalities. It helps to inspect this matrix after defining it in R so that you understand each line in the matrix.

```
cons <- rbind(rep(1, nrow(df)),                       # player constraint
              df$salary,                              # salary constraint
              t(model.matrix(~ team_abbrev + 0, df))) # team constraints
cons[1:4, 1:8] # to inspect the matrix
```

```
                    1     2     3     4     5     6     7    8
                    1     1     1     1     1     1     1    1
                10800 10600 10600 10600 10400 10200 10200 9800
team_abbrevCAR      1     1     1     1     0     0     0    0
team_abbrevNYR      0     0     0     0     1     1     1    1
```

Direction

The `dir` vector represents the direction of each of our constraints. They are typically strings of the form >=, =, and <=. Here we create a vector of four items, and we list them in the same order as we listed the constraints. For example, our player constraint is to have exactly six (=) players, and we cannot spend more (<=) our salary cap, and we have to have at least (>=) one player from each team:

```
dir <- c("=", "<=", ">=", ">=")
```

Right-Hand Side

The `rhs` object contains the bounds on these constraints:

```
rhs <- c(6, 50000, 1, 1)
```

Solution

We will use the `lp()` function from the `lpSolve` package. This allows us to solve the optimization problem as a linear program, which has objectives, decision variables, and constraints. We will use the `max` argument to tell it that we want to maximize the value of the objective, and the decision variables are whether or not to include a player in our solution set. The `all.bin = TRUE` argument tells `lpSolve` that our solution must be binary, or that we can't select 0.8 of one player and 0.2 of another player; we have to include a player or exclude that player entirely.

```
result <- lpSolve::lp("max", obj, cons, dir, rhs, all.bin = TRUE)
result
```

```
Success: the objective function is 94.71
```

How do we identify the actual players that make up our team?

```
team <- df[which(result$solution == 1), ] |>
  select(name, position, salary, team_abbrev)
team
```

```
                 name position salary team_abbrev
4  Frederik Andersen        G  10600         CAR
5     Igor Shesterkin        G  10400         NYR
7       Keith Kinkaid        G  10200         NYR
11      Chris Kreider       LW   9000         NYR
37          Alex Lyon        G   5000         CAR
83        Jack Drury        C   2000         CAR
```

While this is a valid solution for the model within the constraints we specified, upon examination, there are a few problems. First of all, we probably don't want multiple goalies, particularly goalies from the same team, as it is likely that one of them will actually earn zero points and will sit on the bench the entire game. Let's add two more constraints to choose at most one goalie per team and revise the solution:

```
teams_mat <- t(model.matrix(~ team_abbrev + 0, df))
goalies <- ifelse(df$position == "G", 1, 0)
teams_goalies <- t(goalies * t(teams_mat))

cons_tmp <- rbind(cons, teams_goalies)
dir_tmp <- c(dir, "<=", "<=")
rhs_tmp <- c(rhs, 1, 1)
result <- lp("max", obj, cons_tmp, dir_tmp, rhs_tmp, all.bin = TRUE)
team <- df[which(result$solution == 1), ] |>
  select(name, position, salary, team_abbrev, avg_points_per_game)
team
```

```
                name position salary team_abbrev avg_points_per_game
4  Frederik Andersen        G  10600         CAR               15.31
7      Keith Kinkaid        G  10200         NYR               19.30
```

```
9          Adam Fox     D  9400    NYR     12.14
11     Chris Kreider   LW  9000    NYR     13.04
12    Artemi Panarin   LW  8600    NYR     11.84
83        Jack Drury    C  2000    CAR     14.30
```

Does this solution spend all of our money?

```
sum(team$salary)
```

```
[1] 49800
```

Interestingly enough, it does not, and this is not a problem at all. It meets the constraint of being under the salary cap. There is still a problem with this solution, though. Upon further inspection, we see that the proposed solution includes both teams' backup goalies, neither of which are likely to actually play. A more realistic solution would be to filter out the nonstarting goalies. The starters for this game were Antti Raanta and Igor Shesterkin:

```
df_new <- df |>
  filter(position != "G" | name %in% c("Antti Raanta", "Igor Shesterkin"))
obj <- df_new$avg_points_per_game
cons <- rbind(rep(1, nrow(df_new)), # player constraints
              df_new$salary, # salary constraints
              t(model.matrix(~ team_abbrev + 0, df_new))) # team constraints
dir <- c("=", "<=", ">=", ">=")
rhs <- c(6, 50000, 1, 1)
result <- lp("max", obj, cons, dir, rhs, all.bin = TRUE)
team <- df_new[which(result$solution == 1), ] |>
    select(name, position, salary, team_abbrev, avg_points_per_game)
team
```

```
              name position salary team_abbrev avg_points_per_game
1     Antti Raanta        G  10800         CAR               12.70
2  Igor Shesterkin        G  10400         NYR               18.61
3    Mika Zibanejad        C   9800         NYR               12.16
6    Chris Kreider       LW   9000         NYR               13.04
69      Jack Drury        C   2000         CAR               14.30
74   Anthony Greco       RW   2000         NYR               11.80
```

So while the math is correct, we should say that this solution is by no means a guarantee to win a game. It is a very simple strategy and is highly exploitable by professional DFS players. In fact, we would never advocate for using two goalies in one of these games. We generally find a host of solutions once we have added all constraints—for example, use a single goalie, stack lines, and so on. So the questions remain: How can we find the next best? And the next? Or the top 100? Update our constraints!

```
results <- data.frame(P1 = rep(NA, 100),
                      P2 = rep(NA, 100),
                      P3 = rep(NA, 100),
                      P4 = rep(NA, 100),
                      P5 = rep(NA, 100),
                      P6 = rep(NA, 100),
                      points = rep(NA, 100),
                      salary = rep(NA, 100))
results[1, ] <- c(team$name, sum(team$avg_points_per_game), sum(team$salary))
for (i in 1:99){ ## 99 will give us 100 total teams
  cons <- rbind(cons,
                result$solution)
  dir <- c(dir, "<=")
  rhs <- c(rhs, 5)
  result <- lp("max", obj, cons, dir, rhs, all.bin = TRUE)
  team <- df_new[which(result$solution == 1), ]
  results[i+1, ] <- c(team$name, sum(team$avg_points_per_game), sum(team$salary))
}
```

Actual Showdown

Now that we know how to implement and solve an optimization problem in R, consider the full showdown game. For this problem, we need to add in a constraint to select a team captain and adjust the captain's salary and expected points accordingly. The mechanics are essentially the same once we add in this information:

```
df <- dk_nyr_car |>
  filter(position != "G" | name %in% c("Antti Raanta", "Igor Shesterkin")) |>
  mutate(new_pts = ifelse(roster_position == "CPT",
                          1.5*avg_points_per_game,
                          avg_points_per_game))
obj <- df$new_pts

players_con <- t(model.matrix(~ name + 0, df))
cons <- rbind(rep(1, nrow(df)), #6 players
              df$salary, #<= 50000
              t(model.matrix(~ team_abbrev + 0, df)), # >= one player / team
              ifelse(df$roster_position == "CPT", 1, 0), # one captain
              players_con)

dir <- c("=", "<=", ">=", ">=", "=", rep("<=", dim(players_con)[1]))
rhs <- c(6, 50000, 1, 1, 1, rep(1, dim(players_con)[1]))
result <- lp("max", obj, cons, dir, rhs, all.bin = TRUE)
team <- df[which(result$solution == 1), ] |>
    select(name, position, salary, team_abbrev, roster_position,
           avg_points_per_game)
team
```

```
               name position salary team_abbrev roster_position
2   Igor Shesterkin        G  15600         NYR             CPT
13     Antti Raanta        G  10800         CAR            FLEX
19    Mika Zibanejad       C   9800         NYR            FLEX
24     Chris Kreider      LW   9000         NYR            FLEX
181       Jack Drury       C   2000         CAR            FLEX
186    Anthony Greco      RW   2000         NYR            FLEX
    avg_points_per_game
2                 18.61
13                12.70
19                12.16
24                13.04
181               14.30
186               11.80
```

10.15 Lab: Scraping Odds Data to Build Models

In the "Research Block" for this section, we mentioned the research that Gray and Gray did, which uncovered some inefficiencies in the NFL betting markets. They did this by obtaining data for the closing lines for NFL games and then analyzing them against the final scores of the games played. They could have (and perhaps did!) used this dataset not just to publish an academic paper but to try to profit in sports betting markets. What if you wanted to analyze past betting data yourself?

Finding betting data from games (or matches) in the past can be difficult. Some places that store it charge high monthly fees to access the data, as they assume that the users are going to be bettors building models. But there is one place that the authors know of that provides the data: Sportsbook Reviews Online. While primarily an affiliate marketer (which the authors neither endorse nor condemn), they also maintain an archive of odds at `https://www.sportsbookreviewsonline.com/scoresoddsarchives/`. We can scrape this data and do our own analyses.

1. Go to the NFL data link from Sportsbook Reviews Online, scrape the data from the 2021–22 NFL season, and write it to a data frame `df`. Recall the web scraping material from chapter 3 and also recall that you will need the package `rvest` to do the scraping:

```
library(rvest)
url <- "https://www.sportsbookreviewsonline.com/scoresoddsarchives/nfl-odds-2021-22/"
pg <- read_html(url)
df <- html_table(pg)[[1]]
names(df) <- df[1, ]
df <- df[-1, ]
```

2. What do you notice when exploring the data? There are the obvious column names, but some of them may be unfamiliar to you.
   - "Rot" is short for "Rotation Number"—essentially, a key for the team/game when combined with the date. In row 2, instead of saying "Tampa" or "Tampa Bay" or "TB" or "the Bucs" or "Buccaneers," a Rot of 452 refers to the Tampa Bay Buccaneers in their September 9 game versus Dallas.
   - "VH" is "Visitor or Home."
   - "1st," "2nd," "3rd," and "4th" represent the score of that team in those quarters, and "Final" is the final score (sum of "1st" through "4th").
   - "Open" and "Close" can be more confusing. Nominally, these are the opening and closing lines. You will see them listed as the favorite with a number, and then the total next to the underdog. For example, in the "Open" column for the first game (451/452, Dallas at Tampa Bay), you see 52.5 next to Dallas in 451 and 7 next to Tampa Bay in 452. This means that when bets were first accepted, Tampa Bay was a 7-point favorite (e.g., Tampa Bay -7), and the over/under total was 52.5. In the "Close" column for that same game, you see that the total was still 52.5, but by kickoff, Tampa Bay was up to a 10-point favorite.
   - "ML" is the "Moneyline" at close. In this same game, at kickoff, a bettor who thought Tampa Bay would win would have needed to risk $450 to win $100 (e.g., -450), while a bettor who wanted to support Dallas would have received $375 for risking $100.
   - "2H" is the "Second Half Line," in the same format as "Open" and "Close." In this same game, this means that at halftime, sportsbooks made Tampa a 2-point favorite for the second half (and overtime if required) only, ignoring any scoring that occurred before halftime. They also deemed the over/under total for the second half (and overtime, if required) to be 27 points.
3. If you want to use the data for analysis, what tasks need to be performed to clean the data?

Sometimes the team that is the favorite when the betting opens is an underdog by the time the betting closes. For example, look at game 465/466, Seattle at Indianapolis. When the betting opened, Indianapolis was a 2.5-point favorite and the total was 52.5. When it closed, Seattle was the 2.5-point favorite and the total was down to 49. Bettors obviously favored Seattle to see the line shift by 5 points, and there may have been a key injury to one or more Indianapolis players that caused people to shy away from Indianapolis. But our concern here is ensuring we are reading the data into the correct variables. Also, if the teams are evenly matched, the point spread will be written as "pk," short for "pick 'em," or evenly rated. It is equivalent to a spread of 0, so those need to be converted.

Write code that will check for these anomalies and correct for them before writing them into a data frame for analysis.

4. Examine the data for trends. What do you notice, if anything? Perhaps compare it to data from other years to identify trends.

10.16 Conclusion

Many of the analytic methods we have discussed throughout this text can be applied to sports wagering. Through the use of mathematics, a bettor can give himself the best possible chances for success.

The issue with developing complex analytic models for success in sports wagering is that even if one can predict the outcomes of games often enough to be successful, he will find it difficult to find a bookmaker willing to accept his wagers in a high enough amount to gain long-term profits and income that is worth the time invested in building the models. There are, of course, different tricks and techniques that professional bettors use to get their wagers down and accepted, but these are also beyond the scope of this chapter.

10.17 Exercises

1. Write a function that converts American odds to decimal odds.
2. In the 2023 Super Bowl, the underdog Kansas City Chiefs defeated the Philadelphia Eagles by a score of 38–35. Before the game, the bookmakers had installed Philadelphia as a 1.5-point favorite, and the total settled at 51.5. What does this imply the predicted final score would be? What could a bettor do with this information?
3. In many parts of the country, parlay cards are used in the legal (and illegal) betting markets. A parlay card commonly will show point spreads and totals for all the NFL games for a given weekend or NBA games for a given day, and a bettor will select any number of them (usually somewhere between 3 and 10) and make a wager that will then return a certain amount. In the attached graphic, a four-team parlay would pay 10 times the wager, and a five-team parlay would pay 15 times the wager. These are usually huge moneymakers for the person offering the cards because the hold is so high.
   a. What is the fair return for every dollar wagered on a four-team parlay if the teams are evenly matched and both offered at even money (i.e., +100 odds, without juice)?
   b. What is the fair return for every dollar wagered on a four-team parlay if the teams are evenly matched but are both offered at −110 odds by the bookmaker (standard juice)?
   c. Using your answer to (b) above, what is the implied probability of winning all the games on a four-team parlay?
   d. If a person offers parlay cards with exactly four games on them to 16 people, each one of them wagers $1, and all 16 combinations are taken (2 outcomes for 4 games = 2^4 combinations, or 16), what should the parlay card offeror expect to profit? Note below that a winning parlay card returns 10-for-1 and not 10-to-1, so the original wager in a winner is not returned in 10-for-1 (and it functions like 9-to-1).
4. In NFL and NBA games, point spread wagers are usually made on either team at −110 odds. That is to say that one bettor might make a wager on the Phoenix Suns −6.5 points at −110 odds, and a bettor who prefers the other side of the market might wager on their opponents, the Dallas Mavericks +6.5 points but also at −110 odds. A bettor who is betting these games would need to win 52.38% of the time (11/21) to break even. That is, if a bettor were wagering to win $100 per game at −110 odds across 21 games, if he wins 11 of those 21, he will break even. This is proven by the formula $11 \times 100 - 10 \times 110 = 0$.

In a crowded market with many bookmakers, a particular bookmaker may choose to offer a smaller market fee. For example, what if a bookmaker decided to offer each side of a game at −105 odds? Then a bettor who seeks to win $100 per game would need to be successful less often to be profitable: $21 \times 100 - 20 \times 105 = 0$. The break-even point is then 51.22%.

On a given NFL Sunday, where a bookmaker might attract $50 million in bets, equally divided among all teams on games at −110 odds, how much profit would be lost by going to −105 odds? How much more business would that bookmaker have to attract in order to make the same profit as they would have made at −110 odds?

5. Read the DraftKings data for the 2022 NHL playoff game between the Edmonton Oilers and the Colorado Avalanche (provided in the `ISAR` package `dk_edm_col`). Filter to just include the non-captain players in order to keep things simple. Compute a scatterplot showing `salary` on the x-axis and `avg_points_per_game` on the y-axis. Color the points by `team_abbrev`.
6. Find the DraftKings six-player showdown team having the highest (aggregate) `avg_points_per_game` subject to the following: (1) we need at least one player from each team, (2) the team salary must be less than $50,000, and (3) we need six players total. What is the team and the team's expected points and salary? In addition, filter out the nonstarting goalies (the starters were Darcy Kuemper and Mike Smith).
7. Suppose that you are particularly bullish on the Avalanche given that this game is in Denver. Find the best team (as above) that has at least four Avalanche players and report the expected points.
8. The lineup in problem 6 does not include Cale Makar, but assume you really want him on your team. Make sure that both Cale Makar and Nathan MacKinnon are included. You may remove the constraint that the team must include four Avalanche players.
9. Using this same dataset, find the top legitimate DraftKings showdown lineup as we did earlier. Again, only consider the starting goalies.

Index

Page numbers followed by *f* and *t* refer to figures and tables, respectively.

www.ingramcontent.com/pod-product-compliance
Ingram Content Group UK Ltd.
Pitfield, Milton Keynes, MK11 3LW, UK
UKHW051453290926
15471UKWH00008B/1174

9 781958 303078